W9-CAA-205

CHILDREN OF WINTER

ALSO BY JAMES DEMERS

The Last Roman Catholic?

JAMES DEMERS

CHILDREN OF WINTER

How the classroom is murdering the innocence of your child

SARTO HOUSE

NEW YORK

SARTO HOUSE
One Dag Hammarskjold Plaza
885 Second Avenue, 7th Floor
New York, NY 10017
(212) 207-9875
ORDER LINE 1-(800) GO-SARTO

ISBN 0-9639032-0-9

First Printing — December 1993

10 9 8 7 6 5 4 3 2 1

To
Mothers
with
Hatpins

TABLE OF CONTENTS

BOOK TWO A HISTORIC BETRAYAL

THE EIGHTIES & THE NINETIES

PART ONE AMBUSH OF THE INNOCENT

PART TWO TARGET ZERO

PROLOGUE

DID YOU CHECK THE GARBAGE?

IF YOU ARE SOMEWHERE near the middle of your life, you will remember a time when in every village, hamlet, and intersection of this continent the sacred was as familiar as springtime, with as many faces as there are leaves on trees, and it was cherished more than firelight and garden rain. It was a simpler time, some might say a too-simplistic time. But is was not an angry time. It followed a very angry war, and even though man had bitten into the atom, still, God let a garden grow and let us name it. We called it the Fifties.

To some, it was the best of times, to others it was not. Even as the family was being idealized on television in ways that could never be matched or sustained in real life, unseen stresses were preparing to alter our view of home and family forever. And yet, in spite of the Cold War, in spite of the Bomb, in spite of the emotional insecurity that is the domain of youth in every decade, the Fifties left us with an enduring image: the innocence of the under-twenties.

In those days, "troubled youth" meant the guys who split a warm beer outside the sock-hop door. Reality seldom grew any harsher than giving up movies for Lent the year Bill Haley and the Comets hit the screen and you had to spend most of March and April outside the Plaza exit door listening to three hundred friends inside snapping their fingers to *Rock Around the Clock*. A trauma was understood to be the anxiety of choosing between a brushcut and a duck-tail. "Worldly" meant someone who understood the movie *Suddenly Last Summer.*

To be a youth in the Fifties meant dancing five nights a week in the teen room at the recreation center just to practice up for the main event Saturday. You paid fifty cents to go to the dance knowing full well your hard-won quarters would be put to good use, namely, buying streamers for the next dance. In the Fifties, you see, you didn't have walk-a-thons, marathons, or sponsorships. You rarely even had a cause. Contentment was the order of the day as far as social conscience was concerned, non-conformity the only word in the English vocabulary that caused any consternation.

What happened before the dance, on the way to the dance, and during the dance could best be summed up by recalling that one of the burning issues of the Fifties, which commanded nearly as much hysteria as the anti-nuke rallies of later decades, was, "What is meant by necking?"

Trysting spots were dark holes in the pink and charcoal universe of the Fifties. Everyone knew where they were. Everyone knew who went there. If you were over eighteen, you might even understand why.

The pumphouse down by the lake was one place, for example, that one never went to after dark. There was always the danger you might discover who was wooing whom down by the lakeshore. That small building on the water's edge represented the other side of innocence, the dark side, which, like the moon, kept its blush concealed.

Yet God walked, still, in the garden, for the Fifties was the golden age of good intentions and La-Z-Boy chairs. The evidence of a workable industrial society lined our cupboards, popped up our toast and woke us, not with alarms but with music.

The pull of the future was irresistible. It was all Hollywood's fault, of course, how we in the popcorn generation fell in love with the brand of instant overnight success dictated to us by the movies of the Fifties. After all, how many times did you go to a movie back then and see Lana Turner being led out onto a New York balcony where the producer waved his arm and said, "It's all yours, my dear, the city is at your feet."

If you grew up in the Fifties watching Lana win New York, you grew up wanting to win big, expecting some sudden event to solve your problems. Lana would rise from being a make-up salesgirl to being a Broadway star, and we would leave high school and have a car and a cottage and a marriage and respectability just as easily. And all that would happen to us, we knew, at the prom.

Proms were little Lana Turner parties, Anne Blythe smile-a-thons. Kathryn Grayson masquerades. Proms were three hundred Howard Keeles in white collars looking dreadfully uncomfortable.

My last prom was a hideous affair. It ended the Fifties and my belief that all women are created equal. It was, like all proms, held in a school gymnasium, one wall of which was decorated in a three-dimensional paper dragon that took weeks to build and carve and cut out and assemble, the interior of which contained a vacuum cleaner, the purpose of which was to blow pounds of loose confetti out of the nostrils of the dragon at midnight. And so there we stood in tie pins and pimples beneath a paper dragon belching out confetti waiting for the future to strike midnight when all our problems would be solved.

How could people be so naive, you ask? Well, there was no one around to tell us that all proms did was get people drunk and sick and old. Do you know anybody who woke up the day after a prom and was not ten years older?

But during the prom nothing mattered so long as you could dance yourself crazy, sweat yourself from one end of the gym to the other, your shirt front sticking to her dress front, her little cardboard bodice stabbing through the strapless chiffon, making you the envy of the locker room.

The fishnet was a feature at most proms in the Fifties, and there was always a chairman of the decorating committee whose joy it was to announce, to her friends only, that soon the fishnet would be loosened and all the balloons would come tumbling down. You always knew when this was about to happen because a blizzard of crinolines would bunch up in the center of the basketball court dance floor and jump up and down and squeal and giggle, while the guys stood around in caribou antler tie clips, their socks melting into little puddles around their ankles. Then the fishnet would be tugged and the balloons would come tumbling down and the dragon would belch out his confetti and you got it in your hair and in your eye and in your drink and then it was all over seemingly in an instant. And there you stood, with the clock striking midnight. And you had your whole future ahead of you. There is nothing more terrifying than standing all alone on the last midnight of the last innocent party of your life knowing that at last you are all grown up.

Still, the pull of the future was irresistible. If the Fifties could end by bringing us John F. Kennedy, just imagine what the Sixties and Seventies would bring.

Nineteen seventy-two. Already, like an early frost, a lethal chill had insinuated itself into the classrooms of the city. It was, perhaps, the last year of innocence for the Catholic teacher. The right to strike was just there on the horizon. The slip-sliding smile of the politician was showing up on teachers who just one year ago would have left the room at talk of work-to-rule. A profession that had remained virginal a hundred years was now willingly offering itself up for compromise to the highest bidder. The romance of teaching was over.

Late September, a knock came to the classroom door.

"Ronald is missing," the principal whispered, just out of earshot of the class.

A numbing of the heart followed in the wake of that awful word. Missing. Such a simple word. Yet it telegraphed the dread that something was terribly wrong with the universe.

By ten o'clock a full search was underway. I watched it from the second-story classroom window as police cars drew up to a plain wood-frame house directly across the street. There, Ronald had been raised by his grandmother. From the front yard, the police and some volunteers fanned out to cover the streets between the school and the mill in the west end. Several stepped into the adjacent overgrown field to undergo a slow, methodical walk measured off in baby steps, as if the person for whom they were searching was mere inches tall. Now and then, they exchanged glances over the tall grass as if needing to advertise their fear of finding what they were seeking. One police car headed for the International Bridge, where a kid with enough street smarts could easily hitch a ride into Michigan.

As the first day dragged on without any good news filtering back, tidbits of information sifted into the classroom from teachers who had known Ronald in previous years. The picture took shape of a boy who was habitually late, staggering into school some time after 9:15, stopping at the fountain to splash water on his face, then entering the classroom with a courteous apology and an ingratiating smile. He would exhibit an eager responsiveness for the first five or ten minutes after taking his seat, then would doze off, literally drift off to sleep, head resting between his hands. He was twelve in grade six.

The charm he lavished on authority figures hinted at a boy who had no one to negotiate for him. That was, in fact, the case. When he was born, his mother was only fourteen years of age. She deposited him with his grandmother and went into the southern states to live and work. The grandmother did her best to raise him but felt very put upon and admitted she did not know what to do with him. She had been fearful for his health, wondering about his red-rimmed eyes, cracked lips, white blemishes around the rim of his nostrils, consistently foul breath, and his relentless drowsiness.

The second day of the search was more organized, more widespread, with more volunteers. They scoured the taverns and flophouses where Ronald was known to hang out. He had this thing about the company of men and liked being around them, sitting among them in a bar like he was an old man himself and swapping lies, mainly about his mother and how she was to arrive any day to whisk him away like she'd promised.

The third morning at exactly 10:20 a knock came at the door.

"They found Ronald," the principal said, again out of earshot of the classroom.

I returned to the second-story window and watched the grandmother's house across the street. There was a lot of quiet commotion around the woodshed out back. It seems the officer in charge of the investigation had asked for the key to the shed. The grandmother had said Ronald could not be in the shed because it was the first place she'd looked when he went missing. She had padlocked the door when the search party first formed out of fear of possibly losing her new rake. The officer, however, insisted, so she gave him the key.

He removed the lock, opened the door, looked inside. On the left, against the wall, rested three large, green, plastic garbage bags. The first bag was full and was fastened at the top. The third bag was full and it, too, was fastened at the top. The middle bag was not full; rather, it was upside down over something, the open end to the ground. Showing only slightly were the tips of Ronald's running shoes.

I did not watch them carry the body out. It happened while I had my back turned studying Walter. He was Ronald's closest friend. I knew I would tell him first, alone. Then I would tell the rest.

The decision had been made in the office not to break for morning recess but to keep everyone at their desks so they would not have to know the details until they were out for lunch and on their way home to their parents. But that mysterious telegraph system that children operate was working at full click, and before I could sense what was happening, a whisper entered the room and swept from desk to desk.

"They found him."

He had perished inside the confines of the green garbage bag where the airplane glue in his hand would remain concentrated and his grandmother would not see him if she came looking. Not one of us had guessed he was sniffing glue even though all the signs were there—the red-rimmed eyes, cracked lips, blemished nostrils, drowsiness, the need to splash color into his cheeks, the out-of-sync clock that was his body.

I led Walter into the staff room alone.

"You know they found Ronald?" I began.

"Yes."

"You know he won't be back?"

"He's dead. I know," he said.

At the funeral Mass two days later, I confronted the suspicion that somehow or other it might have been my fault. Weeks earlier on the first school day of September, as I walked to work, I had slipped my resignation from teaching into the mailbox, to be effective at term's end. Distracted by my preoccupation with the future, I had moved through September without effort, ignoring the lament from my class that Mr. B., the teacher I had followed, was sorely missed.

The idea that Mr. B., a teacher renowned for his ability to tap into the toughest kids, might have made a difference was consuming my thoughts when the pallbearers entered. It was not until Walter, leading the small white coffin up the aisle, passed by my pew that his words hit home.

"He's dead. I know," he had said, matter-of-factly.

He had been conveying a message to me to do with what I might, the message being that, all through the three days of searching he had known the truth, known where the body was and how it came to be there. As he walked past, I knew that to be true, suddenly, without the passing of thought. Knew it in my heart and in the pit of my stomach.

"... I know."

His message lifted a corner of the shroud to offer a glimpse into a world of violence and despair all but invisible to those adults singularly mandated to ensure childhood was enriched and adolescence secured by positive learning. Already by 1972, teachers were on the outside only belatedly and reluctantly looking in on that world to which children had been exiled by an education system organizing itself into meaninglessness, political professionalism, distancing educators from their very reason for being, parents scheduling their families into surrogate mini-corporations where economics and negotiations substituted for belonging and discipline and our supposed shepherds, so thrilled by their imagined power to make a difference in Nicaragua and El Salvador, turned the feeding of the lambs into a fast-food franchise.

Walter's words about the boy in the bag offered a glimpse into the nuclear winter of a childhood betrayed, a childhood without love, to which teachers and parents bore no more relevance than yesterday's weatherman.

When had this betrayal of childhood begun? Twenty years have now passed since the boy in the bag was found, twenty years since I left the classroom behind. Had I remained, perhaps I would not have discerned the decay of education as it was occurring. Many teachers did not see it coming, were not aware of it happening, and woke up only after the profession had been pillaged of its purpose. The teacher who has survived these last two decades with his integrity intact is a rare creature. Most have retained pride only in enduring. If I were to isolate one characteristic they have in common, I would have to say it was anger. Stand in a school hall today and feel the anger. In teachers. In children. Stress causes anger, they say, but what could be the cause of so much stress?

The Roman Catholic separate school system is the one with which I am most familiar. I taught for it, developed curricula programs for it, and drew the majority of my friends from it. I believed in it totally at one point. Today, there is little left to believe in. In entire regions of North America, one would have to search the archives to uncover anything even remotely Catholic that stands that educational system separate and apart from any other. The increasing and deliberate secularization of Church and school on this continent has vandalized the Catholic home and made off with the rightful heritage of millions. The very name of God is less welcome than punctuation in graffiti. Yet, we know the soul hungers for the sacred.

The systematic starvation of North American childhood has produced a ravenous society devouring itself. A gnawing hunger and unquenchable thirst has produced a race of adolescent terrorists. I believe it is because, when there is a famine of the sacred, violence and despair, like rampaging acids, rush into the void to consume every remnant of the innocence, trust, and joy of youth.

It was not always so.

The symbols of the sacred flourished everywhere as war ended in the Forties, uncountable buds and blossoms in that springtime of belief. Ahead of that wondrous rebirth lay the high summer of Roman Catholicism under Pius XII. We would be through adolescence and into adulthood by the time the days of the Faith began to shorten and the symbols of Catholicism started falling like leaves in the long, unstoppable autumn following Vatican II.

This is the Winter of our Faith. We gather together in makeshift kitchens, huddle for warmth round a picture of the Sacred Heart, flip through our memory albums for black-and-white snapshots of First Communion and Confirmation, and comfort one another with anecdotes intended to ensure the survival, at least in our hearts, of that near-extinct symbol of the Faith—the Catholic child.

BOOK ONE

THE GRAIL

PART ONE

AUX BARRICADES

THE SIXTIES

ONE
DIVINING

"WHERE DID I COME FROM?" the child will ask one day, as a season of blue petals makes the sky appear as near as a burst of violets.

"From God," will answer the parent.

"How come?" or "Why?" the child will ask.

"God made you."

"Why?"

"Because He loves you."

"Why?"

"To know, to love, to serve Him in this life."

"Why?"

"So you can be happy with Him in the next."

To which the child might respond, "Oh, look, a grasshopper!"

In those question and answer days, all of life seemed ordered by the *Baltimore Catechism* to encourage the child to question, "Why?" The answer was always an absolute, an unchangeable truth, a truth existing on its own independent of our experience, interpretation, or understanding. The truth was an attainable, immutable, wordable fact to which one was led by the simple genius of textbook answers that, far from deadening the child's sense of wonder, prompted him, urged, coaxed, practically compelled him to ask again and again, "Why?"

The catechism was designed in 1885 by six bishops gathered in Baltimore to package the doctrine of the faith into a late-Victorian equivalent of manageable sound bites for students and converts. It secured for decades to come fixed bridges of dogma that offered safe daily crossings in the matters of faith between children and their parents and teachers. Its effectiveness in imparting the truths of the faith is legendary.

Known as "the *Baltimore*," this catechism was a treasure hunt, a map to use in the search for the sacred. No child had to be told the sacred was there somewhere waiting for him. The awe, wonder, and gratitude fueling the mystery of each rising of the sun, each twilight, each season of blue flowers confirmed that. We are born dreamers, after all.

Searching for the precious, semiprecious, or downright valueless has been the lot of dreamers since Eden was lost. The forked switch of cherry wood my father employed to find water would twist in his hands until the bark pulled loose, when, walking ever so slowly over the field, he approached a vein of water below the surface. The stick would twist toward the ground to point out the water, just there below the earth.

"Dig here," he would say, or "Drill here," depending on the circumstances of the owner of the field.

They would drill and find water, adding to the number of households among the neighboring hills who gratefully drank from wells my father found.

"Witching for water," as it was called, made him a water-witch to some, but to those of us into whose hands he would place the barkless switch for a tryout, he was not witching but "divining."

The formidable rigor of Madawaska etiquette did not withhold acknowledgment of the gift of finding water from my father, from Izabel O'Mara, or even from a kid who succeeded; the honor accorded was merely a matter of degree. A man of my father's stature with such a record of wet wells was a "diviner." A kid who found water was "lucky." Izabel O'Mara, on the other hand, was "a witch," with or without a fork of cherry wood in her hands.

That a man might find water without a switch, or a child find God without a *Baltimore*, was almost unthinkable. Granted, the water was there, and it was sure to be found with or without a switch, even if it meant tearing up the field from here to the lower forty. God, on the other hand, was there, on His own, just as sure as water flowed underground, but only, it seemed, if the divining was done with a *Baltimore.* Down by the lake, where the Protestants owned most of the shoreline, God's actual existence did not seem so certain. It is not that they believed in God any less, it just seemed in fashion along the boardwalk to talk about God as if a person could find him on their own, without a manual, and that He was not the same to everyone who got that close to Him. He was what you saw of Him, how you saw Him, and very often the whole matter of His whereabouts, His nature, His character if you will, and even the desirability of His company was all a matter of what you made out of what you saw. Down by the boardwalk, God, it seemed, was very much a matter of personal choice. Someone from out of town who did not know better might have guessed George Bernard Shaw had composed *Joan of Arc* while strolling on the boardwalk rehearsing aloud, "Whose judgment shall I judge by if not my own?"

The rabbit-ears atop the black-and-white TV set playing and replaying Kennedy's motorcade, the woman clambering over the trunk, in pink the newscaster said, the women weeping on the grass below the knoll severed the dream factor in many of the last of the *Baltimore* generation. How many of us began viewing the footage sitting down, only to stand upright suddenly at one point, as if the gunman might still be nearby in tall grass beyond the window.

That sudden standing up caused to drop into the dust at our feet so many of the certainties of the postwar years. Those rabbit-ears, pointing, pointing, pointing down to the woman in pink on the back of that car, drilled deep into the untapped river of complacency so long hidden neath the surface of the Eisenhower years.

"From the worm even to the man, there is accomplished the great law of the violent destruction of human beings," wrote Joseph de Maistre in the blood-red shadow of the French Revolution.[1]

When The Great Law is enacted upon the most innocent of human beings, trust in the maker of laws is strained, quite often past breaking. Man against nature, man against man, man against himself are merciful slogans that, like finely woven nets, are extended to catch the falling fragments of shattered belief. Yet, it is so hard to blame nature for the violence that feeds, propels, propagates it. God, then, must necessarily be found wanting if the integrity of our give and take with nature is to remain workable.

"The whole earth drinking blood," Maistre continued, "is merely an immense altar, where every living being must be immolated, time without end, without limit, without rest, even unto the destruction of all things, even to the death of death."

Suddenly, the wording changed, the terms, you might say, preferred in answer to the question, "Why?"

How many young adults shook the dust off their shoes that bleak weekend in November 1963 and began the long walk toward horizons deforested of the certainties of youth? The cherry wood snapped and sprang backward, pointing inward, into the very heart of the one who had clutched so eagerly the divining rod.

"To know, to love, and to serve the truth is the highest goal to which man can aspire here on earth," the new man of the Sixties would state, casually, matter-of-factly, as if shaking off God was no really great matter at all. And of course, the truth, that absolute which now was the focus of life, would be *subjective* truth. With one snap of the cherry wood, the Enlightenment clicked back into focus.

Come December 1963, I resigned from teaching in a well-to-do neighborhood in the city, resigned from a world populated by well-dressed, well-fed children who knew everything, had everything, who not only wanted for nothing, but seemingly thought endlessly about nothing.

Others of my generation, so many others, would live in the streets for the next decade, so many lions in so many streets, no longer seeking, so we thought, but doing.

That was the impulse of the dizzying moment in time known as the Sixties. Do it. Do it. Do. In my jejune omniscience, I, too, set out to reorder the world left so disordered by the God of my *Baltimore* youth. No one, it seemed, remembered, or wanted to remember, that aspect of the Arimathean legend that said the Grail had disappeared because of the impurity of its guardians.

TWO

CATECHISM COAST

EACH TEACHER DISCOVERS, soon after entering his profession, the cipher, the key to unlock the mysteries of the mind, soul, heart of the learning masses. For each teacher the implement is different; to each comes a unique, singular certainty, a Rosetta stone by which to read the past and future of students.

As sure as we read from left to right, as a shoemaker needs a lathe, as a wood carver needs a whetting stone, one student will emerge from among all others to reveal to the searching teacher a prime aspect of character that will act forever after as a guide, a compass needle showing true north, and forever after throughout his career, the face of that student when recalled will act as a bob plumbing true. A point from which the pendulum of a whole career will swing, the point from which to measure all other students, the magnetic center of the teaching universe. Student zero.

I would go north in search of that cipher.

The Polar Bear Express from Cochrane to Moosonee is a single-line, earth-bound shuttle to the Third World shoreline of James Bay and Hudson Bay. There, scattered along river mouths splitting the coast to the far arctic, are the settlements of a life-and-death, no-frills humanity that still has as its prime unit of social currency the nuclear family. Ravaged by disease, poverty, alcohol—oppressed by the relentless chill of the culture to the south—the virtue and value of strength of family would linger on here while disintegration, dismemberment, dissolution, and redefinition afflicted family life in what in warmer climes is still called civilization.

At first glance, the ruins in which the peoples of the coast lived eluded classification. Were these the remnant of some soaring civilization that flew too high, too near the sun, had its wings clipped and been sentenced to sub-zero oblivion? Or was this the seed of a great culture yet to emerge, one that would rise to make nonsense of Wall Street by the deification of some as-yet-unheard-of need of man only the Cree could meet? Or were they really what they appeared to be, just Indians, doomed to house their lives in scabs of tarpaper, cardboard, and plywood on the shoulder of the world?

The glowering shadow of low esteem in which male teachers held themselves in the Sixties faded with the train whistle as, with the prestige of great purpose stiffening newborn resolve, I stepped into the diary of a predecessor. Robert Renison had written:

> I entered a land of yesterday. The twilight of the romance of the Hudson Bay Company still hovered over Ontario's back door.... The Dominion government sent down occasional surveyors. The Indians were left alone. There were only two outside interests, the old Company that came for fur, and the Missionaries who remembered that Indians had souls.[1]

The words had been written upon Renison's arrival in the north in 1880. Almost a hundred years had passed since then.

Midwifery, an aspect of life on the coast in which it was wise to be versed, was the subject of the first day of orientation on Moose Factory Island preparatory to flying north. The delivery into this world of a soul straight from the hand of God (and the flesh and blood of its mother and father) was something of an embarrassment to one who left civilization suspecting God had lost His blueprints for the race. The newborn life was much more likely to hear just, "Welcome to the world, whatever you can make of it."

To one who had so recently queried the value of the regeneration of his species, the Moose Factory landlord offered little solace. He had been on the island seventeen years, came there at the government's bidding to care for an experiment in cows.

"All died of TB," he said, "one at a time. All I did the first month here was dig graves. One day I'd bury a cow, next day an

Indian. Next day a cow, next day an Indian. And after that, guess what? Another cow. Had a devil of a time keeping track of where to place the crosses. Cows don't need salvation. No heaven or hell for them. And I guess that's how it should be. It's not like they earned virtue by making hard choices. They eat grass, make milk, and can sleep standing up or laying down. Still, all in all, I doubt they'd mind knowing a cross marked the spot where they lay down for the last time."

Evening in the village hall, on my second night on the island, a full house sat in silence awaiting lights-out and the start of a movie. Wall to wall parkas and jet-black hair, strong traces of oil, gasoline, smoke. Everyone quite quiet.

Bulbs clicked out and a beam of projector light took shape in the dusty air. The title read either *Peyton Place* or *Return to Peyton Place*—I don't remember which. And suddenly there was—who else?—Lana Turner, bigger than life in her bottled hair and strapped-in figure, getting all tense about some dark secret or other, winding up to slap some daughter's face, if she could just remember whose daughter was who, the future happiness of everyone in the movie's town dependent upon nobody finding out who had been wooing Lana down at the pumphouse.

All this told in giant, full-color, moving hieroglyphics of projected light on a wall above and beyond the heads of a hundred interrelated black-haired brothers, sisters, uncles, aunts, and cousins. They all knew from early on that in life lived in close proximity to deprivation, poverty, alcohol, disease, and death, family lines were bound to overlap or blur now and then, but it did not prevent them from deeply accepting one another.

The flight northwest along the coast in a Beaver aircraft flew briefly into the past with a touchdown at Fort Severn. At a Hudson Bay store, clinging to the mud banks as it had for decades past, commerce was done with a young manager, Terry, and his equally young assistant, Nick. Later that day, after our departure, they would head out the mouth of the Severn in their pointer canoe, towing a two-man canoe behind, heading for the company's campsite along the coast. They would beach the two-seater and the pointer, but, when they weren't looking, the pointer would drift out. They would pursue it in the two-seater. An Indian watching from the campsite said the rollers were five feet out there. Terry and Nick and the two-seater went up, over a roller, and out of sight. Nobody saw them again. Ever. The plane that dropped me doubled back to join in the search. Radio voices would soon call off the search. Out there, a little while was a long while.

In the meantime, I waited out the search on the tarmac of the Winisk Air Force Base.

Alongside the tarmac, a sullen boy scratched lines with a stick in the gravel. His mother, in a green kerchief and red parka, stood looking down at his markings. They were scratches only, less than gibberish. Teenagers boarded the plane. Mothers cried. Fathers waved. The boy with the stick did not want to follow and grumbled menacingly at the engines as they came to life. At last, he climbed aboard. His mother, noticeably, did not cry.

In the settlement, five miles away across the Winisk River, the teacherage I was to live in lay folded on the earth, its walls slowly weathering. I was directed to speak to a man lying under a tractor alongside an assortment of tools—the village priest. He drew himself out from under and stood to listen to my request for a room. That he received it unsmiling with eyes less than hospitable, unsettled me only slightly. That he was a dead ringer for Barry Goldwater, unnerved me considerably. His name was Pepin. He allotted me a room for seventy dollars a month. House rules were simple. The cook was called Alexandria. Don't offer her cigarettes.

The eccentric disciplines of a house run according to the highs and lows of a French Oblate who had not been off the coast in seven years determined that the schoolroom would be my workplace, leisure lounge, and studio from before sunup to long after sundown. I had one brief mandate. Teach English to seventeen Cree students, aged eight to thirteen. Feed them salt biscuits midmorning and mid-afternoon with powdered milk made with water from the river.

The first three of the seventeen to register were Ignace, Andrew, and Celine. Their older sister Jocquin would see to it that they would be first in everything from that day until the end—the first in line for books, pencils, salt biscuits, powdered milk.

The first day after the students' departure from the school steps, a dog with silver hair blocked the stairs. I threw a salt biscuit toward the school bell in the field. He had devoured it and returned by the time I reached the path.

"More," a voice said. But there was no face to match the voice, not anywhere up or down the path. I threw him another to get by. As I neared the priest's house, I caught Pepin watching from the kitchen window. He looked to the dog, then again to me, and shook his head in disgust.

"So?" he said.

"So ... what?"

"So, what happens the day you run out of biscuits?" Then he shrugged and turned his back.

For as long as the biscuits would last, the silver dog would be there at day's end, waiting for his meal. Having guessed the storeroom would feed the school for another generation, I trained him to expect three, no more, but no less. The matter convinced Pepin of my foolishness and he ceased speaking to me altogether.

One blue-black night, an ancient man was carried into the vestibule. Four men, followed by two women, carried his body as straight as an arrow. They lowered him to the floor, placed a rosary on his chest where his fingers were entwined, and folded a jacket under his head.

A grunt from behind my left shoulder ordered me aside. Pepin stepped by, a purple stole around his neck, a breviary in hand, already intoning the Viaticum. The anointing began, and words of the *Baltimore* spelled themselves out before my eyes like letters on a ticker tape.

"*Extreme Unction is the sacrament which gives health and strength to the soul and sometimes to the body when we are in danger of death.*"[2]

Hidden from view, the old man's eyes yielded up their light. By the time Pepin straightened up again, the old man was dead.

The keening began. "Kreening" I call it, Cree keening. Unimaginable sounds giving death its due. Another woman entered to join those crying prayers around the lamplight. Within moments, lanterns were moving up and down the path as the word spread.

The sorrow continued throughout all the next day.

I wondered at the depth of grief poured out over an old man who, dear as he may have been to all he knew, may very well have counted his final days on earth as useless ones and eagerly awaited the journey he was now enjoying.

His body was laid out atop a woodpile in the cellar below the schoolroom, and all throughout the day, as slabs were sawn his length and hammered into a box to house him, I toyed with the need to tell the students about death. The need was mine, not theirs. Except for a few wistful glances out toward the church and the cemetery, beyond where the diggers were at work, the children gave little sign that having a darkening corpse just there beneath the floor made this day different from any other.

We consumed the morning by balling up newspaper between the windows and the storms for winter insulation. It darkened the room. But nothing could darken the mood. Needing water for the powdered milk, I headed for the bank. There was ice on the river that day, not the great slabs that would crash to a halt and block up the river in another week, but a solid crust reaching out from shore that required the heel of an axe to crack it through. The time consumed in doing so permitted a battle to break out indoors. Ignace, realizing that the wood had run out, decided to feed the stove with the paper insulation. By the time I returned with the pail of water, a chain of students under Ignace's command had emptied the windows. Light filled the room once more. But the paper burned fast. Ignace had ordered all school books into the stove, starting with Celine's speller. Celine struck him in anger. He threw in her mitts and toque. The class took sides. War games raged overhead as the final nails fastened the sides of the slab coffin below.

Indulge them in the presence of death, I thought. Allow the old man purity of passage to the other side. As the *Baltimore* says, *"An indulgence is the taking away of temporal punishment due to sins already forgiven"* (L. 33, Q. 197).

Why had Jocquin not stopped them? She was not there. After

the room was cleared and they had gone home, I found her down below, in the cellar with the dead.

She was sitting, when I tiptoed into the basement, in the hydraulic barber chair, a red-leather-and-chrome manifestation of Depression-era America, sitting on a square of cracked linoleum between the woodpiles, its elevated footrest reaching out almost far enough to touch the leg of one of the sawhorses holding aloft the slab coffin.

The old man lay within, on a cushion of moss, his darkened skin appearing even darker against the lace of a hastily cut surplice lining the inner slabs.

She slipped away shyly when I whispered her name. I took her place in the barber's chair.

"By 'the resurrection of the body' is meant ... that at the end of the world the bodies of all men will rise from the earth and be united again to their souls, never more to be separated" (L. 14, Q. 78).

He was carried to the altar railing the next morning by the same four men who had lowered his old body onto the floor of the vestibule two nights before. There was about their manner, as they raised the slab box up onto their shoulders, that calm urgency one sees in gift-givers when they are about to part with a great treasure.

Ignace, Celine, Andrew, and all the others watched from the school windows as houses emptied along the path and friends and enemies streamed toward the church steps. Afterwards, the mourners filled the path as the coffin made its way among them. They wept and sighed and bobbed slowly over the uneven earth beneath their rubbers.

"The chief sins against charity are hatred of God, and of neighbor, sloth, envy and scandal," said the *Baltimore* (L. 16, Q. 93).

A gate opening onto the graveyard split in the middle twenty feet of white picket fence fronting the holy ground. The remaining three sides of the cemetery were fenceless, yet the mourners filed with heads erect and hats in hand through the gate until the grave was surrounded, so all could look down into the hole. They all knew where he was going and where he was destined; still, they all chose to look down into that brief ditch.

"The sins against hope are presumption and despair" (L. 16, Q.

92).

And so, he was lowered down. Covered over. Filled in. The mound patted smooth. A cross planted at his head gathered rosaries onto its outstretched arms as the mourners departed, until ten, twenty, and more rosaries, pink, blue, mint green, black, clear crystal, each suspending a cross just above the earth, formed a curtain, a miniature aurora borealis of belief ever so gently undulating in the cold breeze above the fresh earth.

"The sins against faith are not believing what God has revealed" (L. 16, Q. 91).

And then they left by the gate, many arm in arm, tears spent. Conversation replacing stares. Quite a few stopping by the school steps to collect offspring for the walk home. Many nodded acknowledgments, soft mutterings expressing that it was a fine day. Several smiled. Most insisted on a meeting of eyes with the teacher. Confidently. There was, after all, nothing new in the universe, nothing they needed to know.

"There is a God. The soul of man is immortal" (Appendix 1, Q. I).

The sky that night held every star that had ever shone since the creation of time. By 2:00 a.m., the path was busy with traffic, strollers moving in the dark, just to get out, be with others, voices low, cigarettes glowing then dying in the dark like fireflies. At length, the voices quieted, figures drifted silently, silhouetted against the star-and-ice-spangled river, leaving it to their footfalls to tell the wonder of it.

"We can prove that there is a God because this vast universe could not have come into existence, nor be so beautiful and orderly except by the almighty power and the wisdom of an eternal and intelligent Being" (App. 1, Q. II).

Jane Fonda's celluloid arrival on the Hudson Bay coast was greeted with bemusement by the hundred who crowded the dance hall to watch the ice-bound premier of *Period of Adjustment.*

In near-total silence, the greater half of the village seated between the screen and the projector stared blankly at the black-and-white images as Jane, on her honeymoon, sniffed, squeaked, squealed, and sobbed to her husband about her "little blue zip-ah bag," left, it seems, in the car, which was actually a hearse. By movie's end, "little blue zip-ah bag" was being repeated throughout the hall by old women, ancient men, the smallest children, and teenage girls who could not have known that "bag" meant purse while "zip-ah" was what they had on their parkas, and who had seen nothing blue on the black-and-white screen. The silliness of the government movie program!

The sound of a motored machine drawing up outdoors emptied the hall. Fonda continued to gasp on about her "little blue zip-ah bag." The throng poured down the steps to surround a yellow and black snowmobile revving its motor rhythmically as it idled alongside the path. The first one on the river. What it would do to the fabric of traditional life along the coast would eventually mirror what other modernizing forces were accomplishing in the outside world. Sort of a gasoline-run Vatican II-mobile.

A mere thirty paces from the Hollywood-and-whine unreality of *Period of Adjustment*, a halo of yellow lamplight lay across a yard where Louis Bird was standing alongside his upturned dog sleigh. He was working on the runners. Into wooden troughs running the length of the sleigh, he had packed a mixture of flour and mud. Now, it being frozen rock hard, he was shaving it smooth with a carpenter's plane. To show its durability, he struck it with a hammer twice without leaving a dent.

He had been refused credit at the store for a snowmobile, so the sleigh would have to make it through another winter. Only relatives of the factor could get credit for the new machines.

He bought a typewriter to console himself and was learning to type phonetically. He asked me to read the first ten pages. There, on sheets of brown wrapping paper where line after line played out a near-violent collision of consonants and vowels, was the story of his wedding.

In a village of 172 people, the chances of marrying a woman who was not a near cousin were zero or sub-zero. Louis, determined to seek out and find someone who would marry him for himself and not his blood lines, had made his way to Churchill in the hope of romance. In no time, he was married. After a suitable period of exploring with his spouse in Churchill, he brought her home to his plywood prefab, only to have her discover that she was second cousin to everybody in town. He chose to let her believe this pleased him.

"We can prove," says the *Baltimore*, *"that the soul of man is immortal because man's acts of intelligence are spiritual; therefore, his soul must be a spiritual being; not dependent on matter, and hence not subject to decay or death" (App. 1, Q. III).*

The lure of the traplines would soon empty the settlement. The activity outdoors increased as the day grew nearer. Then the riverbank fell totally silent. Curious, I strolled out into the perfect stillness and journeyed to the store at the far end of the path. Drizzle mixed with snow to make the going a mini-misery. The store empty, I forsook the need for conversation and walked the edge of the river back. Three houses distant from the school, I sensed I was not alone. Dogs were off the leash everywhere. With seven or so to a house, this meant one growl could populate the path with a hundred.

Cutting back toward the school, I encountered a white-faced, black-shouldered hound staring coldly from the high path, almost at eye level. I backed into the wall of a house. A dozen animals gathered to participate. The white face began walking forward, then sort of loped, then almost playfully leapt and drove his lowered head into my stomach. Another dirty brown dog repeated the run, trying to knock me down.

A metal bed rung leaned against the wall. I swung it once. The white face growled. And instantly, the snow lumps of the field came alive. Twenty-two dogs. The snapshot of that yard the instant it leapt to life is imprinted forever in my mind. Whenever I doubt the number, I reach back behind my mind's eye and draw it out. Twenty-two dogs. I can still count them, still map them out on a piece of paper.

How long the seconds lasted while they shredded the air, ran and leapt, all dreadfully playful, I cannot judge. All I know for sure is that I aged, swung the iron bed rung, and acquired wisdom. Then the silver dog appeared. He stood with his back to me, snarling at them. They silenced, scattered. A few vanished back into the snow bowls where they had been curled up and dozing. Others contested the silver dog's motive loudly, wildly.

A woman appeared on a doorstep nearby, cursing and throwing hot water. In seconds, she subdued the fury. Then she looked my way. Just a glance, her eyes touching my face just below my own. She smiled, then laughed, then fled indoors giggling. I had tears on my face, and surprisingly, a prayer on my lips. I dried my eyes and walked home.

"*We can prove that all men are obliged to practice religion because all men are entirely dependent on God, and must recognize that dependence by honoring Him and praying to Him*" (App. 1, Q. IV).

That Sunday, on a walk inland to the muskeg flats, Ed, the Bay factor's assistant, explained how the dogs are made to go hungry three days before the hunt.

"Sharpens their senses."

How they're let loose one day to wear off steam before harnessing them.

Come Monday, they all left before daybreak, dogs pulling heavy sleighs, women carrying heavy loads, plodding through the half-dark early hour, emptying the world of human sound. Only three children remained in school: Ignace, Andrew, Celine.

That Sunday I took God for a walk, intending to go from the spruce and tamarack edging the river to the muskeg flats spreading out through the solar system and beyond.

Halfway to that desert of snow, I came upon a window hanging from a tree. A house window, trimmed in white and suspended from a branch, with eight squares for glass. Where the branch met the tree, seven panes of glass wrapped individually in brown paper and tied in a bundle leaned against the bark. Through the seven squares of empty window, I saw the trail, without footsteps, leading off beyond the stars. Someone lived out there. An individual, unique and free standing, distinct from all other life. Whether one believed or disbelieved that he lived out there, he did live out there, completely independent of the opinions of anyone on the planet, and he was building a house. In the eighth square, I saw myself.

A package of hair ribbon, combs, berets, and hairpins arrived from down south.

Celine wanted her hair combed out. She was half-Indian, freckled. I drew the comb through her sandy hair. It caught on something. A cocoon, nestled snugly in her hair, close to the skin, below the crown. It was extracted carefully in one piece. Ignace and Andrew watched somewhat casually as I sliced it open. A grub emerged. A moth? It did not survive long.

Ignace hurried home at noon, uncharacteristically fast, a bobby pin holding a sprig of hair straight up under his toque. Before one o'clock, his father returned, scowling, speaking deeply, ready, it seemed, to skin, tan, and wear me as boots. Ignace had tied a ribbon to his ponytail.

Had Jocquin not run in, scolding her father, my coastal experiment might have ended that day. In a high-pitched, non-stop stream of scalding rhetoric, she compelled her father to depart the schoolroom. Her voice fell and rose, and continued to whip and snap in the air as she drove her father down the path homeward.

Jocquin, the complete daughter, had it all—wisdom, understanding, counsel, fortitude, knowledge, piety, and fear of the Lord. The *Baltimore* calls those things "gifts."

Unexpectedly, my last lesson on the coast came the next week. A subdued and chastised Ignace, Jocquin's words still ringing in his ears, returned to class with Andrew and Celine. Almost unconsciously and with no great purpose in mind, I used the fourteen empty seats and the three full ones to teach some English words related to arithmetic. All went well until we reached seventeen minus seventeen equals zero. The calculation required the three to leave their seats.

Ignace was the last to stand. Then he returned and sat down again. A battle ensued. It lasted through several logs in the stove. It ended with Ignace, completely resolved not to leave his desk, standing nobly alongside it, tears welling up in his eyes. For most of the next hour, I used chalk, books, cards, shoes, mitts to demonstrate that nothing left is zero. No matter how artfully I drew the formula on the blackboard, the sign "0" drew only silence from him.

At last, tears burst from his eyes. What I was trying to teach him was not just the language of numbers or the function of numbers. I was trying to teach him the unteachable. Ignace could not conceive of the concept of "zero." To him, there was no such thing as "nothing."

After dark, I walked the path separating the two rows of houses, plywood prefabs cracking in the cold. Only the stove pipe from the house of Jocquin gave off smoke. Inside was her father, Andrew, and Celine. And inside also was Ignace, a boy who had never seen a car, truck, bus, or train, a boy who had seen wheels only on toys. A boy who experienced technology backwards. Helicopters, yes, he knew them. Planes, snowmobiles, yes. Radio, yes. Inside that house, in this sliver of a culture clinging to the mud banks of a frozen river, was a boy who could not comprehend "nothing." I had found Student Zero.

"Sanctifying grace," says the *Baltimore, "first makes us holy and pleasing to God; second makes us adopted children of God; third makes us temples of the Holy Ghost; fourth, gives us the right to heaven" (App. 1, Q. IV).*

Ignace, I believe, had never left heaven.

The last walk to the air base five miles away was a silent one. Above the bank receding into the distance, three threads of smoke weaved skyward from the priest's house, the Hudson Bay store, and the house of Jocquin—strings, seemingly attached but unable to pull, lift, or lower God, or move any of His limbs. No matter how straight and true they rose, they always weakened in the effort, wiggled near the top, and gave up. And so it remained until, glancing back a final time, I could see it no more.

"What is man, *Baltimore*?"

Man is a creature composed of body and soul and made to the image and likeness of God [L. 5, Q. 24]. *On account of the sin of Adam, we come into the world without grace, and we inherit his punishment* [L. 5, Q. 29]. *No, God did not abandon man after Adam fell into sin* [L. 7, Q. 40]. *When we say that God is the Creator of Heaven and earth we mean that He made all things from nothing* [L. 4, Q. 17]. *The chief creatures of God are angels and men* [L. 4, Q. 18]. *Angels are created spirits without bodies. Men are created spirits with bodies,* who for a time are children, for a time, have children, for a time become children once again and now and then need reminding that they did not create themselves.

A boy descended from the plane as I waited to board. Beside me, a woman in a green kerchief and red parka awaited him. They remained nearby to watch the takeoff. With a stick, the boy drew letters in the snow.

"I can read," they spelled out.

The woman looked down at them, then, pointing with her finger, she traced the letters in the air above the snow. From right to left. He scolded her impatiently. She could not look at him. Tears came. She lowered her head even more. After a silent moment, he led her away delicately.

"When we say that God is eternal, we mean that He always was and always will be, and always remains the same" (L. 2, Q. 9).

"He knows all things, past, present, and future, even our most secret thoughts, words, actions" (L. 2, Q. 10).

Even where Henry Hudson is buried. Or if he's buried.

"He is everywhere. He can do all things" (L. 2, Q. 10). He can even teach gentleness to proud, impatient sons.

And so I left the land of yesterday, where the triumph and the twilight of the *Baltimore* hovered over the coast, where Indians had souls, were souls, and the Old Company still cheated them on furs.

THREE

ELUSIVE BUTTERFLY

The child's foot does not know it is a foot.
It wants to be butterfly or an apple.
—Pablo Neruda

WHEN DID THE SIXTIES really begin, that "I will not serve" movement that turned our way of life inside out and has been identified ever since as the product of that anti-Establishment decade? When did it end? Some say the Sixties did not end until 1975 when disco beat it to death. Others that it still has not ended. For many, the Sixties began with the death of Kennedy, or rather with Lyndon Johnson trying to squeeze into the slipper of that sleek prince from Boston who had gone to the ball and kept it going for a thousand days. Others isolate the media coverage of Vietnam, bringing the cynicism of the war machine into the living rooms of North America, as the starting point. Perhaps a hockey game or beauty pageant or musical special was interrupted by news of an atrocity far away, which suddenly became an atrocity occurring between the La-Z-Boy chair and the Boston fern in the window. And the Sixties were suddenly upon you. One man pinpointed as the start of the Sixties the high-altitude faux pas of Barry Goldwater proclaiming, "Extremism in the defense of liberty is no vice ... moderation in the pursuit of justice is no virtue." The children of the Thirteen Colonies would have none of that, as it turned out, and good for them, I say.

For me, the spirit of that age, the spirit that, alas, gave us the Seventies, the Eighties, and, God help us, the Nineties, is pinned to the calendar on one specific day in one specific year: May 31, 1967, the day the Catholic Church put to rest the "Oath Against Modernism" and gave us instead the "Profession of Faith."

It would be wrong to treat that date as the birth date of that spirit, for in fact, that spirit was not a conception of the nuclear age. That last day in May did not even mark the reemergence into society or the rebirth in civilization of that spirit, for, the truth is, it had been making its presence felt in the schools of philosophy and theology all through the late Fifties. But on May 31, 1967, it was captured, like a firefly in a bottle. The light it gave off was just the glimmer of the light of human pride, marking the dawn of the post-Christian era. But it was seen by many who had lived through the Fifties in what to them seemed to be the oppressive gloom of the shadow of The Cross. They saw the glimmer of the beginning of the post-Christian era, and Luther and Descartes and Rousseau were seen walking in the city, as if just emerging from the confines outside of Time where they had so long been brooding.

To that human trinity must go the recipe for the accumulation of ingredients of human thought that, bought in bulk, is called "the Enlightenment." Luther, with his attacks on dogma and doctrine. Descartes, with his rejection of objective truth, demanding that all truth, God included, is subjective. Rousseau, attacking the moral law. They walked in the Sixties, and not only did no one hide from them, our bishops ran to them and welcomed them. Liberalism of every degree and shade bathed the Sixties in an incandescence emitting from nehru-jacketed theologians, their happy-face philosophy, and super-secularized sociology. Faith, truth, and law were "all relative and all subject to the conscience of the individual."[1]

Emerging from the white light of media scrutiny trained (with relentless and deadly accuracy) on institutions born of the ages was a new ambition, "to eliminate God from all social life." Seemingly overnight, a new and morbid state of conscience was directed "towards the breaking down of traditions and social taboos, breaking the family, destroying the restraints which (ever) had held our civilization together," leaving only one absolute, "the absolute sovereignty of human reason."[2]

None of this, as I said, was new. It was merely new to the Sixties. It had seen the light of day many times before. At the turn of the century, the very momentum of this accumulation of impulses had threatened to undermine the certitude of the Catholic Church, the longest-lasting human institution on earth, by "waging systematic warfare" upon the Church's authoritative declaration of revealed truth.[3] "Daylight versus dogma" was the slander sloganeers of this new reign of Liberalism propagated. This "war to the death between Christianity and the cult of philosophy" was won by the Church. The liberalism fueling the attack on Church dogma was labeled "Modernism" by the Pope of that time, Pius X. To defeat it, he unleashed the full might of papal authority, that very thing the Modernists had sought to disarm. In his encyclical, *Pascendi Dominici Gregis*, Pius X said of the Modernists, "They disdain all authority and brook no restraints."[4] He described them as "men who are striving by arts entirely new and full of subtlety to destroy the vital energy of the Church."

To protect and defend the vital energy of the Church, Pius X instituted a means whereby candidates for higher orders, newly appointed confessors, preachers, parish priests, canons, the beneficed clergy, the bishop's staff, Lenten preachers, the officials of the Roman congregations, or tribunals, superiors and professors in religious congregations were "obliged to swear according to a formula which reprobated the principal modernist tenets." (See Appendix for full text).

The chief success of this "Oath Against Modernism" promulgated by Pius X, September 1, 1910, was that it educated otherwise unaware clergy of the dangers facing them and did strengthen and fortify the laws of the Church. The means by which that authoritative measure was pressed into actuality are still remembered with shudders today by those who think that being able to call oneself a Catholic theologian has absolutely nothing to do with whether what you are teaching is Catholic. Chairs in theology quivered and shook and have held their professors with something less than convincing security ever since. Theologians from the first half of the twentieth century had at least to pretend that they upheld Catholic teaching or that it was nice if someone, somewhere, did.

Successive popes relaxed many of the restrictions against the modernist school throughout the decades intervening between Pius X and Paul VI, but the "Oath Against Modernism" stood until Vatican II had come and gone.

The forces that hijacked Vatican II did not make the cancellation of the "Oath Against Modernism" a big issue when they rewrote the constitutions emerging from Vatican II. But the intention to dispense with it was not long hidden once the Second Vatican Council ended on December 8, 1965. On May 31, 1967, the Congregation for the Doctrine of the Faith substituted a brief, concise "Profession of Faith." (See Appendix for full text).

It effectively replaced the oath and canceled out what it stood for. The door was open for the "radical transformation of human thought in relation to God, man, the world and life, here and hereafter."[5] This supposedly great step forward was in fact a regression to eighteenth-century philosophy, the Humanism of a century that was to ripen and redden our history books with the French Revolution.

If you do not value the role the Catholic Church has played in the education of youth throughout history, then all of this will dampen your enthusiasm for the twenty-first century not at all. But to those who acknowledge that mankind may not have even survived the twentieth century without the Church and what it stands for, the date May 31, 1967, must take on a vital significance. That it is so little known, so little understood, is one reason why the Catholic world is shaking its head at itself wondering how the Church itself could have possibly gone so very wrong. The cancellation of the "Oath Against Modernism" and the substitution of a simple "Profession of Faith" ensured that a new court, a court superior to the judges and jurors of Christianity, would have supreme authority to pass judgment on all we believed, on the very way we have lived. This was to be the court of individual conscience—"Whose judgment shall I judge by if not my own?" Shaw had made of Joan of Arc a Fabian prophetess for our Modernist era.

Loisy, one of the foremost proponents of the theology that appeared new and threatening in 1910 and which has free reign today, stated of the movement, "In reality, all Catholic theology, even its fundamental principles, the general philosophy of religion, Divine Law, and the laws that govern our knowledge of God, come up for judgment before this new court of assize."[6]

Pablo Neruda caught the entire spirit of the age that began in the Sixties with one image: "The child's foot does not know it is a foot. It wants to be a butterfly or an apple."[7] Since the invention of conversation, there had been voices telling the child that his foot is not a butterfly, not an apple, that it cannot fly nor be peeled for a pie. That it has toes, more often than not five in number, that you can stand on it for a long time once you get the knack of balancing the rest of your body, and that if you happen to have another one just like it you can walk, run, dance, and by strapping skis on them, make snow dust of the greatest of mountains.

I will wager that not one of you over forty who are reading this got through the Sixties without spending at least part of a smoke-filled evening observing some misty-eyed creature apply the macrame of his or her mind to the riddle of what that thing at the end of the leg was. Journeys into infantilism were the hallmark of the late Sixties, where the ever-bottomless pouch of marijuana or cocaine caused to be elevated to the highest intellectual pursuit man's need to engage in the question of whether the four-limbed growth that grew the apple or the five-and-a-half-foot cocoon that produced this butterfly need concern itself even the slightest with regulations for safe flight or the laws governing the picking of apples.

The conviction in the land was that all the standards, laws, rules, regulations of all of history could and would be adapted, shaped, reshaped, and fitted to the intellectual, moral, and social needs of the day. The "spirit of the age" was the elusive butterfly, in whose fluttering wake the dogma and doctrine of the past would be but a *tra-la-la.* An entire generation of priests, nuns, and theologians flew Jonathan Livingstone Seagull Airlines to Khalil Gibranland and smoked the map telling how to get back. Years later they showed up as teachers of theology and sexology.

When did the Sixties begin for me?

It occurred the day I left the coast. The Austin Airways flight into Churchill descended to an airstrip lit with auxiliary lamps, switched on to counteract a power blackout that had left Churchill a dark smudge on the landscape. That night, in a lamplit hangar, a conversation along a makeshift bar became the harder to ignore the more the speaker imbibed.

It seems he was a cook from an air force installation along the mid-Canada line. He was leaving the North forever, he announced to his quiet tablemates. Never to return, not to Canada nor to the Air Force. He was, in fact, off to the United States for a most compelling reason: a clinic there was currently scrubbing up to perform on him, as soon as he arrived, a long-awaited sex-change operation. He made use of the ambience to express how living as a man was living in eternal candlelight, and that he knew when he awoke as a woman he, and not just his name, would be "up in lights."

I did then, as I do now, think changing one's sex a very ho-hum idea. The very notion that one can tamper with an original is the hallmark of mediocrity. Granted, Winston Churchill did improve a Rembrandt by painting a mouse into the corner of the masterpiece, and he also drank a forty-ouncer before tea time without tampering too much with the canvas that was his character.

But had Rembrandt portrayed Churchill he would doubtless not have painted a bottled mouse in his lap. It's all a matter of knowing not to go too far.

Not all the tampering with cells, flesh, bones, blood, and organs since that night of blackout and boredom have achieved anything more than tampering with originals. Like petulant artisans taking scissors to the Bayeaux Tapestry, envious cartoonists taking felt pens to the Sistine Chapel, armchair architects taking crazy glue to the Parthenon, compulsive shoppers picking gloves for the Venus de Milo, the mediocre man must, it seems, constantly reshuffle reality.

Even though I know that long before the lights came on in Churchill, the age of biological meddling had been well under way, nevertheless, the mean reality of the snowbanks of Churchill when the street lamps flashed on marks for me the beginning of the long descent into mindlessness the human race was about to undergo—decades of biological manipulation striving to uncouple us from nature.

The *Baltimore* days had ended. Forever.

FOUR

THE MEDDLING CLASS

HEROES HAVE BEEN SO NECESSARY to the twentieth century that if Tarzan had not been invented, he probably would have been born. As the twentieth century dawned, the Church canonized and Shaw revised the character of Joan of Arc, whose simple certainty triumphed ultimately over complicated bigotry. And Edgar Rice Burroughs invented Tarzan, whose one-syllable world stood strong and firm against the encroachments of civilization. But Tarzan was only the first of the high tree-top flyers to enliven our skies with vigorous virtue and uncommon courage.

When Hollywood failed to transplant Tarzan to New York, America gave birth to Superman, who was merely Tarzan in city drag doing in the skyline what the ape man did in the tree line.

Superman was the first attempt in comic book fiction to paraphrase the Messiah story. Science fiction writers discuss the Star of Bethlehem as a spacecraft that brought Christ to the stable of a humble Mary and Joseph just as Superbaby's spacecrib crash landed in the backyard of Mr. and Mrs. Kent, who took the super-orphan home to learn he was a closet aerialist with a phone booth in his future. But all-American as he was, he only reflected the North America of his day and fought nothing more evil than bank robbers, jewel thieves, and counterfeiters.

In the McCarthy era, when Communism was the favorite enemy of the people, a band of heroes, The Black Hawks, raced jet fighters over the globe to halt the spread of all things Red while other champions of justice in body stockings and racoon masks took care of things at home, not the least inventive of whom was Plastic Man, who could assume all sorts of shapes and sizes and lost interest in fighting crime when he learned how to become a mirror and could study himself endlessly in perfect secular humanist fashion.

It was only natural with the headlines of the Kennedy era spelling out battles of conscience, documenting ecology and directing the preservation of the species, that the most exquisite hero of all rose to prominence. This, of course, was the Silver Surfer, a melancholy tragic figure riding his surfboard through the universe mourning man's inhumanity to man.

And so the comic book heroes had come full circle, the Silver Surfer making no attempt to hide the fact that he was not of this world, his story lines usually ending with a bowed but unbroken hero riding his surfboard through the galaxy in anguished contemplation over the public's refusal to listen to him. Still to come was the far away era of Watergate and Nixon politics, which saw emerge on the comic book market that hero called the Son of Satan, a good boy with the simple certainty that he would someday ultimately triumph over his father, that wicked old horned toad Lucifer himself. But that was still a troubled decade away.

In the Sixties, it seemed as if the whole world had been overtaken by a new class of people—the meddling class. When I returned from the North, I returned to an attitude, the attitude that all life, all thought, all the philosophy and theology of all recorded history had awaited the input of that superstar of the Sixties, the sociologist, to set it aright.

Ah, yes, sociology, the science of the origin, development and nature of the problems confronting society. By 1968, sociologists were well on their way to demonstrating that the greatest problem confronting society was the nature of the sociologist.

My initial week back provided my first encounter with the social worker. She was "working" the staff room at the time, "dialoguing" with teachers who were looking for a moment of invisibility to have a coffee and a cigarette, "relating" to the staff by dropping enough questions to convince them that she not only had all the answers, but all the names of every relative of every student in the universe to boot.

As someone just returning to civilization, I was a natural target for that hallmark of the social worker, that patronizing, pharisaic, elitist attitude that said adults in general and I in particular required "integrating" with the new knowledge of the times.

Clearly there was more wrong with the world than just New Math. There was something bogus about the dynamic at work, the seeming reluctance on the part of the classroom teacher to challenge or, heavens, ignore the output of the social worker, who, it appeared, was sustaining an artificial prominence maintained on the premise that if you talked long enough or briefly enough, talked over their heads or under their consciences, you would keep the teachers unsettled, and they would never catch on that you were just a busybody.

The sociologists moved forward with one prime determination: to unsettle the balance of everyone around them, then run to the rescue. To this curious species of human being must be allotted the gold medal for dismantling in record time that cornerstone of all human institutions, the traditional family unit.

In the world of home and school there was, until the Sixties, one elastic holding the child to the teacher, the child to the Church, the child to the home. If that one elastic lost its tension or snapped or was severed, the social worker would be ensured a long-term influence. That binding tie was one simple directive: *"Honor thy father and thy mother"* (*Baltimore,* p. 106). In the words of the *Baltimore*, the Fourth Commandment commanded us to *"respect and love our parents, to obey them in all that is not sinful and to help them when they are in need"* (p. 107).[1]

Who would have thought that words carved in stone would, through the simple application of the sociologists' rule of time, become flexible, like play dough, silly putty. "Sin" was relettered to spell "behavior." "Virtues" were replaced by "values." "In all things sinful" was replaced by "in all things unusual."

The child, under the guise of problem-solving, was introduced to assessing usual and unusual behavior—what to do if, who to call if. It was a small step from judging behavior to scoring a parent's performance on a scale of one to ten. Enter the child as judge; and without the authority to change what he judged, enter the child as victim. To the service of this exercise in self-centeredness was developed that favorite and sacrosanct tool of the Sixties—the journal.

The journal, as all parents know, is a diary of sorts, a depository of the unspoken thought of the student. It is a totally private world of the written word which, in most cases, the teacher is not to read, unless the student gives permission. Nor is the teacher allowed to correct spelling and punctuation or comment on the neatness or lack thereof. It is a world totally emancipated from rules, authority, standards—an anarchist's daydream.

What follows is a far from untypical use of the journal by a typical writer of same.

Her name was Diane. She was bright, self-sufficient, toughened up to life. At thirteen, she wore a Klute haircut, miniskirt, and high-heeled boots. I figured her a potential runaway and so I took the usual step of not being hard on her, the hope being that the runaway would feel safe in the classroom and postpone her departure from childhood a few days longer.

She was standing looking down at me, suddenly one day. She more or less dropped her journal onto my desk, holding it high and letting it drop so it would slap hard and noisily.

She uttered an unprintable oath for my ears only and walked back to her seat. Once there, she made herself quietly busy, as if the incident had not occurred.

I hesitated to pick up the journal. It was more private than a diary, a safety zone where students could express the unspeakable fears in their lives. All of the class knew the value of the journal and never had they made light of it or attempted to see into one another's pages. But it had always been understood that if a student wanted to communicate on some delicate issue, they could slip their journal into the security of the teacher's top desk drawer and the teacher would read it in total confidentiality.

I opened the journal to the last written page.

"He did it again last night," she had written. "Get help, please."

Turning the pages back toward the front of the scribbler, I read the details she had been recording over the months. She lived with her mother, who had been separated from her father all the girl's life. They took in boarders to make ends meet. One of the boarders had become her mother's boyfriend. They were going to get married, but for three months he had been stealing into Diane's bedroom in the dark, early morning hours.

She was afraid she was pregnant. Her mother knew nothing, or pretended not to know. The girl had confided in no one. Only her journal. Now me.

When class was out, she resisted all my efforts to catch her eye. She had played by the rules, had taken advantage of the journal the way that was allowed. Now it was up to me to resolve the problem.

In the days to follow, the girl continued to attend class and pretended nothing was afoot as various professionals from the school board, at my request, made their presence felt in the neighborhood, her house, the school itself. No one but Diane knew what they were doing. She met with them in the nurse's room and betrayed no notion to her classmates that she was involved in anything but running errands.

Within seventy-two hours, the problem was no more. The man was gone from the house, from the town, having escaped charges only because of the girl. The end of the drama was silent, secretive.

"Would you like to go live with your father?" she was asked.

The question shocked her. She could never leave her mother now that she was so badly needed at her side. She would have to help her through this.

But there was that other reason, that truth. The husband her mother was separated from was not Diane's father. The boarder was her father, and had been the cause of the marriage break up fourteen years before. It was all there in Diane's eyes. That she might be pregnant by her own biological father. And she would need her mother now more than ever before.

This anecdote is included here to underline an admission I must make regarding the social worker of the Sixties. Not all of them were unhinged by their consummate need to meddle in others' lives. In Diane's case, the social worker not only accomplished a vital life-saving, possibly soul-saving, act but used the abominable journal to do it—no small feat, by any standard.

For a brief period of time, I saw the world through the social worker's eyes. I was one of a group of professional educators who had, through the journal of a young teenager, been compelled to spy into the inner workings of a household, no less than if we had descended on that home in trench coats and fedoras to hold a magnifying glass up to a private world. Though much necessary good emerged from it, I could not overcome the suspicion that we had all been acting out a melodramatic TV script, role-playing a soap opera in an overly long sensitivity workshop. That such was not the modus operandi of the dedicated teacher was cause for relief. When it was all over, I was content to return to the teaching world and leave such grim pursuits to that profession best suited to it.

Did I mention sensitivity workshops? Oh, good, I was hoping I would not forget.

The prohibitions of the Commandments fell like dominoes in those role-playing sensitivity workshops of the Sixties. The clear, unequivocal commands straight from the *Baltimore Catechism* were enough to keep sociologists in a whirl for years. Defusing the admonitions was just a matter of workshopping the words honor, respect, love, obey, help, in need. Get someone to role-play mom and dad and child. Don't let it get too serious, keep it light so as not to turn anybody off. And by all means, if there are any short-skirted nuns in the workshop get them to role-play the breaking of rules. You can count on them. It will all be so much fun you need never deal with the prohibitions of the Commandments.

I know a teacher, a grown man, who emerged from one such workshop with tears in his eyes, another who broke down sobbing in the bathroom, another whose marriage did not survive the length of time it took the workshop animator to get her findings presented in a paper to her college professor.

No one escaped the social worker's meddling. No one was spared these Jean Brodies in the prime of sociology's dominance of the professions. Mother, father, child, teacher, priest—all fell under the withering, all-knowing gaze of the nun with one evening course in social work. They left their influence on every profession related to the education of youth. Teachers, nurses, nuns, priests began ignoring the workings of the human soul, bringing all of their methodology to bear on the uninformed but rapidly forming child mind. With the family unit held firmly in the crosshairs, the sociologist allowed nothing foreign to hinder her line of vision, propelling her agenda with a pornographer's disregard for the dignity of the interior life or the mysteries of the faith.

Even so, somehow the foundations of our belief system remained intact within children themselves.

That evidence was brought home one Christmas season.

With a hundred others one December morning, I sat in the total darkness of a silent gymnasium. A door opened, revealing the silhouette of a figure standing as a jet-black cutout against the fluorescence of the hall lights beyond. The figure, in heavy boots, denim jeans, leather jacket, and motorcycle helmet, walked into the room, advancing deeper into the silence until reaching an antique trunk sitting center court, just barely outlined by the light reaching in from the hall. The figure looked down at the trunk, then removed the helmet, white hands on the black helmet visor.

The helmet removed, a teenage girl, Viola, shook her hair free. Then, kneeling, she opened the trunk. From within she drew out a black velvet robe, with long sleeves and a white, ermine-like collar. She drew it over her shoulders and inserted one arm into the arm of the robe. Her hand emerged as a white marble fist from the upstretched arm of the robe. Then slowly the fist opened and a beam of light shot across the room to pinpoint her hand. Iron Butterfly's "In-a-Gadda-Da-Vida" burst from the speakers and the play began, the nativity play—Viola becoming the Virgin as the black robe enveloped her. Then the birth of the Christ Child was enacted in the traditional manner as it had been in thousands of school pageants before. When it ended, the Wise Men moved out into the hall. Viola removed the robe. Donned the helmet once more. Walked back outside. The play ended with a motorcycle revving up and fading into the traffic.

The spell cast by that one child made a lie of the very best efforts of the professionals to demystify Christmas. The sense of wonder left by the traditional representation of Virgin and Child delivered by a girl in a circle of light in the center court of a school gymnasium confirmed for any who may have doubted that there were such things as transcendent realities, that grade school, where the imagination proposes no limits, was the perfect setting to unfold the wonderful story of God-made-Man.

Only with exposure to transcendence can we be fully human, for to be fully human is to appreciate with the heart, mind, and soul that beyond us and independent of us there is goodness, beauty, truth. That there is more than whatever goodness, beauty, and truth we find within ourselves.

Had the presentation of the Christmas story been told by a sociologist, the gym lights would have been left on to prevent any mystery the supernatural might be spinning in the dark. Audience participation would be encouraged, from hand-clapping to singing along, or the whole story would be told as a gymkhana event with bouncing balls and hula hoops to place it within the scope of social evolution, and to eradicate any aspect of the sacred that might linger.

In time, of course, all teachers were bound to meet results of watered-down morality head on. For me, the ability of the social worker to invade every aspect of community life will forever be associated with a wicker picnic basket.

In anticipation of an Armistice Day ceremony, students were asked to bring to rehearsal any national flag that they could find. The next day, a group of boys announced that they had fulfilled the request. But they would not show them to me there, they wanted to perform. We adjourned to the gymnasium where the group took to the stage around a wicker picnic basket.

The idea of drawing a seemingly endless stream of flags out of a basket, rhythmically to stirring music, had been borrowed from *Les Feux Follets*, a Montreal dance troupe who, using tartan rather than flags, had represented in dance how Irish and Scottish immigrants had flooded the globe.

The music began—a military tattoo march followed by "Thou

Hast Left Me Ever Jamie," to which the boys pulled out one, two, three, six, eight flags, all different shapes and sizes stapled end to end. Alas, one of the spectators, who had stepped late into the hall, turned out to be a city policeman investigating the theft of seven flags from atop the roofs of assorted businesses along Main Street. Unfortunately for the boys, the handsaw used to saw down the flagpole above the hardware store still lay in the bottom of the picnic basket.

This minor misdemeanor, which in any other age would have been resolved with detentions and restitution to the wronged merchants, ensured instead that for the next two years each of the boys, their families, their relatives, their doctors, and their priests were subjected to visits from, sessions with, counseling arranged by the social worker who attached herself with the grip of a deep-sea carbuncle, by dint of her status with the school board, upon the institution of the school, family, and the private lives of these students.

An abacus worked in the Orient could not compute the depth of their intrusion into family life. It was the worst form of exploitation, a sociological colonialism in which, for an entire age group, the family was looted, the culture mutilated, to give the sociologist something she wanted—indispensability. A decade before the invention of Trivial Pursuit, the social worker would turn family life into a board game where the child won only by staying one answer ahead of the parents.

Amidst the confusion of the Sixties, few certainties withstood the pressure of change. Anything set by law, anything fixed, would yield to the spirit of movement, to an evolutionary momentum promising change, change, change, be it mutilation of tradition or obliteration of custom. It made possible the torrent of secularism that was about to overwhelm the very laws by which Christian society had protected itself, from conception to the grave. People would be forgetting things of value at an awesome rate.

From amidst that torrent, one boy stands out, pure and perfect, illuminating the shadows into which authority and responsibility were being driven. He portrayed a soldier at an Armistice ceremony, standing on the jutting stage, boots, uniform, and rifle spray-painted gold, standing there motionless for the time it took each breathless child to approach and drop a blood-red poppy in thanksgiving at his feet. But his hair, face, and hands had needed spray-painting, too. The gold greasepaint never arrived, so the make-up girl sprayed gold hair spray into a mixture of flour and corn syrup and applied it.

Curtain time, there he stood, perfectly motionless, as spellbound children of the primary grades approached reverently and stared up at him, staring, staring, staring as the corn syrup and gold gilt ran from his hair, down his face, into his collar, down his arms and chest, down his trousers, over his socks and boots, to curdle in a little swirl of gold sweat around the poppies dropping there, lest we forget.

The confusion of the Sixties smothered the spirit of responsibility and changed society beyond recognition. The age called for complete emancipation from authority. Within the Catholic milieu, this meant a lessening of ecclesiastical authority. But it was not just a matter of no longer welcoming the priest in the school. It went all the way back to link up with Genesis, to the Creator's authority over creatures. That link would be disengaged and the creature uncoupled from the Creator as Evolutionists scorned Creationists into oblivion. We happened on our own, the age insisted. But even a child knows a sound created on a tambourine is not the result of the tambourine changing into an instrument that can strike itself. A creator of sound is needed.

The age called for the emancipation of the universal conscience with which the Church should ever be in agreement. The universal conscience, the existence of which can be proven by nothing outside the insistence of theologians haloed in fantasies of the Enlightenment, will exist in reality only when the Church should not only agree with the majority but lead the majority. The danger of this is quite clear to any child who, partaking in a history pageant, is asked why Pope Innocent III would bless if not instigate a movement so popular and at the same time so tragic as the Children's Crusade.

The age insisted on the emancipation of science in the name of advancement, with every experiment testing man and metal without fear of conflict with the Church. A trip through the child labor days of Dickensian London will leave any child grateful he is not the mere unprotected mechanism of science and progress.

The age demanded the emancipation of individual conscience, whose aspirations and inspirations must never be overridden by any authority, at any time. A brief visit to the attic of Anne Frank, as the Gestapo fulfilled their aspirations on the streets below, will make the child an instant connoisseur of that freedom.

The age demanded the emancipation of the state in such totality that it would never again be hindered by the force of religious sentiment. Walk your class through the basement of the dachau in Ekaterinberg where mother, father, and family of five were riddled with gunfire at the insistence of a godless state, let them watch the Czar, Czarina, Czarevitch and Grand Duchesses being carried out, and they will vote for God in the next election.

The age demanded the right of each individual to apply his own morality to every situation. Chateau Gaillard was the perfect situation to evaluate that. A coveted strategic fortress laid siege to by King Philip of France, it was held by the soldiers of John Softsword of England. To preserve food for the soldiers within, women and children were lowered over the walls to starve on the rocks of the river below, a clash of mini-moralities crying out for a higher moral law. Ask children if the keeper of that fortress was correct in following his own conscience.

The age demanded a reconciliation among all men through the workings of the human heart. But the touchy-feely era that resulted from workshops on the workings of the human heart chilled the heart of the child, who, in his purity, recoiled from suggestions of familiarity not born of family activity.

Against all of these pressures constantly bombarding the child with the message that it was his destiny to be free from of all restraints, rules, regulations, laws, who was holding the line? Who was mounting the defense? Who was sheltering the child, the family, the home? Was it the Church?

It is to the everlasting scandal of that and future ages that the answer is "No."

The spirit of the age demanded that the entire body of knowledge of the entire world be dealt with in language "more meaningful" to the child. Well, then, what language can be more meaningful than the words of Anne Frank summing up her diary with, "In spite of everything I still believe that people are really good at heart."[2]

That statement achieved in our time an effect it could not possibly have had in the year it was written. The diary was a time capsule meant to be opened in the Sixties. It drove sociologists crazy.

If there is one thing that will send the social worker shrieking into the snowbanks, it is a child with a positive outlook. To social workers, the entire human race is dysfunctional, waiting to be fixed. Confront them with a child who is not waiting for things to be fixed, who sees the positive side of a circumstance, and you have a fight to the death between the thinkable and the unthinkable.

In looking back, I can see now it was inevitable, given what I thought of sociology majors, thought-police, and revisionists, that my students should make the most of an opportunity to dramatize their true attitudes in "language more meaningful to the adult." It is also apparent, in looking back, that the "attitude" displayed should bring me into a head-on collision with Parent Zero.

FIVE

THE THING

EVERY TEACHER who has ever smelled chalk dust has encountered a parent against whom they will measure all other parents. On rare occasions, that parent will be an invisible aid in the classroom—their support and encouragement felt, consistent, positive—and firmly in control of the home end of the learning equation. Such a parent does not exhibit a compulsion to become a mini-teacher and will reject all pressure from sociologists to make her one.

All too often Parent Zero will be confrontational, watchful, mistrustful, riding shotgun on curriculum, discipline, and morals. As long as the ultimate aim is a better working relationship between teacher and student, teachers should count themselves lucky if they have one kind or the other. The parent who continually condescends to the teacher, as she would to any well-paid babysitter, is the parent who is of no value whatsoever and therefore dangerous.

Parent Zero was for me both the first type and the second. She entered the ring guns blazing over the matter of that thing which has been forever a cornerstone of the calendar year of educators, "the school play."

The whole fracas would not have come about if the staff had not fallen victim to a malaise common to staff rooms in the month of February. Teachers who have held unchallenged sway over their students for the six months since September suddenly, for no apparent reason, start being challenged by one another. People take sides; the staff room becomes a battlefield. Obsessive, vicious, vindictive, and totally personal war games are played out at the cost of intense mental, emotional, and spiritual anguish that lasts through the darkest days and weeks of winter. Then the season bleeds away. Someone opens the staff room window to catch the drip of a melting icicle in the palm and suddenly no one can remember what the battle was all about.

As a veteran of many Februaries spent lunching at my classroom piano to avoid the trenches, I have come to a conclusion that may have been obvious to you all along. In winter, people and teachers do not get enough fresh vegetables. During all those months of grey snow, dry skin, and grey skies, they do not get enough fiber. Yes, that's it. It's all about fiber.

In the case of February staff rooms, the wise principal knows that the only way to avoid war is to plan a science fair for right around Ash Wednesday so warring teachers can let off steam by literally exploding things at one another in the gymnasium. Watching students reinvent electricity or find 371 sources of alternate energy in a compost heap has a humbling effect on grown-ups.

My principal was not into science fairs. She chose instead to combat the bleak moods of February by "requesting," as a natural consequence of the impression made with the obedient soldier and a lot of corn syrup on Armistice Day, that I present a play.

Having interrupted my teaching career for a total of three years to pursue the life of an actor, I had no trouble agreeing that, compared to the science fair, the play was "the thing."

"The thing" that resulted in this instance, to my complete surprise, was about to talk back to the system that, as far as I could see, was inside out, upside down, and backwards.

It was, after all, the high noon of that era in education when universal standards were banished; students learned at their own rate and advanced in standing whether they had mastered the subject matter or not. The teacher was compelled to endure years of improvisation, deadening the senses to universal realities as education degenerated into state, provincial, regional, municipal, neighborhood experiments. Nuns caught up in this new way of doing things would soon impose it on the Church.

"The thing" was about to tap the mood of children caught in the midst of all of this.

The performance was the definitive role-playing-in-the-round-sensitivity-workshopping exercise so dear to the Sixties, the same theatrical device which, when placed in the hands of such people as priest/sociologists and theologians, would produce the mediocre claptrap and melodrama that has turned the once exquisite Immemorial Mass into a Punch and Judy show.

It consisted of short vignettes strung together to reenact moments in history when injustices had been inflicted on children by the adult priorities of the age. It was called *Children of Winter*, and it was basically your average guerrilla theater free-for-all played out against a recorded background soundtrack. What no one anticipated or understood then was the effect produced on an adult audience by children who took like ducks to water to the tradition and discipline of theater, tradition and discipline no longer being offered anywhere else.

It was performed on February 24 in the small gym for the assembled school. A repeat performance that night was to be for parents. The reaction of the daytime assembly ensured that come seven o'clock the gymnasium held standing-room-only, wall-to-wall parents. I would learn later that Parent Zero had come to the performance expecting to see, in reference to the title of the piece, children in gaily colored snowsuits having the equivalent of a teddy bear's picnic on the tiny stage. She did not see that.

The gym went black. A glowering, green-tinted semi-gloom revealed the stage hung with shredded meat-packers' cheesecloth. To the anthem of the Sixties, "Also Spake Zarathustra," two dozen young actors in black enacted the six days of Creation, a tambourine marking the coming and going of God during those days of labor. Upon the creation of Adam, a mature senior student, from a dark corner of the gym, sang in a deep, bluesy voice, "Where did I come from?"

The scene dissolved into a mass of bodies then configured a mill wheel, which they pushed and turned in slavery to some unidentified directive. Through the audience streams of crusaders, in white body scapulars and red crosses, carried aloft on his *sedia gestatoria* the pope, who blessed the Children's Crusade. Over the top and down the back of an upright piano anchored on the lip of the stage, an avalanche of children were seen being lowered screaming to the rocks on the river below Chateau Gaillard, the "river" being a long trolley that drew them, weeping and wailing, out of the gym as they pleaded with the audience for succor.

Again they emerged in a pocket of semi-light, this time the slums of industrial London, where they were born, married, and died near machines they serviced. In response to a voice calling out "Olga, Maria, Tatiana, Anastasia," actors rose from the melee and, as the children of the Czar and Czarina, descended the steps into the basement of the dachau in Ekaterinberg where they were shot. They were carried out, limp and silent, through the audience as the girl in the corner sang "Where do I go?"

Woven in among the darkness, flashing lights, pockets of illumination, a tempestuous soundtrack, and the keening of the singer was the narration of the unending flow of vignettes by a young "Anne Frank." As the scenes unfolded, she was pinpointed in an attic of light above the stage. As it drew to an end, she read aloud from her diary, "In spite of everything, I still believe that people are really good at heart." Then she left the attic and exited under the raised arms of Hitler Youth, who saluted her and history itself with the chant "Ahmen ... Ahmen ... Ahmen ..." Then the lights came on. The children were gone. A tape recorder, some cheesecloth, and a piano were the only evidence that anything had transpired. It had lasted twenty-eight minutes.

Ever wonder what it would be like to stand in a gymnasium jammed with silent, expressionless parents, as their eyes search the room, looking for you? Ever see your entire career pass before your eyes as two hundred parents looked on?

Few teachers have developed solid careers without at least once hitting an "Uh-oh!" February 24 was for me "The Big Uh-oh!" It was that nightmare come true—you know, the one where you wake up in church in your underwear!

There was applause. It did last for a long time. The kind of applause you hear at a movie when "The End" finds you drained and stupefied in your seat.

The mood was not hostile. It was something else. It was as if two hundred people had suddenly woken up to the fact that the prom had ended twenty years ago. A whole new generation walked the earth. And it had a point of view. But whose point of view was it?

Next morning, Parent Zero withdrew her children from school. For fourteen consecutive days, letters to the editor filled the city paper with reactions to the event. Some advocated running the teacher out of town on a rail, others to giving him the keys to the city. "Teaching hatred. Anti-parent. Dangerous," ran the letters. Then the editor assigned a staff writer to go see a repeat of the play, a command performance that the journalist reviewed as "not only good theater but great education." I shudder to think what the occasion would have generated in later years when teachers would fall like ten pins for exhibiting any spark, initiative, experimentation. But there was still credibility left to the teacher's role in 1969.

The school board requested another showing for concerned or merely interested parents, and board reps sat in on it. Following that, schools were closed one afternoon for a fourth showing so city teachers, under pain of losing a day's pay, could come and see it for themselves. A national magazine featured it coast to coast. The CBC documented it for "The New Majority" series.

All in all, I would say the school board handled it very well. There was none of the ridicule directed at parents that would mark confrontations in later decades. The school board, I would learn, took its cue from the demeanor of the students when the lights came on. What they could see then was that the explosion of creative energy that had traumatized the community was a controlled one. These were not children pulled out of shape by a mindless, undirected need to act out their hostility. The actors were just normal children with one telling difference: they had embraced wholeheartedly the rigorous discipline common to theater and reveled in the tradition that sets theater apart from rock performances, athletic competitions, or, yes, science fairs.

The school board gave its support to a two-year continuation of the experiment, funding part of the rent on an empty Mormon church to be used as a school theater center.

But the entire event had touched a nerve among parents. Just what was being taught in matters of religion and history? The fears resulted in the perception that the child knew something the parent did not; that the child was being taught what the parents were never taught and did not approve of; that the child was being set against his parents by what he was taught. That *Children of Winter* was a brazen way of saying to the parent, "See?!"

This suspicion may have been magnified out of all proportion by one small oversight. A cynicism was read into the piece that was not intended when, to the glee of a television cameraman, it was discovered that the "pope" floating in the *sedia gestatoria* over the heads of the audience was chewing gum.

Then, as now, I sympathized with those parents and educators who were rocketed out of their apathy by the *Children of Winter* affair. An entire generation of parents was just beginning to realize that the sacred heritage passed on to them from their parents was not only not being passed on to their own children in the schools, it was very often being contradicted. In that very bastion of religious upbringing, the Catholic school system, so hard-won in tax battles directed by good Catholic bishops, community by community across North America, the most pristine articles of the Faith were no longer being coveted and taught as the sacred patrimony of Catholic children.

Teachers, especially those nuns and clergy still serving in the field of education, were showing a definite lack of concern for the mysteries of the Faith. The sacraments were being treated as little more than eloquent formulas which might, under the right circumstances, stir the soul and perhaps even carry it away. But so could "Desiderata." The prophecies of the Old Testament and the miracles of the New were being treated as dramatic but "poetical imaginings." So why not read Khalil Gibran at morning prayers? The sacred writings of every religion were being spoken of as valid experiences of an "extra-ordinary nature." So why not incorporate quotes from the Koran into calligraphy lessons? All religions were now considered equal in value from the point of view of salvation. So why not have three Australian bushmen carrying the great serpent of their Dreamtime to a newborn baby in the Outback on a card that reads "Season's Greetings"?

Those seemingly innocent signs spinning out from the Sixties' counter-culture were causes of alarm gone unnoticed by parents for too long. By the time parents began suspecting that the immutable truths of their faith were being assimilated to the Sixties, the amateurish church of pop-Christianity was accepting Jesus Christ Superstar as a neurotic, long-haired, alienated loser with a heart of gold institutionalized on Broadway and eight-track stereo. Christ's work in founding the Church was just a matter of someone taking himself very seriously. Uptight but relative. As for His instituting the sacraments—heavy, man. And besides, the Christ of Faith was not the Christ of history. The needs of the faithful had made Christ out to be something not proven by history.

With respect to the imagination, the Sixties did not excel at all. In terms of the possible advancement of the human mind, heart, soul, the Sixties were not an accomplished period at all. In spite of the color, noise, movement, the Sixties were monotonous.

The appearance of a laid-back, godless naturalism filling scribblers begged the questions, "Who is holding the line for Catholic doctrine? If no one is defending Catholic doctrine, what will become of it? If no one is teaching Catholic doctrine, what are they teaching?"

The sensation caused by *Children of Winter* reflects perfectly the moment reenacted in communities throughout North America toward the end of 1969 by parents electrified into realizing that the Catholic schools were not Catholic any more. Catholic parents, in small numbers at first, suddenly looked at their grade six or seven children and realized they knew next to nothing about the Incarnate God who had destined for them the Kingdom of Heaven.

"Ecology" was "the new road to Salvation." "God" had been "reduced to the role of a careful farmer."[1] Church was just mediocre entertainment. The very mention of the interior life drew dull, dead stares. The whole of the supernatural had been made subject to the peace-beads philosophy and bell-bottom theology of the age. But added to all that was an attitude frighteningly close to being institutionalized in the sociology department of school boards—that the very concept of the "family" had been the subject of "revision." It was no longer the prime ingredient of community life. A new axis had been formed threading the child to the specialist, to the never-never-land of counselors and care workers out there somewhere beyond the brutal confines of home, where he was misunderstood, unfulfilled, and not spoken to "in language meaningful to the child." The "family" had a new identity. It was something that served the child or abused the child. With the family subverted, the child was cut off from submission to laws, authority, government. With Church authority belittled, now the child was "liberated" from "sin." And grace.

Now that the supernatural had been demythologized and all religions made equal, the prohibitions of the Fourth Commandment were not taught. If tradition itself was merely an overrated device for ensuring status quo, then it could be discarded as oppressive; it is not then a matter of moral obligation to obey parents and lawful authorities. In the processes of revising society itself, we shall uncover the true meaning of lawful authority. Then, the morning after we will reinvent the universe.

The Catholic mother, who, somewhere near the back door of 1969, grabbed her coat, skipped down icy porch steps, and hurried to the school to demand of Sister how these ideas could possibly have slipped past the directors of religious education, was in for an awful shock.

SIX

HATPINS AND HERESY

THE CATHOLIC MOTHER reaching for her coat is a veritable logo of separate school education in the Sixties. You can see her now as she ties a scarf over her hair, dodging traffic, entering the schoolyard with nerves in a knot, butterflies rattling rosaries in her innermost self, dreading but daring to ask, "What is going on?" She fears, with a fear unlike any she has ever felt, what she will hear as an answer.

To even the simplest questions, it seemed, the voices in the religious education department were forever changing their answers. Everyone talked about feelings, about getting in touch with them, as if truth had some capacity to mutate in order to satisfy certain momentary needs or emotions of any and every individual.

"Do your own thing" meant "do your own dogma." It, dogma, according to the former priest and his wife, the former nun, who were now the directors of religious education at the school board, was ever-changing anyway, evolving. The principal, Sister herself, had been towing the same line ever since she started to wear short skirts, as if evolution was so inescapable it even determined hemlines.

Yes, she would purr into the phone, there was movement in the Church, the Holy Spirit was at work. Sure, it might be painful to those who grew up in the old *Baltimore* days and dealt with God as something "up there," but the sign of the Holy Spirit at work was change, movement.

The fascist, like the pussycat, disarms our resistance by purring.

Catholics accepting that the pope is the latest vicar of Christ in a long line that leads all the way back to Peter think of Peter as the first pope. This means the Catholic must accept that on the very day the Church was founded, in the face of the very first crisis, the savage act that caused the life-giving sacraments to issue from the side of Christ, the first pope ran away. In fact, all the men ran away—except one. Eyewitness testimony tells us that the eyes witnessing the birth of the Church on that ugly hillock outside the west gate of Jerusalem were women's eyes. All we know of that history-shaking event we know from those women and that one man. All that was passed on to the early believers in that new age of redemption, we know from those terrified, traumatized, grief-stricken women and one man. Throughout the whole two thousand years of Church history, it has ever been so. As surely as every child of the Church for two thousand years—paupers, princes, and popes—came to the Church from the body of a woman, the belief in the man who died on the cross that day and rose from the dead came through women. It has ever been so. "Faith always has and always will come through the mother." "Nothing can replace the education given by a mother," wrote Maistre.[1]

Christianity and western civilization came from a mother's womb, from the greatest lawmaker to the most avid law-breaker. The Church is not called "She" for want of a better word. And we know what She believes because the only man at the foot of the Cross was a writer.

The panting, disheveled, and angry mother entering the school foyer, sizing up the distance to the principal's office, worried that she'll not go through with it, afraid she'll lose courage and go back home without demanding answers, has the clay of Calvary on her heels, the scent of the murdered God in her nostrils. What she sees before her in that school corridor is the Darkness at Midday.

It could only strengthen that mother to recall that every pope to sit in the Chair of Peter had to pass through a woman's womb to reach it.

The Catholic mother has ever been the guardian of authentic Catholic education. In 1916, the French school, Ecole Guigues, in Ottawa, Canada, was caught in the middle of a political controversy having to do with the long, never-ending squabbles over language and religion in education. The French fought to have their children taught in French and the Catholic faith taught in the tongue of "the oldest daughter of the Church." In a crisis of changing regulations deliberately generated by an anti-French, anti-Catholic lobby, the Ecole Guigues faced the prospect of having its status and curriculum taken out of the hands of the teachers and parents. A clash of ideologies boiled down to a clash of authority when, on January 5, 1916, the authorities came to take possession of the school. The police, expecting trouble, ringed the school. They had heard there was to be a demonstration. It was not long in appearing. Remember now, this was Ottawa, Canada, a city proven statistically to be colder than Moscow in winter.

What the policemen saw coming down the street was a mob of nineteen mothers, shoulder to shoulder, dressed in the long skirts of the day and enormous broad-brimmed hats echoing the *belle epoque*. The mothers advanced through the snow and slush, step by determined step. The police linked arms. When the mothers were a mere fifteen paces away, without losing a beat, they reached up, on a given signal, and withdrew from their hats those long, lethal hatpins of the day. On another signal, still moving forward, they held their poinards like bayonets in front of them. And they charged. The stupefied police broke ranks (one policeman had five puncture wounds in his belly). The mothers broke through the lines, stormed the stairs, seized the school, and barricaded the doors behind them.

The mothers literally held the authorities at bay for days while neighbors threw food in through the window, until the new regulations were overturned and the school, language and curriculum were in their hands once more. They are known in Canadian history as "the Hatpin Mothers." They are also known, quite properly, as "the Guardians."

But all the hatpins in the world could not have helped the mother who woke up in 1969 to the reality of the ideology that had usurped the teaching authority in Roman Catholic separate schools. The primary Catholic truths—the Divinity of Christ and His mission as Messiah—were no longer being taught.

To open a window on that dangerous time, it is necessary to rely on the vision of its writers. The *Canadian Layman*, a Catholic journal that began publishing in the early Seventies to alert parents to the threat within the schools, presented in its pages a call to arms by informed Catholics and professional educators, a broad spectrum of some of the best Catholic minds of the era, who had as their common denominator their belief in the once trustworthy, reliable, and orthodox teaching of the separate school system. Their names for the two decades following Vatican II have been high on the roll call of that resistance movement of orthodox, conservative Catholics which by 1992, no longer just an underground movement, began numbering bishops and cardinals among its number: Sean O'Reilly, William de Marois, James Likoudis, William Marra, Monsignor Eugene Kevane, Francis J. Conklin, James Daly, and a remarkable writer from Hamilton, Canada, Sister Mary Alexander. To see, feel, and taste the struggle to keep Catholic schools Catholic in that era, one can do no better than to let them speak for themselves.

The reality about to be confronted by the Catholic mother rapping her knuckles on the principal's door in 1969 was admitted by Robert Hoyt of the less than conservative *National Catholic Reporter*. Writing for that publication in 1970, Hoyt stated, "It is simply true that the religion texts of today are vastly different ... progressivist views dominate the most Catholic religious and theological training...."

Those religion texts included the *Dutch Catechism*. In 1967, having been reviewed by concerned cardinals, it was found to have omitted or ignored eight vital areas of Christian doctrine. The U.S. catechism, *Christ Within Us*, passed three million copies in distribution only to have Church approval withdrawn after fifteen years of exposure to Catholic students.[2]

"... In consequence," continued Hoyt, "the Catholicism of tomorrow will be something new on earth ..."

Something new on earth? What? How?

"... And all this has been accomplished ... by ways and means that eluded standard ecclesiastical safeguards...."[3]

How could they possibly elude "standard ecclesiastical safeguards"?

William de Marois, in a retrospective of the era written in 1975, explained that the innovators "seem to have successfully entrenched themselves in our ecclesiastical structures, particularly in the educational and catechetical fields...."[4]

The Catholic parent, suddenly realizing "something new on earth" was already in existence, must have shuddered at taking into her hands the driver's manual for this "something new."

The new course for religious education in Canada was called *Come to the Father.*

To the complacent Catholic who had been looking the other way for the last five years, *Come to the Father* was to be a rude awakening.

Sister Mary Alexander did not buffer the shock. In a searing analysis of *Come to the Father,* she pierced the fog and illuminated the stark details of the teachers' guide.

"Authors of the *Come to the Father* series are insistent the Divinity of Christ be hidden in grade one! Creation and Christmas, miracles and angels and explicit references to the Divinity of Christ are all taboo in grades one and two." The parent is warned "not to mention the name of God too quickly or too often at moments when you and your child are filled with wonder at something."[5]

Filled with wonder? Without God? What kind of family life did the pathetic designer of this manual experience?

Grace was eliminated. Original sin discarded. The supernatural abolished.

How did this thing get printed?

The explanation can be found in the words of Robert Hoyt.

"Liberal theologians dominate the public prints, the Catechetical training centers, the publishing houses, the professional associations, much of the Catholic bureaucracy; they praise each other's books, award each other contracts, jobs, awards and perquisites."[6]

But how did this ... thing get into the schools? Who could allow young, forming minds to be exposed to such anti-faith information?

Come to the Father was adopted by the bishops for use in Catholic schools in 1966. By 1970, the Catholic child had been exposed for four years to a religious education program that was indeed "something new on earth."

Using a system of evaluation compiled by the Papal Commission of Cardinals, the *Come to the Father* series scored a total of fifteen points out of a possible five hundred awarded for doctrinal content. The result was appalling. The *Come to the Father* catechism was only three percent Catholic!

Imagine the terror in the heart of the Catholic mother on her knees in the hatless Church of the post-Conciliar age without as much as a hatpin to prick the disbelief that engulfed her. She knew now what the "something new on earth" was. You can fool some of the people some of the time, but the Catholic mother, who if she had only one wish would wish that her children live and die in the Faith, has instincts made keen by the wisdom of all those saints her gender has given the Church and she can smell the abyss even in the dark. Even in the dark, she had sensed something was not right in the souls of her children since around the time she stopped wearing hats to Mass.

Is it not odd how mothers, preoccupied by the mundane and menial chores of motherhood, are so quick to see the big picture once danger compels them into focus? The big picture was detailed with alarming clarity in the March-April *Faith* magazine editorial of 1974.

"We have now in the Church, the presence of open and cynical heresy, and it does not matter from which quarter it comes, it is our obligation to rally authentic Catholics to refuse and resist it, and that without the slightest fear or respect of any person whatsoever,"[7] wrote William de Marois.

To the Catholic mother, the emerging faithless, graceless monolith aimed at overwhelming her offspring with a new ideology, a new religion of self, had as its reason for emerging from the shadows of academe nothing less than the devouring of her children. Moloch was back. They were decorating the tophet. But how? Who let him in? Who lowered the drawbridge? Where had they parked the Trojan Horse?

PART TWO

BRICK ROADS

THE SEVENTIES

"Up to now, what aspect a life without God a world without faith would assume was known only in theory."

—Cardinal Joseph Ratzinger
The Ratzinger Report

ONE

HANDMAIDS OF THE REVOLUTION

THE IDEA that an ideological movement could set out to shape a new age by capturing the minds of youth has fueled revolutionaries for as long as there have been children. It is one of the fundamentals of the socialist and fascist state alike.

Pius XI recognized it as one of Mussolini's prime directives. With the full power of his office and force of his personality, he resisted it. To Nicola Commine, Rumanian minister to the Holy See, he pinpointed the conflict precisely.

"The rights and prerogatives of which I am the depository are of a divine nature. They have been entrusted to me as pope, and I cannot depart from them in any way. The essential problem in my disagreement with Mussolini concerns, primarily, the education of youth. On such a question no compromise is possible. I have been threatened with reprisals and wrecking. I am ready for anything. I would even withdraw to a monastery if I am forced. But I will never abandon what I believe to be my mission. Never! Never! Never!"[1]

But in the Sixties, someone, somewhere, abandoned that mission, the mission to teach the Divinity of Christ and His mission as Messiah.

Who?

"It is impossible to determine," writes James Hitchcock, "how the decision was made to teach this new kind of Catechism [*Come to the Father*, in Canada, and *Christ Among Us*, in the United

States]. Clearly it was not made by the bishops. Even more clearly it was not made by popular consensus, since many laymen have also shown themselves quite disturbed over Catechetical developments."[2]

In an open letter to bishops in 1973, Sister Mary Alexander wrote that they "relied upon the professional expertise of those Catechetical directors, consultants and specialists whom you [the bishops] and the Catholic taxpayers have rewarded so munificently for their labours."[3]

William de Marois underlined how the Catholic taxpayer was sidelined: "The bishops simply 'did not have the time' to study the materials or did not have a diocesan director who was capable of doing it. This means they have approved the Catechism in a general way without being aware of the content."[4]

Can there be any more just demand on a bishop's time than that of ensuring that Catholic children are taught the Divinity of Christ and His mission as Messiah? Who would contrive to distract a bishop from this most fundamental responsibility?

In discussing the origin of the new catechism, James Hitchcock alludes to the answer: "It [the decision to write a new Catechism] seems to have originated from a kind of underground consensus of a limited number of largely anonymous individuals in theology schools, publishing houses and classrooms, who decided among themselves that a new catechetics was needed and what kind."[5]

"A certain element [of this middle bureaucracy] has exhibited signs of irresponsibility," Sister Mary Alexander wrote, "or of wilfulness, or of what could be interpreted as contempt for ecclesiastical authority and specifically the authority of the bishops."[6]

"Few of these persons," Hitchcock stated, "are accountable to the community of believers, and few have received any kind of mandate from that community."[7]

"And yet," explained Alexander, "these shadowy figures have a stranglehold on Catholic religious instruction."[8]

Who comprised this middle bureaucracy? Who were these anonymous, totally unaccountable individuals in theology schools who decided a new catechesis was needed and what kind? Who could have such contempt for ecclesial authority, and specifically the authority of bishops? The answer requires a little looking back.

The peace, love, and flower-power spectacle of the Sixties was very much an off-Broadway show that ultimately took uptown by storm.

It was mirrored with sparkling clarity within the Church, but remained unnoticed behind the clouds of satisfaction rising from sparks ignited in the world-wide do-your-own-thing laboratory that the Sixties became.

Individualistic theologies sauntered out of schools of learning and streamed toward the nearest open spaces, where the shadows of towering authoritarian, dogmatic structures could not block the Aquarian sun. There, out in the open, the liberated-thought alchemists acknowledged one another, saw their strength, and, as children are wont to do at summer camp, began sharing knowledge of the weaknesses of their authority figures back home. What they discovered decided them on a simple consensus—it was within their power to dismantle the towers of authority so that never again could shadows be cast on their playtime.

The list of names of theologians, nuns, priests who lost their innocence in that supposedly innocent decade now comprises the membership of those dissenting organizations and associations that are in full and complete control of the bureaucracy in North America of a Church barely thirty years old that has replaced the once-mighty Church of Rome. Veterans of guerrilla war waged against the Magisterium during and after Vatican II, they continually heap honor on themselves as former Che Guevaras who challenged the ancient regime and leveled it.

The dissenters who stormed Rome in the Sixties showed little imagination in clearing the Rock. With breathtaking savvy, they simply copied what had proven so effective in centuries past. Such "King of the Castle" games have victimized the innocent for as long as there have been castles with keeps. In the year 1212, there was Chateau Gaillard. In our own time, the Paris-educated rulers of the Khmer Rouge, having taken Phnom Penh, drove two million urbanites into the countryside. To eradicate all memory of the culture it was replacing, teachers, doctors, scientists were put to the sword, the gun, the garotte. Anyone who could recall anything of Cambodia before the fall was hounded into the dust.

Having plotted their revolution, our dissenting theologians stormed the fort, lowered the certitude of dogma over the walls to the mercy of the tides in the world below, and raised the scarlet flag above the ruins. Anyone who harbored even the slightest preference for the certainties so long held was hounded from credibility, maneuvered on a long march, and driven into the desert.

For two decades now, they have been in complete and total control of the agenda played out within. Driven from the citadel, the faithful, from the desert, look with longing on The Rock.

But the entire rebellion against the Kingdom would have fallen short of revolution if the theologians inking the presses had not been relieved of the mundane, banal legwork of revolution so eagerly assumed by the liberated religious, enticed by the rhetoric of revolution from their psalters and breviaries.

The leaders of the feminist movement long ago stated that their ultimate success would be the achievement of the reign of secular humanism. So much for any possible link between the feminist movement and the reign of Christian humanism that is John Paul II's battle standard. Yet, this clash of starkly opposed ideologies was apparently too subtle to be distinguished by the superiors of religious houses in North America. There, the feminists' success in gaining mastery over the rudderless age was evident from the beginning: the abandonment of religious habits, the introduction of individual stipends that severed the dependency on the mother house, the welcoming into convents of, not the confessors who had shaped saints in the silent confessionals of centuries past, but self-styled experts introducing Zen, Yoga, TM, and sensitivity workshops.[9] Are they doing yoga in your sanctuary yet? How about Tai Chi? They will.

No more determined force has faced the Church in two thousand years of hope and heresy than that army of pawns comprised of the liberated sisterhood, who unleashed two decades of violence against anything dogmatic, hierarchial, and sacramental.

Here the movement activated a missile lying dormant in one human factor—sexuality. To activate the rebel religious, the movement had sold them a bill of goods aimed at generating in them the anger of the unjustified victim: non-sexuality was equated to deprivation. Abuse. The result was to prove that hell indeed hath no fury like the suitor scorned. The "liberated" religious, in a holocaust of doctrine and dogma, set out to revise the very Word of God. They seemed programmed to dismantle the very nature of the Kingship of Christ as detailed by Pius XI in 1925's *Quas Primas*. The wounds on the hierarchial, dogmatic, and sacramental Church caused by that particular projectile were inflicted before anyone could comprehend what had launched it.

If Isaias testified that the child "born to us" would be called Wonderful, Counselor, God the Mighty,[10] then Isaias would have to be a prime target of revision. The attacks on the Infancy Narratives aimed at portraying the birth of the Christ child as merely the birth of another child in schools and church basements by so-called experts brought there by the liberated sisterhood stunned the laity, not only by the virulence of their insidious reinterpretations of the Gospels but because no bishop stood up to oppose them, no bishop stood up and put a stop to it. What, one might ask, was the bishop doing at the time? Was he out of town on business? At a tribute dinner for some other bishops? Giving notes to the biographer contracted to write the bishop's memoirs when retirement was achieved? What was the bishop waiting for?

Jeremiah foretold the "just seed would rest upon the son of David," that he should be "wise and shall execute judgment and justice in this earth."[11] Laughing at papal infallibility would, by a reverse process, undermine authority, so dissent, always dissent, became the rule. The Call to Action petition, published in the *New York Times* in 1974, advertised their dissent for all the world to see. Where were the bishops the day that issue hit the street? At Yankee Stadium throwing the first ball? At a tribute luncheon for some other bishop? What were the bishops waiting for?

If Daniel announced the Kingdom that the God of Heaven found would "never be destroyed" and would "stand forever,"[12] then the modern sisterhood would spend endless energy marketing the theologian's revision of the meaning of the words "never" and "forever." In a raucous chorus of "I will not serve," they proposed that phrases like "eternal life" were not only meaningless but harmful to the individual's self-image and the sense of mastery he must have over his own choices.

If Daniel said, "His power is everlasting power that shall not be taken away and his kingdom shall not be destroyed,"[13] it was absolutely necessary for the sisterhood to explain that, after all this brouhaha with Old and New Testaments and what not, God and Christ were simply names for a cosmic reality, that the universe is power, and that, no, it will not be destroyed for it is too big to be subject to outside forces and too well-ordered by its own consciousness in matter to self-destruct, but that it might, in time, eons of eons of it, simply wear down. God's power became a cosmic reality, a dynamic of the sun and the moon and the stars; one had only to look to see the signs in them saying just that. Rocks and pebbles and grains of sand had not only consciences but spirits. All creation was of itself and by itself and whooppee for all of that!

If Zachary prophesied that Jesus would enter Jerusalem as the merciful king, and the prophecy was fulfilled and witnessed and recorded by the evangelists themselves, who saw the Son of Man riding into Jerusalem on an ass as "the just and savior,"[14] then the sisterhood would get busy right away workshopping with people on how Jesus was really unaware of who He was until the moment of baptism, or unaware at least of who He came to think He was. That He was misguided, naive.

If, after His so-called Resurrection, it was imagined by the Apostles that Jesus had mandated them to baptize all nations, then it was important to coax priests into putting baptism off for five or six months after birth—wait until there grew a goodly number of babies on hand to make the ritual worthwhile so that people could realize that baptism was not that important, that it was a social thing and that it was all right to risk the baby's soul for six or even seven months. That nothing bad would happen if they failed to get the baby baptized. That it was just a ritual after all and served the rather unhappy purpose of separating us from other people who did not believe in Christ but rather in Buddha or followed Muhammad. It was just another obstruction to universal brotherhood.

If Jesus in his last discourse spoke of the rewards and punishments that will be the eternal lot of the just and the damned, it was because He was simply drawing imagery for his talk from the nearby Valley of Gehon where the garbage of Jerusalem burned day and night. There is no such thing as the flame that will not die; it is just a metaphor for backing the wrong horse. In the end, hell would be empty and everyone would go to heaven whether they thought it boring or not because we are all destined to be one.[15]

If the Council of Nicea defined and proposed for Catholic belief the dogma of the Consubstantiality of the Only-begotten with the Father, and added to the Creed the words "of whose kingdom there shall be no end,"[16] thereby affirming the kingly dignity of Christ, then it was only because the Council was held in the age of kings and empires. What we needed, according to the liberated religious and the conquering theologians, was a new Creed.

What we needed was to point out to people that kings exist only in England and a deck of cards.

In the face of all this, which has been continual for the last two and a half decades, we might as well have asked, "What were the bishops waiting for?"

Were they unaware that such things were going on? Away in Rome on business? For thirty years? What did they say when they were told? Did they mouth the ultimate buffoonery of, "I did not dare to dream that such a thing was possible?" Or were they at home surrounded by secretaries planning their own retirement dinners?

What were the bishops waiting for?

One characteristic of the usurper's strategy was that it always portrayed itself as creative, positive, and forward-looking.

A prime conceit of the movement was its conviction that it had the means to cause the Church to adapt to the intellectual, moral, and social needs of today. But this necessitated sidestepping the *sensus fidei* of the Church that has proven again and again the wisdom of not marrying itself to the spirit of the age.

To perform this subtle footwork, they employed the time-worn tactic of distracting the Catholic from what the spirit of the age actually demanded by insisting on the necessity of returning the Church to the simple form it possessed in antiquity.

With the entire human energy of the Church directed to look for ways to capture the seed of Christian worship as practiced in antiquity, the movement, at the same time, enlivened a manifesto not antique at all but one itemized as recently as 1861.

It might be said that the very constitution of the movement can be found in Pius IX's *Syllabus of Errors*, that pope's cataloguing of heretical beliefs: proposition 7—the prophecies and miracles of Holy Scripture are poetical imagining; propositions 16 to 18—all religions are equal in value from the point of view of salvation; proposition 55—complete separation of Church and state; proposition 76—that "the Roman Pontiff can and ought to conform with contemporary progress, liberalism and civilization."[17]

It was what Leo XIII called "Americanism" and what Pius X called "Modernism." The three errors of Modernism would be the very pavement on which the mosaic of *Come to the Father* and *Christ Among Us* (the new catechism for the United States) was blocked out: "Naturalism" would pervade the texts—a subtle emphasis highlighting natural laws and natural order existing on their own, independent of any outside cause, mainly God; "Rationalism" would determine the learning process, the only valid knowledge being that reached through the natural reason of man; "Liberalism" would cause to be excluded the acceptance of any authority above one's own, especially God.

All teachings of the Church would be revised in light of this earthly trinity.

William de Marois identified as one of the "more notorious leaders of this revisionary program"[18] the Reverend Gregory Baum, who, writing in *Faith and Doctrine: A Contemporary View, 1969*, stated quite matter-of-factly that what was called for was "the reinterpretation of the entire teaching of the Church in the light of the new focus."[19]

Whose new focus? Gregory Baum's, of course.

Baum epitomizes the "theological expert," the "reactionary proto-schismatic,"[20] entrenched in the ecclesial structure in the educational and catechetical field, dominating the public prints, the catechetical training centers, the publishing houses. For almost twenty-five years the Paulist Press has published the *Ecumenist,* devoted exclusively to printing the thoughts and plots of Baum. A convert from Judaism, describing himself as having descended from a long line of atheists, once an Augustinian priest, now an ex-priest married to an ex-nun, Baum has had his dreams and schemes in close proximity to the world of education and catechetics throughout his days as adviser to Archbishop Polcock of Toronto (for whom he was a *periti* at the Second Vatican Council), as teacher of theology at the University of Toronto, and as the writer of twenty-four books, all aimed at the "reinterpretation of the entire teaching of the Church in the light of the new focus."[21] His part in orchestrating the Canadian bishops' dissent from *Humanae Vitae* at the Winnipeg Conference of 1968 and his freedom to do so will forever cast the shadow of scandal over the bishops who "did not have the time" to read what he successfully maneuvered them into signing. The recent demise of the *Ecumenist* because of hard financial times will be little comfort to those Catholics who are left to clean up the mess Baum made in the offices of the hierarchy of the Church in North America.

When the bishops in North America—who looked the other way while these out-of-control, old, hippie "experts" and their "Gimmee-an-A" pompom theology looted Catholic doctrine and dogma—will have gone to their frightening judgment, left behind for the children of the next decades will be the wasteland of the Faith their negligence brought into being.

The list of names identified as the "shadowy figures" who successfully piloted their revisionist beliefs under the guise of Catechetics onto the desktops of Catholic primary, secondary, and post-secondary schools is a veritable litany of renegade clergy who, during and after Vatican II, acted as if ecclesial authority were a joke. "Former nun" and "former priest" again and again appear in the media blurbs used to introduce them to the talk shows or newspaper columns where Church-bashing is a favored time-consumer.

The renegade religious left empty convents and truncated vocations in their wake by adhering in the fullest to that pivotal betrayal of *Humanae Vitae*. In 1968, Pope Paul's encyclical on conjugal chastity was the target of dissenting theologians at a bishops' conference in Winnipeg, Manitoba. The critical revision of the meaning of *Humanae Vitae* was worded to propose that whoever was unable to "pursue a line of conduct in keeping with given directives" could "be safely assured that whoever honestly chooses that course which seems right to him does so in good conscience."[22]

Bishops who attached their signatures to the *Winnipeg Statement* drawn up by such "experts" mildly complained that "the episcopal gathering was called upon to approve the virtually unrevised document" in a "hurried-up procedure."[23]

The Catholic mother observing her children doing homework on the very night of her rude awakening might very well have wondered what degree of negligent behavior would seduce a bishop into being railroaded by a "hurried-up procedure" when the very soul of a child was at stake.

On that and the seemingly endless sleepless nights to follow, as the determination grew to combat the theft of her child's very chance for eternal life, the Catholic mother would have been mercifully fortified by these words of William de Marois:

> Parents are and must be the first teachers of the faith to their children....We must defend our historic patrimony of the traditional Christian faith....We must see to it our children are steeped in the heroic and prophetic tradition of the Saints, both those of the past and those of the present....If we are not prepared to man the barricades in defense of the Church and our children, even against disobedient bishops, if need be, then we are merely taking up space in the Bark of Peter....It is our common responsibility for the preservation and propagation of the faith—not just bishops and theologians.[24]

But, oh, the damage that had already been done by all those unveiled, unzippered dissenters!

TWO

HAVE-A-NICE-DAY THEOLOGY

THE VERY EXISTENCE in a Catholic classroom of a religious education manual that did not teach the Divinity of Christ and His mission as Messiah lost forever for the bishops the confidence of the parent in their authority and integrity. That we still had bishops at all by the time the Seventies were under way testifies to the difficulty alarmed Catholics encountered in their efforts to wake Catholic taxpayers up.

Mesmerized by change, by the deceptive new simplicity of Church ceremonials, and by increased access to the sacraments, most Catholics shrugged the warnings off and joined with the revisionist ex-nun, ex-priest promoters of the new Church in labeling the call to arms the shrill work of extremists and fanatics.

But no hurdle was more burdensome to the concerned Catholic parent than the accusation that they were not in tune with "present theological trends." If one asked for a clarification of the word "trends," it would be explained that this happy-face lingo referred to "Vatican II renewal." The "trends" of course were "the direction the Church has taken in recent years."[1] The onus for any lack of understanding of the new direction or lack of compassion for its implementors was placed squarely on the challenger. The parents of the party of the first part, the child, raising their voices in defense of their offspring, found themselves treated as inferiors to all other interested parties. The parent, it would be said, had failed in "not integrating into daily life the renewal of Vatican II."[2]

But no one—neither the shocked parents, the guilty bishop, nor the smarmy-faced, glad-eyed revisionists—could deny one incredible fact concerning *Come to the Father*. Papal approval of the new catechetics had not been sought, although Rome had made this mandatory. The implications of that fact were inescapable. William de Marois spelled it out:

> What the Church in Canada is confronting is a radical cleavage, a parting of the ways between those who still adhere to the Roman Catholic religion in its traditional integrity, including respect for our communion with the Petrine See and our filial submission to the authority and government of the Holy Father and his supreme jurisdiction over the universal Church on the one hand—and those who are committed to the revisionist option, which implies the gradual secession of the Church in Canada from its papal obedience on the other.[3]

In short, the Church was not Roman any more.

To believe that such an appalling betrayal of the sacred heritage of millions could have been so successfully enacted one must accept that a master strategy of smoke and mirrors was constructed to relieve an entire population of its birthright. Hard as it may be to countenance, that is exactly what transpired.

The appearance of disorganization, of spontaneous expressions of uncoordinated belief or disbelief, has been the hallmark of revolution ever since the invention of the lie. To this day, we are still expected to believe that the *Marseillaise* was marched all the way to Paris without someone with a game plan conducting the voices, that the women's march on Versailles was an impulsive display of undirected energies miraculously kept from disarray, that Desmoulins and other pamphleteers of the Revolution were just letting off steam.

"By their fruits you will know them" has seldom been a more accurate description of human undertaking than when applied to the catecheses produced by the revisionists, those superior minds, those experts in and out of their ordained cloth who decided the truths of the Church needed "reinterpreting" in view of the "new focus."

Christ Among Us and *Come to the Father* were a triumph of what de Marois calls "the great blurring."[4] The "spirit of the age" that could not tolerate anything permanent—that was the real "spirit of Vatican II." The revisionists might very well have taken their cue from Belgian's Cardinal Suenens, who said of John XXIII, "He made the supernatural seem natural."[5] *Christ Among Us* really meant Christ was just one of us.

That, of course, was precisely the point and the aim of the new Descartes and Rousseaus now penning pleasantries for the minds of the unsuspecting innocents in grade schools of the continent. So Christ was presented as "a classic example of adjustment" to one's environment, "an easygoing, good-natured Person experiencing all the natural drives on the level of mediocre specimens of humanity."[6] In wording endlessly promoted as "language more meaningful to the child," anthropomorphism was put to the service of clouding over the demarcation between matter and spirit.

In the *Christ Among Us* and *Come to the Father* milieu to which the child was ever so cautiously introduced, the baptized Roman Catholic was no longer distinguished from the Hindu, the Muslim, the Baha'i. The child Jesus was no more special than the infant Dalai Lama. To all who denied or rejected or even vilified Christ, we were to be compassionate. Any other attitude was self-serving, extreme. Not in the "spirit of Vatican II."

Only the humanity of Christ was presented.[7] Miracles, the signs that people might believe, were out, out, out.

In patronizing, forever correct, non-sexist language, the words of the Gospel were put to the service of whitewashing the dark side of Roman Catholicism, sidestepping guilt, reward, retribution, heaven, and hell.[8] Jesus, apparently, came to earth to be the subject of endless, sentimental, pre-adolescent, campfire, feel-good, get-in-touch-with-yourself sing-alongs.

De Marois called it "patty cake" progressivism. "Simplification, insufferably patronizing to children of normal intellectual endowment," he wrote of *Come to the Father*. "So it is anti-educational. You do not teach by frustrating the student's desire and capacity to learn."[9]

In every type of education today, except catechetics, the "in" thing is to follow the lead of the pupils. In catechetics, "parents and teachers are adjured to stay strictly within the limits prescribed by the lesson plan," pointed out Sister Mary Alexander, and they are ever advised to strive to speak in "language more meaningful to the child."[10] As if parents had no natural access to such a thing!

"The new Catechetics," said Sister Mary Alexander "is dull and dead. It has no living faith to offer."[11]

"The truth is not sterile," says the *Catholic Encyclopedia*, "but always serves to nourish devotion, to bear fruit."[12] That it cannot be "reinterpreted in view of the new focus" without boring everyone to death is what *Come to the Father* and *Christ Among Us* proved.

That there is a God, that He is separate and individual, existing on His own, whether we know of Him or not; that He is One God in Three Divine Persons; that the Second Person of the Blessed Trinity, the Son of God, became man at the will of the Father and suffered and died for us, overcame sin and opened for us the gates to eternal life, is not even alluded to. That Catholic adults could keep Catholic children in a classroom six hours a day and not be bursting to tell them these wondrous things, and claim all the while they were simply integrating the lessons and spirit of Vatican II, must remain one of the greatest lies of the dark, distorted age in which we live.

As early as 1973, the gifted Sister Mary Alexander prescribed a fourteen-step plan for correcting the miasma of Modernist mediocrity that polluted catechetics. I include it here in its entirety as it appeared in her *Open Letter to Bishops.*[13]

> 1. There must be a complete reorganization of personnel, goals and methods in the teaching of catechetics. Only those whose faith is strong, and whose loyalty to the Holy Father is unquestioned can be trusted here. No one has a right to lead Catholic children and young people astray.
>
> 2. Only degrees or diplomas granted as the result of serious study in institutes which provide an education comparable to that provided in the Pontifical Institutes ... should be recog-

nized.

3. Close supervision of the courses should be maintained.

4. In addition to the provision of academic courses in religious education at graduate level, practical courses conducted by qualified persons whose faith and teaching ability is above average, should be provided for persons who have strong faith, normal intelligence, and a strong desire to make Christ's Church better known. You do not have to be a genius to instruct others in the faith; you do have to be a good, practicing Catholic who believes what he is teaching. N.B. While degrees of sanctity cannot be scientifically measured, faith in the sense of sincere adherence to the teaching of the Church, and a desire to conform to that teaching, can be adequately evaluated.

5. These thoroughly Catholic centers for the preparation of religion teachers should be set up under the auspices of the bishop of the diocese, who should accept personal responsibility for the way they are conducted.

6. Standards for admittance as teachers or students should be strict. Our young people deserve the best. Only those able and willing to achieve the established goals should be considered as teachers. Parents and other interested Catholic lay people should be on the Board controlling these Institutes.

7. Courses in Church History, general literature, and cultural movements should be provided for those interested.

8. We should have reading circles, question periods, publications, radio and TV programs which provide definite answers to definite questions, and which would really train people to discriminate between what is true and what is false.

9. Only persons with a good general background, teaching ability, strong faith and personal competence should be allowed to teach in seminaries, or to take charge of religious instruction in Teachers' Colleges.

10. Care should be taken that only those of exemplary lives, a satisfactory standard of general culture, and a strong faith should be placed in charge of Newman Clubs, or University chaplaincies. In addition, the incumbents should be self-sacri-

ficing, hardworking people who have the ability to communicate with young people but who will not be dominated by the young. They must not use their position as an opportunity to recapture their own youth.

11. School Board elections should be preceded by honest campaigning. Candidates should be made to reveal their aims and goals, and those who wish to safeguard the faith should stand for office.

12. If proper religious formation could not be provided in schools in any section of the Diocese, the possibility of establishing schools conforming to the true aims of Catholic education should be explored.

13. Before the new committee sends in its report to the Bishops regarding the *Come to the Father* series, its basis should be broadened. Those who have felt that this series is unsatisfactory should have an opportunity to discuss—on equal terms—and in front of bishops and parents, the points on which they condemn this catechism. Also the committee should be really representative. The so-called experts should not be the judges. People who have some special reason—financial or otherwise—for supporting any text should be very circumspect.

14. We should have nothing to do with courses in comparative religion. These at best can only be a neutral historical presentation which disregards belief in the Divinity of Christ, the truth of dogma, the infallibility of the Church, etc. Young people taking courses of this sort would be in great danger of having their faith weakened. There is a series of sketches in the Grade 6 text of *Come to the Father* which illustrate what I mean.

Pierre, A Swiss Calvinist comes first. There is a little Hindu girl whose religion is described. There is a Jewish boy, and a Mohammedan. It can be seen that to find a common factor in their religious belief, each child would be stripped of everything except belief in some sort of Supreme Being, and it might be difficult to define this Supreme Being in terms which would admit the Hindu child. Hilaire Belloc says there is no common denominator that will include every shade of Christian belief, even when we exclude the Catholic Church. It is a mistake to think that the more inclusive the circle of Christianity the larger the religious freedom. The opposite is true. The higher the numbers included in the problem, the lower the highest common factor. When we step outside Christianity, the common factor becomes very small indeed. However, in their eagerness to enclose all mankind in the charmed circle of the Church established by Christ, the authors of the Grade 6 text include a final figure, Natasha, the little Russian girl. All mention of God or religion is omitted. Natasha has nothing that was explicit justification for the page of pictures. She belongs to the Young Pioneers, and goes to camp each summer.

By broadening down from precedent to precedent, we end with a number of children who all belong to some group which congregates together for its own ends. There is your comparative study of religion.

There is the constant factor presented as a goal in the *Come to the Father* series.

"And by the way," Sister Mary Alexander added, "I understand that the Canadian and American delegations at the Religious Education Conference in Rome, 1971, attempted to have the word Catholic replaced by Christian!"

We did not adopt Sister Mary Alexander's plan, alas for us. So we had no defense against what was to follow.

If the Catholic parent thought they could counter the neo-naturalism infiltrating every lesson of the "new" theology by dusting off the old *Baltimore* and, by kitchen lamplight, introducing the call—"to know, to love, and to serve Him in this world so as to be happy with Him in the next"—to teach them the unrevised beauty of the Decalogue, the Pater Noster, and the Creed, they had yet to learn that in the revisionists' arsenal was another quiver of bright arrows aimed to shake, shatter, and reduce to dust that very bedrock of the Catholic Faith.

THREE

SEX AND THE SINGLE CHILD

The bells of hell go ting-a-ling-a-ling
For you but not for me.
O death where is thy sting-a-ling-a-ling
O grave thy victory.

—Brendan Behan, *The Hostage*

ALL OUR LIVES we have known the phrase "the gates of hell." It lingered as a colorful metaphor in song and sonnet long after we had stopped believing in heaven, hell, and saintly bishops. In flights of fancy, for which Irish playwrights and poets are justly famous, the phrase winged its way back into our psyche, perhaps causing the mind on sleepless nights to wonder where, if it did exist, it might be located.

The Catholic mother knows. The day after her rude awakening, she more likely than not stood at her living-room window staring at it, across the street.

Picture Pope St. Pius X, that great saint and great pope who was excoriated by Modernism's elite for his vital determination to see children receiving the Blessed Sacrament in communion upon reaching the age of reason, and imagine what the news of sex education in the schools would do to the heart of that wise and gentle man. Pius X, in 1914, unable to effect any deterrents to the great battle about to begin, died as war thundered its way into the twentieth century. He was called the first casualty of the "war to end all wars." The purity of the child he fought so hard to protect was to be the first casualty of the sexual revolution's war against children.

"How many there are who hate Christ, who despise His Church and His Gospel, rather out of ignorance than depravity!"[1] said Pius X when stating the purpose of his pontificate.

Now, Holy Father, it is out of both. The unthinkable has overtaken the thinkable.

Make no mistake about it, it is the same philosophy Pius X defined, confronted, and halted dead in its tracks in 1907 in *Pascendi Dominici Gregis,* his encyclical against Modernism, that is responsible for introducing the sex education programs in the schools.

"Modernism," said Pius X, "is nothing but the union of the faith with 'false philosophy.'" "The spirit of [Modernism] demands the emancipation of science, which must traverse every field of investigation without fear of conflict with the Church ... 'the emancipation of the State which should never be hampered by religious authority ... the emancipation of the private conscience whose inspirations must not be overridden by papal definitions or anathemas and the emancipation of the universal conscience with which the Church should be ever in agreement, so as to bring about that radical transformation of human thought solemnly promulgated at the French Revolution."[2]

"It is a philosophy," says James Likoudis, "without divine absolutes—a philosophy scorning transcendental values—a philosophy that mocks God, but has plunged pell-mell into a new idolatry—the sophisticated worship of sex, the divinization of orgasm. It is a philosophy that, in effect, glorifies the Sensual Man, the Sensual Woman and is bending every effort to mould the Sensuous Child."[3]

Anyone who would have predicted in the Fifties that such a philosophy would ever be able to invade Catholic schools would have been considered badly in need of an analyst. What then, today, when sex education programs dominate the curriculae of grade schools, can be said about those individuals who brought it about and service it? Considering the ravages of the sexual revolution, how could anyone want to cheat children of even one year of freedom from that dreaded mess?

The great Catholic voices crying in the wilderness of the Seventies drew strength from one particular voice, who, on this occasion, at least, was nothing if not specific and decisive.

"We must realize," came a voice from a far country, "that we are living in times when human animality is degenerating into unrestrained corruption; we are walking in mud."[4]

The voice was Pope Paul VI's. The year was 1973, five years after the renegade religious had made dissent from *Humanae Vitae* a matter one could commit "in good conscience," since the Church's stand on sexuality, as you will remember Gregory Baum proclaiming, needed to be reinterpreted in terms of "the new focus." Paul VI, you may recall, did nothing about that act of betrayal.

The new focus was a thing of wonderment to some, apparently. Francis J. Conklin noted that one "activity" for six and seven-year-old boys and girls was a "tour of the boys and girls lavatories."[5]

What restless mind among the newly liberated religious-sexologists managed to squire that obsession onto the list of primary school things to do? Imagine the discussion among the sex-ed planners that would follow such a suggestion? How, I wonder, was the lavatory inspection proposal introduced to said planners? Was it drawn out of a hat? Submitted to an anonymous question box? Or was it worded in a bull session?

"I think we should ... I thing they should ... Don't you think they need to ...? You know, something I've never seen is the inside of ..."

One must wonder if notes were sent home informing parents that "Tomorrow __________ will be shown a boys' urinal," or "Tomorrow __________ will be shown that there are no urinals in the girls' lavatory."

No? Why not? Did the Gestetner run out of ink printing all those notes for home about bake sales for Biafra, clothes for El Salvador, swimming schedules, ski trips, library visits, tours of the dog pound or mail-sorting room or old folks home, canned goods collections, clothes for Nicaragua, shoes for Cuba, socks for Angola?

One must wonder what kind of intrusion occurred during the sexologists' own years of innocence that they decided that to ensure a healthy period of personality growth and psycho-sexual development—the "oh yeah?" period of childhood—had to be made into the "oh!" period.

The "oh yeah?" period is recognizable to anyone who has spent one day with a seven, eight, nine, ten, or eleven-year-old. Children will acknowledge the newness of an idea or an activity and then almost immediately go on to something, or back to something, that intrigues them. It is the innocent age of learn-by-playing that interests them the way physical or mental games interest them. It is an age of naturalness, when knowledge is acquired as the child requires it. It is an age when a built-in system of defense and deflection protects them against knowledge to which they are not inclined or which they are not ready to assimilate. No special education is needed to understand it. It is a period of latency that has been sensed, worked around, dealt with in every culture in every tent, tepee, wagon train, suburb, and condo in history. Above all, it is a period of grace, in which the natural instincts of the child are toward modesty, a time in which the child can play at being a leader or a follower before his character determines one or the other; it is a time when chastity is at home in the flesh as well as in the mind. It is a time when the heart can know unadulterated purity.

It is a time when parental love, to use the words of Francis Conklin, knows "an indescribable tenderness for their children, an inexhaustible patience with their children's weaknesses, an unceasing watchfulness over their activity."[6] It is the time when all members of a family know that they are a family. Conklin captures the tenderness, patience, and watchfulness of that unit in words that should be inscribed on every fridge door: "The family is a natural school with an inviolable charter written by the hand of God on the heart of the parent and the child."[7]

What possible creed would produce such rapacious salesmen as would crave to shatter that school? Salesmen who did not accept that a latency period exists or salesmen who knew it existed and violated it anyway.

Robert Louis Stevenson's *Treasure Island* was all about a boy and buried treasure. Regardless of what other heroes and bandits populated the pages, the reader knew in his heart that Jim Hawkins and gold doubloons went together like islands and oceans. And it was destined from page one that Jim would find them. Yet, Jim already possessed a treasure—his character. He was more responsive to justice or injustice than he was to dreams of wealth, yet pirates were willing to risk the boy's body, soul, and character to get their hands on real doubloons.

Luckily for young Hawkins, an old survivor, Ben Gunn, protected the treasure, securing it at a safe distance from thieving hands so that when they uncovered the chest it was filled with sand. Jim's share of the reward, one was left to conclude, would be his when he was mature enough to handle it.

Sex education in the schools is an act of piracy. Sexologists insinuating themselves onto the beaches of childhood might just as well have worn the skull and crossbones on their briefcases. It would be easier for them to prove that man is an island than to prove that what is called the latency period, the period of hidden treasure, does not exist.

Anyone who has raised a child, taught a child, seen a child, or been a child knows that from the age of approximately six to approximately twelve, a treasure is very much present, increasing in value month by month, year by year. Yet, a gradual stockpiling of wisdom, fortitude, piety, and a strong sense of self-preservation allows the treasure to remain unseen, and the child will instinctively throw anyone off the track or detour them through the labyrinth of his child imagination if they isolate him and start digging for gold.

Occasionally the ownership of this treasure will overcome the child with wonder, and he will think out loud, asking questions about it: where did the treasure come from, what is it worth, and what will he do with it? If answered with responsible honesty and candor, the child will value the treasure more and be happy to let it remain hidden, increasing in value until it is no longer possible to keep it from view. Then he must learn how to be a good manager of his worth.

The dormant sexuality, the sleeping treasure of the child during this period, leads to a deepening love and understanding of the character of their child by parents. The emotional development of the child during this period is a wonderland of options, but directing attention to it cancels the options. Wrong responses to the child's questions—inappropriate stress focused on what, to the child, is his own treasure—usurps the initiative to ask and learn born of wonder. It is a time of tides, ebbing and flowing to the gravitational pull of the very core of the child.

Can you imagine anything worse than contradicting that natural flow with a regimented timetable, a formula, a schedule? Sex education in the schools is an oppressive agenda imposing interior exile on the sole inhabitant of a treasured island, and imposing on paradise a glacier of our making.

My suspicion is that adults who deny the existence of the latency period must have hated their childhood, remember it as totally impoverished, or, having been visited by pirates, have now become pirates themselves.

"Much of a child's moral development is at stake in this period," writes Dr. Melvin Anchell, internationally recognized child expert and psychiatrist. Unfashionable though it might be, he takes his argument from Freud:

> It is during latency that the mental forces are built up which are later to impede the base sexual instinct. These mental forces or dams include disgust, feelings of shame, and the claims of aesthetic and moral ideas.
>
> These mental barriers are inborn; however to be effective later in life they must be strengthened during latency. The sex education given to six to twelve-year-old students interferes with proper sexual maturation by keeping the sexual impulse stirred up, disrupting both sexual growth and personal and cultural achievements. The six to twelve-year-old student who has not been sexually disturbed is normally a most responsive individual and among the least likely to be involved in socio-

pathic behavior."[8]

Ah, but the insistence on experimenting with children, for playing doctor, for prolonging under a microscope the most infantile obsessions with sexuality, did not come from the children. The eagerness with which the anatomical differences between little girls and little boys was maintained as a subject of scrutiny week after week did not come from the children. The determination to dabble in a non-stop delirium over body functions did not come from children. It came from people acting out their own need for in-depth psycho-sexual therapy—dissenting nuns and ex-nuns, priests and ex-priests.

Monsignor Eugene Kevane, director in 1973 of the Notre Dame Catechetical Institute, Middleburg, Virginia, came straight to the point: "The question whether the dissident priest and religious is the driving force behind this type of programs is a serious one."[9]

It was not for nothing so much energy was burned up by dissenting theologians maneuvering to out-maneuver the bishops on *Humanae Vitae.*

"Most active in the desacralization, demythologization and humanization of contemporary Catholicism are the theologians who have dissented and maintain their dissent against *Humanae Vitae,*"[10] writes Likoudis.

Is it possible the promoters of sex education to young children are drawn from the ranks of the Catholic clergy who abandoned their vocations in droves following Vatican II? What kind of childhood did those people have? What forces could produce such an intense obsession with genitalia that children have to be a captive audience to its expression?

The renegade religious, former nun, former priest, have no apologies to make, of course, to the Catholic priests and religious brothers currently up on criminal charges of sexual abuse against youths in their trust. Or do they?

Something new on earth? The direction the Church has taken in recent years? Theological trends? The new focus? Language more meaningful to the child?

Did the 1968 Winnipeg Statement not say that if people could not pursue a line of conduct in keeping with the given directives, they could be safely assured that whoever honestly chooses that course which seems right to him does so in good conscience?

Does this mean choosing to invent, promote, and partake in Dignity, a homosexual association that does not advocate celibacy and chastity and is banned from using Church facilities by the Vatican, is doing so in good conscience?

Does this mean that the seminary dean experimenting with his priestly function by buying drinks in gay bars with money from the collection plate is doing so in good conscience?

The phrase "in good conscience" made possible the acting out of an adult sexual delirium in lesson plans of the grade school sex-ed program in Catholic schools. Sex fantasies written and promoted by ex-nuns and ex-priests being played out with children in the classrooms. An entire industry driven by and for pedophiles now has its pup tent pitched in your child's school.

Very often the "language more meaningful to the child" is a euphemism for language that won't alert mom and dad. And so suddenly, somewhere between 1966 and 1969, curriculae started spouting such cute and inoffensive titles as "Family Life" or "Family Living."

William A. Marra categorized these programs, such as *On Becoming a Person,* in an article called "On Becoming a Plumber": "... the anatomical and physiological details of the male and female bodies ... so thorough, so all-embracing, so minutely detailed in films, texts and diagrams ... as well as the biological details of coitus, conception, pregnancy, and so on.... It would be more accurate to entitle the curriculum, '*On Becoming a Gynecologist, Urologist and Obstetrician.*'" He adds, "If the school officials of this nation spent the same time, energy, and ingenuity to teach reading as they seem willing to teach sex education, we should become a nation of Rhodes Scholars."[11]

How could such a curriculum trend be enacted side by side with the traditional Catholic teaching on purity, chastity, and modesty exemplified by the Virgin Mary and lived out by the countless saints whose lives played such a large part in classroom content of old? You would know the answer if you'd visited a Catholic classroom in the Sixties and Seventies. The Blessed Virgin, St. Joseph, and all the saints had been demoted, their very existence in the history of the Church relegated to the same waste bin in which archaic curriculae had been filed—times tables, phonics, penmanship.

To teach sex education in the Catholic schools, Catholic teaching had first to be denied. Francis J. Conklin explains: "Herein lies the scandal of the Faith, the Catholic Family, the child and the world.... The litany of Our Lady has been replaced by the litany of the 'religious' sexologist: the two are incompatible."[12]

The success of these sexologists in bumping aside religious priorities was staggering. Catholic boards and teachers, for the most part, acted as though they too had bought the new and all-purpose sex instruction kits the way they would blithely accept a new box of colored chalk. The pillars of Catholic education began to crumble into dust as if they were that chalk.

"It is not surprising," said Monsignor Kevane, "that *Becoming a Person* already in certain places is being taught in Catholic schools in place of religion class....This is the final denouement of the idea of Catholic schools in the United States, and the ultimate term of the fateful departure from the original purpose for which the Catholic Bishops established the Catholic school system in our country." This clarion call by Monsignor Kevane was issued in 1973.

"*Becoming a Person,*" he continued, "is sex education as part of a guidance program that largely prescinds from the Catholic religion, approaching this entire matter of human sexuality as if it were a secular subject."[13]

The holiness of purity, chastity, and modesty, the holiness of married life, the holiness of heart and home had been replaced by blueprints for carnal knowledge.

Again we must ask the question, where did this obsession with genitalia come from? In a blunt backhand to the self-righteous meddlers who had propelled the sex-ed mandate onto the desks of children and who treated it with the deference one might have reserved for manna from heaven, Conklin identifies as the culprits the liberated religious from convents and presbyteries.

"Sex," he writes, "[is] to be taught by the celibate, for the celibate now possesses a greater knowledge and competence of sexuality than the child's parents!"[14]

Their neo-Freudian pan-sexualism was, in the words of Sean O'Reilly, "one of the baleful fruits of Modernism."[15]

By 1975, the middle-aged ex-religious playing doctor in the classrooms of the nation was a pathetic sight, blinded to the heights from which they had fallen by a hodge-podge of notions on sexuality, perfectly personifying how a "little knowledge" could manifest itself into a truly "dangerous thing."

FOUR

PARENTS, FIRST AND FOREMOST

"WHOEVER WOULD TAMPER with the Divine institution of family," says Conklin, "violates the most sacred rights of parents and children."[1]

Defending the unassailable right of parents not to be hampered in the performance of their duty to educate their children, Conklin says, "Sex-education ... is a flagrant attempt by the state to arrest control of the child from its parents and to inculcate through the public school values and attitudes alien to home."[2]

Says Likoudis: "... the sex educationists of our time ... in denying 'de facto' the primacy of parental rights in education and the consequent freedom, independence and integrity of the family, indeed fight God."[3]

The very existence of the sex educationists in the classroom shouts rather loudly that, in their opinion, parents are negligent, failures, and incapable of judging the interest level of their children in sex. That "opinion" seems to have been adopted by school board and teacher alike. It represents the absorption of parental rights "by the disruptive intervention of the school," says Likoudis, an intervention which, "whether parochial or public is an intolerable abuse."[4]

Vatican II's *Declaration on Christian Education* states:

> Since parents have conferred life on their children, they have a most solemn obligation to educate their offspring.

> Hence, parents must be acknowledged as the first and foremost educators of their children. Their role as educators is so decisive that scarcely anything can compensate for their failure in it.[5]

The means by which sexologists drove their sex-ed agenda into the schools relates to this very same Declaration: "By taking one sentence ... out of context, ignoring the rest of the document and indeed its whole thrust." That sentence, Sean O'Reilly points out, was: "As they advance in years, they should be given positive and prudent sex education ..."[6]

To remove from parents the opportunity and obligation to give positive and prudent sex education within the context of home and family is nothing less than committing an act of piracy against the home and family. To insist that all parents are happy to relinquish that obligation is to assault the very integrity of every family represented in every school. It is to deny that Catholic parents have "the grace of state to fulfil that right and obligation." It is to hold in contempt the "inalienable right and obligation to educate their children, this includes above all religious and moral formation," which, O'Reilly points out, is "carried out as much by non-verbal as by verbal communication" and is "infinitely more important" than mere information.[7]

The sexologists, of course, had from the earliest stage of the game operated on the premise that sexuality was completely separated from religious and moral formation. The idea was to separate Church and state early in the child's mind. It was left to our very own dissenting liberated renegade religious to devise curriculum formulae that would, in the mind of the child, uncouple sexuality from procreation. The more explicit the classroom sex education, the farther away it would appear to be from anything experienced at home or at church. The effect on the child's mind could only be traumatic.

"Sex education is organized naturalism, that is, animalism," said Conklin. "It would have little children associate marital love with chickens and dogs copulating." "The magnitude of this crime against children," he added, "is incalculable."[8]

The force that has made the Catholic schools an unfit place for

Catholic children springs from a philosophy four hundred years old. Its spirit is rebellion; its expression is revolution. Luther's "down with dogma" became Robespierre's "down with Christianity" became Lenin's "down with God in general." Then, as now, its target was the education of youth.

The forces at work shredding the integrity of the Roman Catholic separate school system have as their goal the complete reign of secular humanism. The formula for accomplishing this was simplicity itself; it merely required a complete contradiction of the intentions of Pius XI in *Divini Illius Magistri* and was accomplished by switching two words: "to make the Catholic schools a (fit/unfit) place for Catholic students ... it is necessary that all the teaching and the whole organization of the school and its teachers, syllabus and textbooks in every branch, be regulated by the (Christian/anti-Christian) spirit ... and this in every grade of school, not just the elementary, but the intermediate and the higher institutions of learning as well."[9]

This anti-Christian element is spelled out in detail by Francis Conklin: "Sex education is an attempt by the state to influence and control the child: in the religious order it denies the things of God; in the moral order it denies the life of virtue; in the family it denies parental authority and competence; in the educational order it denies the plurality of creed, culture and custom."[10]

No wonder the feminist movement targeted the orders of religious women. Lured out of their habits, then out of their convents, then very often right out of the Church, the Catholic nuns succumbed to what their saintly predecessors in previous decades and centuries would have recognized as the very bankrupting of the interior life: out went religious habits, in came individual stipends, degrees in secular universities, appointment to secular professions—all necessary advance footwork for the conquering movement. Why? Monsignor Kevane explains:

> Impossible in a special way would become the position of religious teaching Sisters faithful to the principles of the Magisterium regarding religious life. How would it be possible to them to teach, under duress, programs so clearly in conflict with their basic principles of approach to children and young

people?[11]

The success of the neutralize-the-nuns strategy was so effective that Cardinal Ratzinger was forced to admit: "By the year 2000, religious orders for women in Quebec will be a thing of memory only."[12]

This tragedy is not the work of some aggressive sexologists working from beyond the walls. The drawbridge was lowered under cover of the chaos thrust upon the Church by the manifold interpretations of Vatican II shouted from microphones in seminaries and churches by the renegade dissenting religious. These were the same revisionists who drew their inspiration from the foremost agitators of Liberalism, those who gave grief to Leo XIII and Pius X (Loisy, Tyrell, *et al.*) This was the same movement which emerged from Vatican II totally free of the constraints on teaching imposed by *Pascendi* and has enjoyed uninhibited reign over the Church and schools ever since. William de Marois unmasked their agenda by identifying the goals of the movement specifically: evaporating sacerdotal and religious vocations, ravaging the discipline and dedication of so many religious orders and congregations, making a noisy vaudeville of divine liturgy, producing a breakdown in moral integrity among our institutions, sapping the morale of the faithful, and seriously eroding the vitality and cohesive unity of the Church in her institutional discipline and ministry.[13]

In place of all that, the victorious renegade religious preached and propagated from grade school to seminaries an adolescent obsession with genitalia. "In short," said Conklin, "a phallic religion." A religion that presents sex to children as "a normal biological function that is acceptable in whatever form it manifests itself."[14]

"Training in sin," he called it.

Imagine then what must pass through the mind of the eroticized child who returns home, sits at the kitchen table, and imagines the school lesson acted out by his father and mother to bring him into the world. The unspoken home lesson demonstrated minute by minute in how the parents live together, work and relax together, seek out and partake of each other's company in the home, do little things for one another, sidestep what would not please the other, the ongoing building and maintenance of a love relationship—all this will never carry its true weight again.

The cold chill emanating from the end of the table where the newly eroticized child is seeing the parents anew has sent shivers through mothers and fathers from coast to coast for over two decades now. They would learn all too late that the teacher's manual turning their family into a deep-freeze had no suggestions for defrosting.

The parent who thought right up to the last that it was all some phenomenal accident of a system gone wrong, that the religious could not possibly have had a hand in it, were to learn about the near-incomprehensible degree of involvement of that very class of educators.

FIVE

POLKA-DOT PRIESTHOOD

IN 1973, Monsignor Eugene Kevane wrote: "The *Becoming a Person* SIECUS [Sex Information and Education Council of the U.S.] Sex Education Program offers strange and deviate mentalities an unfortunate opportunity to lay their hands upon the children and young peoples who are the hope of the Church of the future."[1]

"It is a philosophy of hedonistic materialism," says Likoudis, "that justifies in the classrooms of the nation the dehumanizing aberrations of pre-marital sex, contraceptive birth control, divorce, abortion, sexual perversion and totalitarian population controls."[2]

That is the *Playboy* philosophy, now grade school curriculum.

Even so, it would represent a quantum leap for believers in this philosophy to go from mouthing the words to teaching primary school children how to make genitalia mobiles out of ping-pong balls and empty toilet paper tubes to hang from the ceiling of the classrooms over their tiny desks. Yes. It has come to that.

A landslide of lunacy has swept over Catholic schools engulfing teachers, children, and parents in an obsession with genitalia that has surely seen no parallel since the phallus-worshippers of the ancient world. Picking over the rubble, one would be hard pressed to uncover any nugget of nonsense more telling than the following: a workshop for teachers given by a sexologist who must have learned anatomy by fantasizing over old gladiator movies.

It occurred in the Essex County Roman Catholic Separate

School Board, Windsor, Ontario—Detroit's sister city.

Parents were placed in one group and teachers in another. The parents were kept busy in discussion. One parent, no doubt suspicious of why parents were set apart from teachers, passed himself off as a teacher and sat in their group. And this is what he saw:

"The teachers were offered brown bags (the parents were not). Inside the bags were 'aluminum foil, a pack of pipe cleaners, two ping-pong balls, two marbles, a few straws, a roll of cellophane tape, some string.' The articles were for 'grade-school children,' and they were to be used in constructing 'male and female genitalia.' All of these items were presented in a paper bag for little girls. 'Little boys also got some balloons.' The string was to be used to make hanging mobiles for over the children's desks."[3]

The materials were intended for a "methodology, the teaching-learning transaction and sex education and family living" outline, for use by professionals and group leaders in the teaching field.

The mind behind this dalliance was Dr. Michael A. Carrera of Hunter College Institute of Health Sciences, City University of New York, who suggested the above materials would be helpful in "understanding the male-female reproductive system."[4]

Now, I have never seen what kind of automobile Dr. Carrera drives on his search for ping-pong balls and pipe cleaners, though I have no trouble guessing what kind of mobile hangs from his rear-view mirror. But one thing I hope he is prepared to answer is the question from little Freddy, who is absolutely certain to ask, "Did they play ping-pong in Eden?" or "Did they shoot marbles in Ancient Rome?" or "But Grandpa says they didn't have cellophane when he was growing up!" How then did the race survive? How did the Celts, Gauls, Huns, Moors, Incas, Chinese, Polynesians, propagate their race without a sex specialist from an Institute of String and Straws to give them a methodology? And of course Freddy is bound to spend part of the day wondering, "When do Mommy and Daddy get to play ping-pong?"

Who conducted this lunch-bag lunacy? An outpatient from a clinic for the terminally infantile? Heavens no. This brown bag buffoonery was conducted by a Catholic priest, the Reverend Leo LaFreniere, O.M.I., who wore a giant polka-dot bow tie to pose for photographs.

To LaFreniere goes the credit for bringing the initial "Family Life" and sex-ed programs from the United States to Canada. The LaFreniere philosophy dominated teacher education for the Catholic school system for decades. Fundamental to that philosophy was separating sex instruction from Catholics' morals and a denial of the reality of the latency period, that time of hidden treasures. In fact, to LaFreniere and his colleagues, the latency period was a red herring, a Freudian notion, something that did not survive the leap from hypothesis to actuality. To the child between the ages of six and twelve, LaFreniere provided full and sexually explicit instructions.

"In the New Society," writes Sean O'Reilly, "it is essential that sexual activity and gratification be divorced as much as possible from procreation....In the 'reformed' Church of the dissenters ... such a divorce is indispensable ... in preparation of the right climate of opinion ... for the abolition of celibacy."[5]

Is it any wonder parents were outraged at such irresponsible meddling with their children? Is it any surprise that these religious sexologists with their condescending attitudes time after time revealed themselves as shockingly immature, with ideas of sexuality more akin to lewd games played at Boy Scout camp? Is it any wonder parents went screaming to their bishops demanding to know how such a movement was allowed to usurp the parental prerogative, make finger games of the traditional teaching of the Church, and subject their children to the sexual dementia of the renegade religious? Alas, when they reached the bishop's door they were in for the shock of their lives, those parents who had patiently, with stiff upper lip, endured "the direction of the Church in recent years," trusting that the bishops had it all under control, that when the spoiled, elitist delinquents currently giving clergy a bad name had it all out of their systems, the bishops would restore some sanity to the Church.

What they got, those parents shaken to the very foundation of their marriage by these A,B,Cs of debauchery, was condemnation, vilification, and slander.

"There can be no doubt," said Archbishop Plourde of Ottawa,

"that the ['Family Life'] program as a whole can help a child to a better understanding of self and others."[6]

The unmasking at the highest level of the dioceses of supposed shepherds completely in thrall to the sexologists and their foot soldiers, the dissident religious, would shake the very foundation of their faith, shatter whatever tenuous ties exist between home and school, and in time threaten the very survival of the Catholic school system as a system different and apart from any other. It would represent to parents a virtual betrayal of the home, family, and faith by the hierarchy of the Church in North America.

What could possibly be the source of an agenda that would capture the hierarchy of the Catholic Church?

What possible agenda could represent so much power that the shepherds of the Church would feed their own sheep ping-pong balls? What could these particular educators be after? What really lay under the X that marked the spot? In all of the seven seas, there can be no greater distress than that of parents dismissed as crackpots, fanatics, and nut-cases because they insist the latency period exists, and consider an abomination what the bishops of the Church have authorized be taught their children. In the wake of this Medusa, parents clinging to the raft of sacramental matrimony, scanning the horizon for signs of rescue, were about to see the Bark of Peter flying the Jolly Roger.

SIX

SOMETHING NEW ON EARTH

THE SORROW DEEP INSIDE that comes to the Catholic today who hears the priesthood denigrated by so-called clergy of the modern Church was also known, but only in minor ways, in earlier days. Mostly, it might have been a matter of the good Father doing a little tippling with the shot glass now and then, a flaw found in the most ardent of Catholics and therefore, easily forgivable. Irascibility, difficulty in concealing appreciation of a particularly attractive lady, or a propensity for favoring one family in the parish over all the others were the twists and turns of human nature in even the most responsible priests, and the Catholic was skilled at eventually learning to ignore them. There can be few relationships in the history of mankind as curious as that between the celibate Catholic priest and the carousel of weak and worried sinners who rode, year after year, round and round, up and down to the music of their souls, souls he grew to know so well. The celibate priest, a living victim willingly immolating himself daily so that he will not reach heaven alone, answerable to God every moment of every day for those around him and, as if that weren't enough, sworn in obedience to answer to and obey his bishop.

What better directive to his priests, religious, theologians could a bishop give than the following:

"We must put ourselves in a state of defense, repudiation and renunciation of so many exhibitions and manifestations of modern debauchery; and not surrender either out of acquiescence or fear of what people will say to the pollution of the surrounding immorality."[1]

The Bishop of Rome, Paul VI, said those words on September 13, 1972, to his bishops. I say "his" bishops purposefully. For, no matter how carried away a bishop becomes with delusions of his own importance, it is only when he is in communion with Rome and in obedience to his own bishop that he has any authority in the Catholic world.

What, then, was the reaction of the bishops of the United Sates and Canada to the prospect of sex education in the schools, which Paul VI equated with erotic literature, obscene entertainment, and pornographic magazines?[2]

Far from finding their bishops eager to defend their rights as the first teacher of the child, parents storming the bishop's palace learned all too abruptly that they need never look to the bishopric for assistance in the defense of traditional family prerogatives.

The bishop who emerged from Vatican II was a weakened creature, mesmerized by media attention, beholden to his adviser experts, and committed to expanding a bigger and better bureaucratic machine to handle his newly realized status as a high-flying executive.

The appalling reality parents had to learn to face was that bishops don't become bishops because of intellect, intelligence, or holiness. They become bishops because some other bishop has trained them to be the kind of bureaucrat he wanted to succeed him. Holiness and common sense have nothing to do with it. They are simply office managers. Bureaucrats beget bureaucrats.

What Vatican II gave them was what bureaucrats love most—more bureaucracy, with countless new roles to be filled with even more bureaucrats.

Those newly created bureaucratic roles were filled even as they were being created by the dissenting, renegade religious. The bishop became a queen bee surrounded, shielded, protected, and fed by the buzzing minds of the expanded hive while they contentedly hatched their plots.

"Liberation" for many a nun or former nun, priest or former

priest, meant freedom to spend the remainder of one's earthly life conniving for power in a diocesan or archdiocesan chancery. On a solid salary, of course.

What could possibly be the outcome of the seats of diocesan power falling to the renegade, liberated religious? James Hitchcock offers some insight.

"Radical Catholics ... too often seem excited and mesmerized by the drug culture, the rock culture, the culture of total sensual fulfillment. Their vision of religious renewal appears to be simply that of assimilating religion to this counter-culture usually in stumbling and amateurish ways."[3]

"We have the spectacle," wrote O'Reilly in 1973, "of apparently orthodox Catholic clergy and teachers joining forces with the ungodly hierarchy of SIECUS, Planned Parenthood and Zero Population Growth, to promote, nay to compel, adoption of explicit classroom instruction of sexuality and indoctrination in secular humanism.... Such programs have two things in common: they have excited opposition from informed, concerned parents, they ignore or misinterpret the teaching of the Church."[4]

Materials for sex-instruction programs all over the continent had been inspired and furnished by the Sex Information and Education Council of the U.S.[5] But the real merchandise being marketed was the mores of the movement crystallized in SIECUS, "an ideology directed at overturning personal family and societal values as well as Catholic faith and morals."[6]

In the *Social Justice Review* of December 1971, James Likoudis identified sex educationists and theorists of the "Sex Revolution."[7] At the top of his list was Dr. Mary Calderone, one of the founders of SIECUS, who he called "the madam of sex education."

"Who has been more effective in peddling the sex-ed mania in our schools?" he asks.

Next comes Dr. Lester Kirkendall (who "also sits on the Board of Consultants of that vile magazine, *Sexology*"), Dr. Alan Cuttmacher, Dr. Albert Ellis, Dr. David Rubin, and Isidore Rubin (by this time deceased). Other propagandizers of a permissive society listed by Likoudis include Professor Hans L. Zettenberg (Chairman, Department of Sociology, Ohio State University), who proclaimed sex education in schools to be the vehicle for shifting the consequences of sex from "taboo and fear" to "reliance on contraception." He includes also *Look* editor J. Robert Moskin's words in his indictment, "Religious taboos no longer work in a society with a welfare economy and a contraceptive technology."

"*Playboy, Look,* Mary Calderone, and Zettenberg are all exponents of the Contraceptive Society," added Likoudis, "and it is their anti-life hedonism with which millions of children are in the process of being brainwashed through governmental sex-ed programs blueprinted by SIECUS and Planned Parenthood Zealots."

The candy with which the child is lured into the shadows of hedonism is situation ethics. "Whose judgment can I judge by if not my own?" Let the student decide. Play up the child's curiosity in power. Situate him as an individual faced with a choice; let him be the ultimate judge of what is legitimate sexual expression. Remove from the child's reach the option of learning that God's law applies to political and educational considerations. Fatigued by the trauma of Godlessness, the child will allow you to dismantle and put away his old toys—reason, faith, charity, authority, and redemption by divine grace. Thus is the child offered a bag of sweets, "in utter hostility to the truth of man, the truth of God, to Catholic and civilized order," wrote Likoudis.

The sexology peddlers, the dabblers, holding parents at arms' length while experimenting with their children, took no heed of the admonition of Victor Frankl.

"The more we concentrate on sex and sexual techniques instead of on the person we love, the more we become neurotic ... sexuality is disturbed in the exact measure in which intending it and attention to it takes over.... Whoever sees his salvation in a refinement of 'love' techniques will only be robbed by it of simplicity, unconcerned naturalness and artlessness...."[8]

Something new on earth—the sensuous child? Who will pay the awful price? Louise W. Eickoff, psychiatrist, has no doubts.

"Sex education apart from parents, in school, is dangerous, for it destroys the in-built natural safety devices of personal, private, ultimate, love connections that protect the individual from society, from evil and from harm.... Sex-ed programs are wrong because they take the vehicle straight from the showroom to the motorway, leaving it in the charge of one who has studied a general handbook but has no driving experience."[9]

Tomes will no doubt be written in decades to come about the forces that seduced the Catholic religious out of their allegiance to the Magisterium and into the promotion of sex toys and tools. But, as I said before, it doesn't always take a rocket scientist ...

Tay Legacy was a counselor for the Sault Ste. Marie separate school board in the late Sixties and early Seventies. She wore as many professional hats as there were people in search of headgear. She was not thought of as a nurse or as a psychologist, she was simply "Tay" or "Mrs. Legacy." Anyone lucky enough to have needed her advice or enjoyed her friendship would attest to her unfailing ability to cut through the dross with unerring focus when a child's welfare was at stake. She was the best friend a child or a teacher ever had, and she had no time for fools.

One lunch hour, after listening to a conversation in the staff room about the chaos into which religious orders had collapsed, she was asked what she thought of those nuns who were currently flashing through *Come to the Father* parent-teacher showdowns or *Becoming a Person* sex-ed seminars in the latest shades of make-up and the hemline of the week.

She glanced at everyone individually in silence as if they should have known better than to ask, took a puff of her cigarette and cleaved the exhaled cloud of smoke with three words.

"Great escape artists."

In her view, there were two kinds of religious. Those who left home because they were holy, and those who left home to escape responsibility for siblings. There were two kinds of religious who quit the religious life. Those who quit it because they were holy, and those who quit it to escape responsibility for defending the convent against the seduction of contemporary culture. There were two kinds of survivors of those who left the convent. Those who survived the outside world because they were holy, and those who survived by escaping the responsibilities of chastity and celibacy. There was only one kind of liberated religious who survived the betrayal of celibacy, those who set about to get revenge on the institution that once sold them celibacy in the first place. And they escaped responsibility for sexual activity by adapting the contraceptive mentality.

"Sex-ed," she said, "is a blueprint for the great escape."

"It is all part," Likoudis said, "of the permanent revolution marking the course of history since the Renaissance ... nothing less than a fight against God."[10]

Eroticism is acceptable not just as an exceptional aspect of life but as a lifestyle itself, is the message being played out, the message of the adult magazine rack. It is an assault on young minds that, once the bishops were neutralized, had no defenders but their maligned and vilified, outraged parents, now alone without any Church to help them.

In 1970, Francis Conklin wrote:

> The silence of the Church has been correctly construed as tacit approval of public sex education.
>
> The bishops and priests responsible for this sex education, this sabotaging of the family, are solely responsible for the bitter passions their action or inaction has incited among Catholics: passions akin to civil war strife.
>
> Their action [bishops and priests] for which they must answer before God, has called forth no burst of charity, zeal or converts to Christ's Church; rather it has excited the enthusiasm of the professional sexologist whose occupation it is to traffic, among the young, in those very things the Church has always warred against: the concupiscence of the flesh, the pride of life and the devil.[11]

Feed the lambs?

"Where the severity of superego [conscience] was reduced," wrote Anne Freud, "children produced the deepest of all anxieties, (i.e.) the fear of human beings who felt unprotected against the pressure of their drives."[12]

Where sex education had been introduced, she noted, the same corruptive pattern of social change has been observed: an increase in the need for pornography, an upsurge in wanton, destructive aggression in the community, public displays of foul language anywhere and everywhere. Chaos on the motorway.

But no one was more able to take the pulse of the time better than the stunned, disoriented parents who discovered suddenly their children were strangers—cold, insolent little adults who held everyone in reproach, but reserved for their parents a special emotion: contempt. A child sentenced to a living death in the age of reason, made hostage to "strange and deviate personalities,"[13] becoming the victim of the deadliest of all imaginable sins. Pulling the bell rope at the gates of hell. Altar boy to the "divinization of orgasm."

"... So terrible is the temper of our age, so terrible the desecration and work of decreation,"[14] wrote Conklin in 1970.

And it was just the beginning.

SEVEN

CHARIOTS

THERE WAS SOMETHING rather casual about the Seventies. It was as though, once everyone accepted that the only thing to fear was fear itself, nobody seemed to worry any more. So much had changed in ten years.

Back in the Fifties there had always been that one reality—that it would all end with the Bomb someday. As long as we believed and felt and breathed each morning the reality of the Bomb, we could be gentle with one another. There was only one anxiety, that being, "When?"

Bomb-shelters were built with all the home-project sense of a family getting their own summer camp at last. But the Cuban Missile Crisis came and went and, lo and behold, there were alternatives to the Bomb. Multi-leveled, multi-faceted anxiety rose up and overthrew the banality of resignation, and people once again began to toy with riddles, scorn the wisdom of the ancients, and hopscotch all over fables of lost worlds. And before you knew it, it was 1975. The Garden of Eden had grown over with no one to trim the hedge. All the gardeners had scrapped their clippers at Vatican II. Now it too was closed off forever behind the flaming swords and flip-open phasers of Captain Kirk and Erich von Daniken. And dreamers who grew up swooning over Atlantis and Mu and heaven and hell found themselves naked in a decade of dry bones where Atlantis became Thera and Paradise became Titicaca and Nazca became an airport, and phrases like "ultimate rendezvous" had more to do with a new TV special than with anything everlasting. We had been afraid for so long, we had lost our sense of fear. Our sense of respect. Our sense of wonder and awe.

Nixon didn't cause the loss of order in governed lives. He just gave it a face. "I am not a crook," said the poor man, but by then a lot of us had turned down the volume.

Paul VI did not cause the collapse of authority in the Church. He just gave it a voice. "Is that a good thing? Or a bad thing?"[1] he said when told that only in the Soviet Union was the principle of authority still intact.

Charles Manson did not cause the abolition of the sacred, did not give birth to the anti-life, anti-God, anti-family mood of the Seventies. He just gave it his grin.

In the spring of 1975, I was contracted to direct an educational program in what very well might have been the only setting in the world where authority still reigned over tightly ordered lives in an anti-life, totally secular, non-family situation.

As a pilot program in therapeutic recreation, I took into a minimum-security correctional center a video-drama program. It was designed, ostensibly, to give tools for expression to inmates but, in fact, was just an excuse for some government department to spend a lot of money on portable video cameras, which were all the rage just then.

The survival of the principle of authority here was dependent on one directive—consistent inconsistency. Keep the inmates on their toes through practiced unpredictability. The inmates were never to know what was coming from one minute to the next. Keep their spirits broken by humiliating them in moments sacred to them. Devalue all they held of value; keep them constantly reminded that compared to what they would have endured in the old days this was a "country club." Controlled, authorized terrorism—the same dynamic that had seized control of the average parish since the end of Vatican II.

Keep the faithful mesmerized by sleight of hand, keep them wondering what they might lose next. Consistent inconsistency. A new liturgy each Sunday. Belittle what was sacred, uproot tradition.

It was a skill I could not acquire.

The monotony, banality, and sterility of the setting was absent of any reference to womankind, womanliness, motherliness, femaleness. Those women serving functions within sight of the inmates rarely exhibited any womanliness. They were imitation males—a woman guard, a vice-warden, a kitchen matron—more demanding than men in the same roles, more unpleasant than men, more condescending than men. Like the imitation priests running all over the sanctuary each Sunday, burning off ambition once veiled and coiffed in the cloister.

That institution was a grim mirror to the sterility descending on the Church, a lifeless Church from which the fertile, nourishing, mothering face of God through the presence of the Virgin Mary had been excluded. The new order of the sanctuary had banished from the liturgy and from the house of worship any reference to the unending, unconditional security of a mother's love. What the faithful would get instead was the unpredictable agenda of ball-and-chain liturgical drudgery under the watchful eye of imitation-male wardens. The faith had been imprisoned.

That same agenda, the anti-fertile, anti-nourishing, anti-love agenda—the secular humanist agenda of the feminist movement—imposed the same sterility on the Catholic classroom by shoving the Faith aside, demoting the family, dismantling parental rights, and introducing the Planned Parenthood, zero population, sex education formulas.

In a motherless, fatherless, loveless environment, genitalia are imitation weapons, instruments of rebellion, fantasy explosives for fantasy rebellion against the mother, father, lover who is not there. To incite such a captive audience by inflicting erotic film or conversation upon them is cynical, perverse. It is tarring the wheels of a chariot of fire. Showing a sex-health film to inmates amounts to inciting a storming of the fantasy barricades which, with repeated frequency, grow closer and closer to the real ones. Sexual acting out in prison is rebellion by a one-man assault force on the loveless machine into whose belly he has been swallowed. By 1975, teachers in grade schools had come to understand that.

The headlines spelling out sexual assaults by children upon children following the imposition of sex education in the schools are familiar to everyone, sickening to everyone. They serve to inflame already alarmed parents, titillate the media, and compel sexologists to demand even more and more detailed educational programs.

I failed miserably at teaching in the lifeless setting of that "country club." The only predictable member on a staff of professional chameleons, I was an outlet for pent-up needs. A supply trunk in the project van when it was checked out one day at the gate contained a smiling, folded-up inmate who apologized profusely for trying to take advantage of me as the guards led him back up the driveway to the "club." Two inmates who went missing during rehearsal for a taping were found by the vice-warden under the rubber mats in the gym closet having sex. White mice brought in for a Sesame Street-type video production ended up crimson smears on the concrete floor when they bit the inmates. A cameraman focusing his lens on two smiling "buddies" performing an alphabet skit glanced away momentarily only to discover when he looked back that one buddy had bitten the other's earlobe off.

At last, warned by an inmate not to eat with the staff on a certain day because of what one apprentice was to do to the food, our team was ordered off the premises never to return when it was learned we had had advance warning.

Who could have dreamed the "country club" was merely teacher orientation for what the schools of the Seventies had become?

Finally, after eight years of sex education, the parents were acknowledged as having a role to play, after all. A child leaving school after being immersed in the sexologists' first decade of experimenting was indeed "something new on earth." Now, he truly needed parents. Come the late Seventies, the one thing parents were allowed to do was pick up the pieces of their children's shattered psyches. That singular function for the grieving parent was identified by Anne Ross in her review of Wilson Brian Key's *Subliminal Seduction*. The title of the book became a buzzword for *Playboy* jokes lobbed out at TV audiences with relentless banality on talk shows throughout the Seventies. Ross, however, recognized the reality of the destruction at work.

"... People are being driven somewhat brutally from their

churches by the intentional use of the 'image.'"[2] The studied violence against the child in school committed through the secular humanist directives of the sex-ed programs was merely paralleling the studied violence against the faithful that the revisionist movement was enacting in the churches of the Seventies.

Ross itemized the evidence:

> The Cross minus the Corpus, the ugly altar vessels, the spurious banners so artfully worked to present the feeling of disorganization, the tabernacle, when finally located, that looks like an oven from an old coal stove, the church-in-the-round when annulation of seating "proved to be" psychologically disturbing in group tests, the gross diction in some of the Gospel translations, the wording in the new Lectionary that there was only "one" sacrifice, the overstressing of the word "memorial."
>
> All of these are not accidents of choice: it is a calculated shock to drive Catholics into a shell of fear.[3]

Just as the words, symbols, and monotony of the sex-ed program drove children into a paralysis of disbelief. Too late, parents realized the wording emanating from the pulpit, the bulletins, the bishop's letters were contrary to something vital to belief, to Faith.

"It is enough," said Ross, "that our 'instinct of Faith' has warned us something is very wrong."

Too late the compulsion to correct erroneous concepts, distortions. Lulled into complacency by two decades of ever-expanding communications media, most parents failed to recognize, let alone challenge, the abuse of that key to truth—the written and spoken word. Not for North America, in the post-Conciliar world of Catholic Churches and schools, the passions "*Filioque*" aroused in a distant place and time.

Children bombarded with education in sex divorced from matrimony, parenthood, and family were then left to deal with the result of using the names of sexual parts at the supper table. Parents attempting to maintain propriety in table talk were glimpsing the tip of the great transition completed through one decade of sex education in the schools. The school was a fantasy world where the child could get whatever he wanted without fear of reprisal while the home became a war zone with the ugliness of reward and punishment. The parent became the enemy. Fantasy and mythology were the offerings of pedagogery. Good and evil was just a Lucas-Spielberg hang-up. The empire of secularized childhood did not have to strike back. It reigned supreme. Suddenly, the face of childhood was not joyful any more.

EIGHT

THE ROAD FROM UTOPIA

NINETEEN SEVENTY-NINE. Nothing would empty a living room faster than a Jimmy Carter press conference, mainly because Carter looked like the kind of guy who could laugh at a Nancy and Sluggo cartoon. By 1979, even the funny papers weren't funny any more. A sad realization for the generation that grew up with Li'l Abner, suffered through his bashful marriage to Daisy Mae, and his bewilderment at the birth of his son, Honest Abe.

It wasn't easy to find replacements in our childhood mythology for Marrying Sam or Moonbeam McSwine. Equally disconcerting was the entire range of mysteries left unsolved by characters who drifted forever out of those balloon-filled frames of the Saturday Color Comics issue without as much as a token explanation of their most noteworthy and memorable peculiarities.

And so we may never know if Popeye replaced Spinach with Olive, if Steve Canyon ever got around to proposing to Mitzie, or if Wimpy showed up to pay for all those hamburgers on Tuesday. Did Dick Tracy ever get Flattop to justice? Nobody I know knows. In spite of public opinion, Archie continues to choose Veronica over Betty, and no one has yet solved the riddle of why Wee Henry has been bald all these years.

Some things we do know, however. Mary Worth changed her name to Betty Friedan and started lecturing. Ella Cinders masquer-aded as a Playboy Bunny, then penned her tell-all exposé under the pseudonym of Gloria Steinem. Marrying Sam lost his license and grew old as chairman of the Senate Watergate Committee. But whatever happened to Red Ryder and Little Beaver? Did they live happily ever after out there on the range where no one could bother them? Did they open a dance studio in Reno? Or did they join the Oblates? Pogo's swamp is now a parking lot for Florida's Disney World. Mandrake pulled the ultimate disappearing act. And with the exception of Frank and Ernest, the Wizard of Id, and BC, the funny papers have fallen to the likes of Scamp, Hi and Lois, and Emma Lou.

Gone are the days when Joan Baez would sue Al Capp for maligning her in caricature. Gone the prophetic Terry and the Pirates flashing American Eagle tattoos before blue-faced ladies of the Orient. Modern cartoons in the press and on television, with their barren, single-line offerings, are not only not even junk art, they make the early Disney sketches look like they were lifted from the ceiling of the Sistine Chapel.

It is time to dust off traditions. Time to stop the potter's wheel from throwing relentless mediocrity into our lives. Time to seek out the gem-cutters in our midst and polish diamonds.

When an entire continent can adulate a bewigged, cloth pig stuffed with foam whose ravenous appetite for romance with a frog is a veritable metaphor for our lack of self-esteem, it is time to start rummaging in the past, to rediscover the disciplines of the wise and try them out on ourselves. I mean, it's not just that the funny papers aren't fun anymore, it's the world. The world is tired of itself, run ragged by the unharnessed troika of Naturalism, Rationalism, and Liberalism.

The Supreme Being invented by Robespierre lasted less than sixty days. Because his "something new on earth" grew tired of Robespierre and of itself. A world without a past to fall back on grows too tired to sustain itself. That is the fate of Revolution. Unless they cut the past adrift, it is not revolution but only rebellion. Then, when the future stares them in the eye and says, "Now what?" they wither, because they have no past to draw from.

The new world, new focus, new age of the renegade revisionists began to run out of steam when the burden of reinventing the liturgy every Sunday taxed even their most fervent revolutionaries. They could not even sustain the monotony, banality, mediocrity their invention was destined to be. For when they tired of inventing the future they had nothing to fall back on. They had dethroned tradition. Why?

Professor James Daly, president of the St. Athanasius Society, categorized the Catholic dissenter as having "an unrealistic fear of an embarrassment over 2,000 years of Christian history. And a drive to seek solace in a fantasy world furnished with the illusion that we are just emerging from a supposedly pristine period of Apostolic purity, with our historical plate clean.... a fear of the 'dark side' of Roman Catholicism with its insistence on the reality of sin, death, damnation."[1]

The impulse to push the reject button on notions of sin, reward, and responsibility caused the revisionary to roll out the red carpet to the salesmen of sinless sexology and pain-free self-indulgence, and to replace responsibility with technique and tools and toys.

The dissenting clergy's betrayal of children goes hand in hand with their betrayal of the evidence of history. As Daly also pointed out, "the assumption that the Apostolic period was one of uncomplicated bliss is unrealistic and unfounded. Far from being more tolerant and indulgent, early Christians were committed and unyielding, fiercely intolerant of heresy in their own ranks and uncompromising in their opposition to the gentile civilization in which they lived."[2]

Daly takes the infantilism of the renegade religious a step beyond the "great escape artists" of Tay Legacy. He characterizes their fear of history as "utopian, betraying a desire to return to the womb."[3]

Like great escape artists and infants everywhere, it is left to others to clean up the mess.

The degree of change in the teaching profession since I left the classroom in 1973 was brought home to me in 1979 when a living, breathing personification of the banality of sinless sexology sat opposite me at a teachers' conference dinner table. This individual, a male teacher about thirty years of age, was one of those supremely confident individuals who look you straight in the eye with the absolute assurance that you have never met anyone in the world quite as dear as they are. You know the type—he dresses in layered clothing, long flowing coat, several scarves, so that even when standing perfectly still he appears to be in motion, his blank, purportedly innocent gaze the eye of the storm his clothes enact all around him.

He listens to conversation with empty-eyed simplicity as if he were just emerging from a supposedly pristine period of purity with a slate clean even of chalk dust. Uncomplicated bliss is the style of life he determinedly projects. Let's call him Chad.

"How did the trip go, Chad?" someone down the table asked.

The "trip" was a weekend excursion to the Tyrone Guthrie Theater in Minneapolis on which he had taken his grade ten class.

With precision-worded brevity Chad detailed, then discarded, the points to be made about a bus trip with thirty teenage students and the summer camp atmosphere on the floor of the hotel they inhabited for two nights. All of this told as a prelude. Programmed into the telling was the anticipation of something wonderful he could not keep to himself one more minute. The "something wonderful" was dragged out of him by a woman in blue down the table saying, "And...?"

We were then treated to the spectacle of this thirty-year-old informing the table of how his students had helped him select, out of a possible three choices of men they'd encountered in and around the hotel, the one that should be his "date" for the theater.

As the only stranger at the table I was accorded a glance from Chad that said, "... but of course my class knows ..."

They had made their selection based on what "Sir" had told them about his preferences. The Choice not only accepted the proposition but waited patiently while the students made sure Chad was properly attired for the big date.

So successful was the date, in fact, that Chad and his guest took a room on the floor above for the night, but their idyll was frequently interrupted by the "shivaree" the students enacted outside their door.

We were not spared the telling of how the students watched

from the bus window as Chad exchanged goodbyes with his discovery, nor the titles of some of the sing-along numbers the students used to console him on the long bus ride home. You know the "There's a Place For Us" repertoire?

Now, I may not be the most sophisticated person in the world, but the "uncomplicated bliss" born of this pain-free self-indulgence made me momentarily feel that I, alone, at that table, was from the dark side, the domain for the uninformed, where sin and death still interfered with one's need to fulfill oneself. Comfortingly, no ovation followed his telling. The teller of this amazing tale, his voice expiring out of sheer pleasure, basked in the silence that now overwhelmed the table, assuming, apparently, that it represented awe and wonder. He had, for the moment, ceased tooting his own horn, but now his lungs, a veritable calliope of self-praise, emitted melodious confirmations that what he had related was not only the total truth but that it had happened to him, because of him, and above all for him.

Thankfully, the whole house of ever so delicately arranged cards he had erected amongst us came tumbling down when the woman in blue, in a voice as cold and unfeeling as a guillotine blade, said "... And ...?"

That, of course is exactly the point, isn't it? What, after all, can possibly be the fruits of such totally unabashed exploitation of youth, such near-incomprehensible pride in silliness? Complete and utter self-centeredness can only produce a black hole in the self, the gravitational pull of its interior so dense no light can escape it, nor survive in it. It has only one function—to pull everything nearby into the darkness as well.

Once, on a train, I met people on their way home from Utopia. They were all seventeen years of age, returning from a summer work program in the bush for which sixteen-year-olds were not old enough and eighteen-year-olds considered over the hill. They filled a quarter of the train car. Upon boarding they raced to the window to bid farewell to a line of camp "counselors" mooning them from the field alongside. Immediately noticeable was the enormous quantity of alcohol they were alternately imbibing and concealing from the porter's view. The ratio of boys to girls was perhaps five to three. The language that was sustained at a level of half-drunk hysteria for the hours ahead reached degrees of obscenity never encountered before anywhere at any level of society. But most curious of all was that it did not cease. The stream of pornographic utterances neither let up nor paused for the duration of the trip. An hour, it seemed, before deboarding they began their farewells. What transpired in that period was one of the most unusual sights one would ever expect to encounter on a train. Passionate, prolonged kisses engaged at least half the number in a macabre performance without any exception made for gender. Among those so engaged there seemed no hesitation. Those not partaking in the ritual showed no interest in the happening at all.

Occasionally, in the intervening months, that peculiar ballet would reemerge in my mind's eye begging explanation. So far I have found none. I can only apply to the riddle details of the summer camp that were overheard that day. From the conversations in the train car, it was clear that none had communicated with their parents for seven weeks except by letter or an isolated call by short-wave radio. Alcohol was present from the first day to the last. The only one not seventeen years of age was one counsellor, nineteen, one of the mooners outside the window. The responsibilities of the participants had forestry as the common denominator and wilderness living as the goal. They lived in both tents and camps.

The main conversation, made up of many little conversations that came and went, concerned plans for "getting" their parents when they reached home. Two girls plotted loudly how it would only take one week back home to have mom and dad where they wanted them for the balance of the year. Quite apparent was that they all originated in homes one would call "good" or "monied." Even more curious than the event they represented was the puzzle of just how those homes would appreciate the return of a summer culture that uttered as its anthem the most unsettling of obscenities—music and lyrics, I have no doubt, by *Lord of the Flies.*

It is of absolutely no value to anyone to pretend that society is just going through a necessary adjustment following the sexual revolution. Simple common sense recognizes that something has gone terribly wrong.

It was brought home to me by an incident I more or less happened upon on the grounds of a private boys' college. A wallet on the asphalt of a shopping mall lay directly in my path as I stepped from my car one evening. Credit cards identified the owner as a staff member at St. Andrew's College nearby. I drove to the address on campus and, having parked and walked not twenty paces from the car, collided with someone running wildly in the dark. Behind him, in the distance, a man was calling out for him to stop. It was the groundskeeper doubling for a watchman off work with the flu. The building in whose open door he stood revealed itself, as he switched on the overheads, to be the college chapel, standing in a field apart from the dorms. He searched the interior then came to a halt near the lectern of the altar. Then he walked slowly down the aisle, out and down the path until he stood before me. In a voice soft and faraway, filled with disbelief, he said, "He defecated in the Bible, in the open Bible. It's there, on the lectern. In the Bible.."

It is pretty certain that defecating in an open Bible on the altar of a chapel in a religious boys' college is not a prank. It is something else, something the word "obscene" does not cover. Yet, in that geographical region in 1984, it was not as surprising as it might have been.

It did cause me to make notes on some of the mini-dramas experienced in the process of piloting a drug-awareness program in twenty-eight schools over a period of ten months.

The region was forty by forty miles square, within one or two hours driving distance of a city of three million—a common enough setting in North America. The age group encountered was the twelve to eighteen set, in a region hosting multiple school boards, a burgeoning economy, and falling under the jurisdiction of no less than three separate police forces.

Incidents of drug abuse were wall-to-wall, commonplace, and always blamed on "peer pressure." Of course, evidence that more than peer pressure was at work cropped up everywhere.

A ten-year-old seeing a plastic model of a marijuana plant said,

"My mom's got one of those in the porch."

A girl, perhaps twelve, drawn and haggard, asked tearfully, "If Mom does dope, can I make her stop?"

A teenager from a nearby high school was waiting when I exited a grade school one noon hour and extended money to buy "stuff." When I shook my head he offered his girlfriend as an extra inducement. Not until his girlfriend caught up to him did he learn I was not "Sir." He had mistaken me for a teacher at the school.

One grade eight girl failed to show up to do her part in an exhibit for a Thursday evening, standing-room-only parents' night for drug education. She was found drunk on a park bench outside the school.

A senior gave in to his parents' endless pleading to quit drugs. He did. Then he inhaled butane from his father's lighter and died at the foot of the bed.

After overhearing two grade eight girls plot to "get" a male teacher, I followed them down the hall. They came upon him conversing with a woman teacher. One girl positioned herself down the hall as a witness while the other, saying sweetly "Excuse me ..." slipped through the space between the conversing adults. She brushed her breasts against the male teacher's folded arms then proceeded to join her friend. By the time I reached them, the "victim" was sobbing that Mr. X had touched her breasts. I approached Mr. X and the woman teacher and related the details as I had observed them. The "victim" girl, enraged, without a trace of remorse, vowed she would "get" me if it took her all her life to do it.

A comic book store on the main street of a town in the heart of this region was an intersecting point for businessmen along the street who met regularly to engage in an adult pursuit of Dungeons and Dragons. Within blocks of the store stood a school where I was to spend two weeks during the pilot year of the drug program.

First day at the school I noticed a circle of boys in the yard, grade seven probably and eight, shoulder to shoulder, turned in, mesmerized it seemed by something occurring in their midst. When they entered at the bell, there was chaos in their voices, something uncontrolled, akin to hysteria, a near-palpable tension filling the corridor.

I was to spend that week with the eleven-year-olds. A grade six class. The first impression was that these were not children. They were wizened, pronouncedly mature, serious, angular faces. Sharp, chiseled, stern. One girl had a copy of *Old Whores* on her desk, a paperback joke book.

The outgoing teacher offered some advice. "When they're bored," he said, "let them draw pictures of the game landscape."

The game was *Dungeons and Dragons*, the landscape, a papier-mâché terrain covering three stacking tables set end to end along the side wall.

It was the second time in as many days the game had popped up in conversation. The previous day, scouting locations for a segment of the pilot program, I had entered the comic book store. The proprietor had released a deluge of commentary expanding on the upcoming session of *Dungeons and Dragons* he and the other merchants had scheduled for that night.

Looking down at the elaborate homemade game terrain, I recalled the newspaper headlines of the recent year concerning youths who had taken the game too seriously. No, I decided, there would be no "game" while I was in the room.

Instead, I launched a word-association game to introduce the drug-abuse topic. A hand went up. A blond girl asked to go to the washroom. As I said yes, I became aware of a stillness in the room. Not only were the other twenty-nine not moving, they were almost not breathing.

Continuing with the word game, I was interrupted again by the girl returning. In that brief instant away she had changed from slacks to cut-offs.

Mere moments passed, and she asked to leave again. Again the silence descended. This time she returned wearing an elastic halter instead of her sweater.

Twenty minutes into the first controlled discussion she left again. Upon her reentry, the entire class sat in stony silence awaiting my reaction.

And then I saw it, that thing that I had sensed earlier, something that did not belong among children. Although the girl walking across the room was no taller or older than the others, she was now distanced from them by years of knowledge. She towered over them, contemptuous of them, of their youth, perhaps of their innocence.

Her cut-offs had been cut even shorter. She could have had herself arrested on Main Street.

Her walk, her attitude, her glance were obscene, not because of the lewd intention of her movements or the haughty angle of her head, but because the girl still had the form of a child. There was nothing grown-up or even adolescent about her body. This was a child in everything but the mind.

The bell cut short the performance. They poured outdoors, a stampede without shape or structure. After moments reassembling my thoughts I approached the windows and looked out.

The circle had formed again in the yard, boys shoulder to shoulder, trance-like, eyes fixed upon some object of attention in their midst. Elsewhere, pockets of students looked my way, watching.

Then it happened, suddenly. A football shot through the air connecting with the back of the head of one boy in the circle. He fled in pursuit of the thrower. In the split second it took for the others to close ranks, I saw into the circle. She was there, among them, that blond child, on her knees.

What to do?

They were back indoors seated and staring my way by the time I had accepted it as true.

Something alien to childhood had entered that school and was acting out its lewdness through these children.

I decided to let them be kids again for just one day. When they returned from lunch, I was ready to let them try.

I fixed to the front board a three-dimensional sci-fi mask sculpted out of colored art paper. I explained a few tricks of folding paper and laid out supplies for them to do likewise.

The instant reaction was childlike enthusiasm. By three o'clock, after two hours of intense concentration, one wall of the room displayed thirty sculpted paper masks. When the class drifted out of the room and homeward, they were docile, listless.

I called a passing teacher to take a look at the wall, an African woman who returned to Soweto each summer to teach. Staring down at us was a demon with thirty heads, glowering, coveting that room.

"That damn game," she said, shaking her head.

The season had barely passed when, in a town just outside the region, two children were found murdered in a grade school. A twelve-year-old admitted to leading his two neighbors, a little boy and a little girl, into the empty building outside of school hours. The girl he strangled in the girls' washroom. The boy in the boys'. The girl revived herself but he heard her as he was strangling the boy. He returned and ended her short life. He claimed he had been commanded to do it by "a force" he was accustomed to playing with.

An exterminator, I thought, anti-life, anti-mercy, anti-purity.

Soon after, I encountered a young man of sixteen, seemingly productive, still boyish in his charm. He confided to me about a game he played with his nineteen-year-old pal.

The older fellow owned a car. Together they made a pact: to use the car at least once a day to have sex. Their target—only grade-eight girls. And they had to be virgins.

They would hang around schoolyards, car parked on the street. The younger one would attract the grade-eighters with his innocent looks, while the older one provided the mystery-man-behind-the-wheel effect.

He assured me it was a foolproof operation. He boasted of the schools and the grade-eight virgins they had conquered. He laughed unreservedly over the phone calls he would receive from them after and he called them "pathetic." After all, it was his rule to only have sex with virgins.

Sociologists, psychologists, sexologists had had this region for their professional playground for two decades. Needless to say, the busiest intersection in that forty square miles was just outside Family Court, where Utopia intersected with the dark side.

NINE

PHANTOM

IF A CITY gets the Main Street it deserves, then Yonge Street in the late Seventies was whispering sordid nothings about Toronto, Canada, to those who lived and visited there. Body-rub parlors had made prostitution a storefront business. City Council, like councils in major cities across North America, was paralyzed by fear of transgressing boundaries of a nightmare of lunatic excess of its own making. The much-touted inviolability of individual rights so dear to the heart of city politicians that decade had allowed Toronto's once-great Yonge Street to become a wide-open purple sore on the face of a city bruised into numbness by the boldness of the sex industry.

In the shadows of the trade, a neon-speckled surf of cocaine swirled up and back against this malevolent playground of pimps and pornographers. Crime had at last found contentment in this inner city. Now Toronto could stand toe to toe, stiletto by stiletto, with other hardcore cities of the continent.

It might have gone on forever had a small photo not appeared one day in the city paper. A shoe-shine boy had gone missing from his usual corner on Yonge and Shuter Streets. Emmanuel Jaques, aged nine, child of Portuguese immigrants, was last seen ...

The story was unfortunately familiar enough in the Seventies. The use and abuse of children by the sex industry had made alarming leaps into the newspapers in the Netherlands, California, the Philippines, Rio. A network of pedophiles had actually grown emboldened enough to have a representative legally agitate the courts for the age of consensual sex to be lowered from fourteen.

They adopted the slogan "Eight is too late."

Children disappearing seemed to be reaching epidemic proportions. Adults hardened by years of news items on radio and television seized up as rumors of child snuff films circulated. A society wherein Christian morality had been dethroned was choking and gagging on its own vomit.

Then the shoe-shine boy was found. On the roof of a Yonge Street theater complex. In a garbage bag. His killers, after photographing him and subjecting him to every twist on sodomy they could devise, drowned him. Two men held his head down in an overflowing sink while a third man watched the door. Then they put him out with the trash on the roof of the old Pantages Theater, where a decade later *The Phantom of the Opera* would enthrall sellout crowds.

Like countless others in the city that week, I went to the church where the funeral was held. It seemed most of Toronto was there in the streets, by their numbers saying to the Portuguese community and especially to the devastated immigrant family, "This is not what we are like."

The street was blocked from horizon to horizon, an entire city impaled on a spike of grief, as the little white coffin floated up the Church steps and inside to the funeral Mass. Meanwhile, across the city taxi drivers took up collections, CB-radio operators organized a cash drop. Donations poured in, coins and dollars and checks saying, "We are not like this." Yet, everyone there in the street that day could have asked, "Who is waging this war against childhood? Where is it coming from?"

From dawn to dusk, the battle rages on. Innocents fill the trenches, their virtue spilled in death in an endless stream of sacrifice while supposed educators and protectors rack up credits in sexology, and school boards pay thousands to bring in some dysfunctional ex-religious has-been from academe to blather on about penises and vaginas and vulvas to gymnasiums overflowing with blank-eyed teachers. Priests and nuns with too many or too few weekend courses in psycho-sexual maturity go over the wall, marry each other, and return to inflict on entire school boards the wonder of beings who have just discovered orgasm. And bishops endorse courses in sandbox gynecology so kindergarten children will understand intercourse years before their minds, bodies, or souls can comprehend it.

The small white coffin returns to view at the Church door, floats down the steps toward a silent, endless mob. The eloquent are speechless, the glamorous dressed in grey. The toughest laborers melt into their shoes. The gentlest concoct violent oaths. Still, the coffin moves, its muted voice transmitting waves of forgiveness.

We are the dead. Short days ago we lived
Laughed, loved and were loved. And now ...[1]

Pale harvest from our fields of sin, the solitary white kernel of youth enters the crowd and is lost from view. The crowds fade back to where crowds come from. Day darkens. Neon flickers to life. Bishops go to dinner. Committees gather in gymnasiums to study new color illustrations for grade one of penises, vaginas. Ex-nuns share an enlightening experience with a lesbian outreach subcommittee. An ex-priest meets alone with a school board chairman to plan how to silence parents protesting sex education. And so it goes. For life, after all, is a celebration, and we, in the new Enlightenment, are fully alive. And there will always be someone, somewhere, who will put out the garbage.

BOOK TWO

A HISTORIC BETRAYAL

THE EIGHTIES & THE NINETIES

PART ONE

AMBUSH OF THE INNOCENT

ONE

THE CULT OF THE PRESIDER VERSUS THE FAMILY

WHATEVER VIRTUES our North American bishops may or may not exhibit, one impression endures—Vatican II was their Woodstock, and they will go to their graves, as many of them already have, steadfastly refusing to acknowledge that they have done to the Church what my generation did to that farmer's field in upstate New York—left it unusable, untillable, a great smear of clay in once fertile acreage.

In the last chapter of my 1991 book *The Last Roman Catholic?*, I describe an occasion on which, in search of the treasures of the Church discarded in post-Vatican II desecrations, I found a statue of Mary, with empty sockets where her hands should have been.

"When you wrote about the statue of Mary without hands," wrote a reader from California, "my heart jumped."

"Two years ago," she continued, "we had an earthquake. A priest friend told me that in a religious book store in Los Angeles, the only part of the statues that were broken was the left hand on all the statues of the Blessed Mother. We knew it had some meaning ...

"We've heard that it's the Blessed Mother that is staying the hand of her son from punishing the world at this time. Jesus is at the right hand of the Father—Mary must be next to Jesus (figuratively). It would be her left hand holding back that of Jesus."

Now her left hand is not there.

God speaks to us in ways we can understand. The writer of that letter was pierced through with the simplicity of Catholic truth.

She trembles without reasoning why. Sleeps fitfully wondering why. Forgets the names of her loved ones even as she sews their costumes for a school play, not knowing why. She is just reacting from the strength of her faith to the danger in the wings.

Left on our own, our lives would be a one-act wonder, played out in the conflict and conquest called Faith. But we are not solitary life forms. We lead or follow others who have less or more faith than us. The second act is called Hope. But luckily for us, it does not end there, for we have an author who comes to us with a third act. Charity. And from Him we take our cues.

We live the lines He feeds us.

"Love one another as I have loved you."

"Love your neighbor as yourself."

"Do good to those who hurt you."

"Bless those who persecute you."

In the early Nineties, these directions would be tested to the breaking point by *The Interim*, a fearless weekly paper hammering out danger, hammering out warning from its cramped and crowded downtown Toronto offices. In late 1991 and early 1992, *The Interim* took the lead in challenging the educators and supposed shepherds of the separate school system on their new sex-ed program, *Fully Alive*.

Father John McGoey, a specialist in Catholic Family Life Education with more than a passing acquaintance with *Fully Alive*, provided for *The Interim* a necessary overview of how it reached the classroom. With words dipped in lightning, he drew a bleak blueprint: "The serpent slipped into paradise through the Church."[1]

The "serpent" he identified as SIECUS/SIECCAN—the Sex Information Education Councils of the United States and Canada, the twin offspring of Planned Parenthood International.

Since the *Fully Alive* program existed only in Ontario, the response to *The Interim* would be led by Bishop John O'Mara of Thunder Bay, head of the Ontario Conference of Catholic Bishops. O'Mara's attack on *The Interim* shocked Catholics. Threatening lawsuits, demanding Catholic advertisers withdraw from *The Interim*, pressuring schools to no longer participate in this singular pro-life paper and thereby robbing students of much-needed confidence in activism, banning the distribution of *The Interim* in Catholic churches—he left no stone unturned in attempting to destroy *The Interim*.

Beneath the surface of this tirade from an infallible mini-pontiff was the howl of complaint of the bishops of Canada caught between the sheets with Planned Parenthood. The bishops were now to receive from parents what Rome had been receiving from them for decades: contempt and rejection. Catholics started searching for back issues of *The Interim*. What they found there was a thorough and professional examination of that little *Fully Alive* acorn and how it grew.

As McGoey wrote in September 1991:

> The serpent undertook to sell a so-called Christian program through the National Councils of Catholic Bishops who authorized their representatives to take seats on the SIECUS/SIECCAN boards. Planned Parenthood was big on those boards, subsidized with millions through government taxation.
>
> Eventually, a whistle blew, though just a tweedle. A few prophetic bishops, alerted by bad news, reluctantly accepted what was going on. Most generally stood by while the majority decided that less damage would be done their personal prestige if they allowed it to continue.
>
> Had they terminated it immediately, as they should have, their mistake would probably have been seen as an honest one. Now, in view of the relentless onslaught of the plague of AIDS in which the medical establishment distinguishes itself by deception and lies, it [the silence of the bishops] will be seen as a cover-up of appalling ignorance to the point of dereliction of duty.
>
> By the time the first plague ever to exist simultaneously in every nation of the world peaks in its final explosion, it will be obvious just how much the abandonment of Catholic moral-

ity will have contributed to it.[2]

Responding to the bishops' accusation that their critics were irresponsible and ill-informed, Father Alphonse de Valk, editor of *The Interim*, published in February 1992 a supplement that placed *Fully Alive* and the conflict in clear perspective.

"*Fully Alive*," he wrote, "is the first Canadian attempt by a large school system [some fifty-two Boards of Education with approximately 500,000 students] to offer an alternative to the destructive Planned Parenthood programs which are offered as solutions to social programs when in reality they only aggravate them." He pointed out that he had read all twenty-one volumes of the *Fully Alive* texts for grades one to seven (three volumes per grade), "doing my best to keep an open mind and approaching them with sympathetic understanding as representing a commendable effort to guidelines of the Catholic faith."[3]

De Valk prefaced his conclusions with the simple reality that "taking issue with *Fully Alive* does not mean attacking bishops or Catholic schools. We support both and we support them wholeheartedly. But wholeheartedly does not mean mindlessly."

De Valk acknowledged that *Fully Alive* had "the makings of a true alternative to the subversive Planned Parenthood approach," but that "... its religious pedagogy is inadequate as a defense of the family today, and its sexual explicitness undermines the rights and works of parents who conscientiously carry out the tasks given them to do by God, on the one hand; then, on the other, contribute little if anything of worth to children of parents who don't care, while quite possibly being psychologically and spiritually dangerous to the child."[4]

De Valk pointed out that "while the Curriculum Guideline of 1983 [for *Fully Alive*] projected a program based on Pope John Paul's teaching on sexuality and sex education in the light of faith, the light of faith was reduced to a minimum."[5]

Explicitness, it seems was amplified to a maximum. But it was not the detail with which the text illustrations seemed obsessed that was the issue, but the very fact that sex was being taught at all.

Long before *The Interim*'s *Fully Alive* controversy drew the bishops' anger, the gifted and eloquent Dietrich von Hildebrand had contributed some of the clearest prose ever penned on the sexual aspect of human nature in his book *Sex Ed: The Basic Issue I*, a rejection of sex education programs. Wrote Hildebrand: "Apart from its depth, sex possesses a unique intimacy, intimate things call for a veil; they appeal to bashfulness. But we should realize that bashfulness is not identical with shame. Shame is the right response to things that are ugly: we are ashamed of certain actions which are not only morally evil, but also specifically mean and petty."[6]

Dr. William Marra, who followed Hildebrand's work with *Sex Ed: The Basic Issue II*, took aim at the graphic detail of the programs.

"This power to offend bashfulness and pierce the veil of modesty is to be found in all cases of indecent exposure of one's naked body to an innocent, in dirty jokes told especially to make innocence blush, and in the tasteless public sex instructions where the combination of description, diagrams, and analyses of behavior is enough to violate the spirit of any child and to induce fits of hurt weeping."[7]

Hurt weeping. Those words cause the heart to jump in recognition. Parents who have spent sleepless nights questioning its cause suddenly will see a light going on.

The student, Marra summarized, "has been rudely, crudely violated in a spiritual sense, he has been spiritually molested."

I would be remiss if I did not interject at this point and offer you the following firsthand account of how coarse, superficial, and boring human beings can be when they overturn "noble shame" and live out their days in the extreme opposite of "holy bashfulness."

Jojo was a high school teacher given to frequent loud condemnation of her parents, who, it seemed, constantly plagued her with inquiries about what she was doing with her salary paychecks. She claimed to be completely detached from the goings-on of the world, but secretly ran a Ford van shuttle service to and from Toronto's El Mocambo, inviting musicians out for a weekend at the commune in Cayuga where she lived (this was 1975).

Two men and seven women lived in the commune. Those with jobs turned their paychecks over to the commune. The others worked the farm. This meant growing and drying and selling "herbs." Planting "herbs" might mean sowing marijuana seeds around the base of the white guardrail posts along the highway where a policeman, steadying himself to focus binoculars on the farm, would never think of looking. The other source of income was for two of the women to marry and divorce Rastafarians, who paid handsomely for this quick route into Canada.

"Secrets" were not allowed on the farm.

"Secrets," said Jojo, "are merely weapons we store up to use against one another." This naturally meant newcomers to the farm family were required to tell in explicit detail their most valued sexual fantasies.

To ensure no secrets lurked anywhere, the door to the bathroom had been removed so that guests playing crokinole on the living-room floor would not be deprived of the goings-on in that multi-purpose cubicle. Anyone who wished could join anyone else in the shower at any time as long as he or she did not neglect his or her turn at crokinole.

All seven women had had sexual relations with the two men, and on one long, slow night in the previous months had circled the crokinole board expectantly while the two men, yielding to the necessity to shed all secrets, went upstairs and had sex with one another.

The evening of my visit, while the two men circled and smoked and tried crokinole with their big toes, Jojo, in a violent outburst excoriating her parents for challenging her choice of lifestyle, worked herself into a foaming (literally) lather and had a breakdown on the bathroom door. (It was now the coffee table, i.e, herbal tea table). She was squeezed into a van and taken to the emergency room, where she quickly recovered, but it meant her high school class required a supply teacher for three days.

A craving for power has mutilated and left unrecognizable the Catholic Church in the last half of this century. Dissenting religious and theologians did not discard the authority they rejected.

They assimilated it and found they liked the taste of infallibility. The militant sexologist's drive into the classrooms and into the earliest age groups is a grab for power. School and family are strapped onto the operating table. Those playing doctor wear, as surgical masks, the shield of "scientific" or "social" purpose.

And they are not doctors. They are the sexual revolution's "useful idiots" acting as a vehicle for the invasion of perverse sexology. In his characteristically delicate manner, Hildebrand muses: "Although it is sometimes very difficult to escape the suspicion the unconscious influences of sexual repressions are operative in those priests and nuns who rave for these sex education programs, let us in charity assume that such is not the case, and that their belief, that destroying the mystery of sex will aid purity, is itself held purely and in good faith. Nevertheless, this belief is sheer nonsense."[8]

A self-anointed class of spoiled, self-indulgent ex-nuns and ex-priests, having gone completely unchecked by their bishops, now act out, at the expense of the grade school children under their authority, those self-same sexual deliriums that drove them to shatter their own vocations. They have simply picked up in middle age from where they themselves left off as curiosity-driven tots, displaying the hallmark infantilism of camouflaging sex as a game or a project.

The results of such dangerous meddling are everywhere in newspaper headlines for parents to see. Hildebrand explains:

> Destroying the mysterious character of sex, presenting it as a merely biological affair, instead of in its God-given ultimate connection with spousal love, far from diminishing man's appetite for a brutal sexual satisfaction, will only foster his yielding to it.
>
> What these misguided teachers actually will kill is, not the temptations to impurity, but the sense for the depth and the mystery of sex, and its deep interwovenness with spousal love, they will kill the true authentic God-willed attraction and charm of sex, for the desiration of this mystery, for the horror of impurity. They will kill holy bashfulness, decency and modesty. They want the children to be informed about every

possible perversion. Can we imagine a more stupid idea! Have they forgotten that St. Paul said there are things which should not even be mentioned among us?

This sex education is a crime committed against the soul of any youth. By enforcing a laboratory view on his mind, it condemns him to an endless boredom. Man waging war on what is human. And this is done by priests and nuns, who let themselves be impressed by Dr. Mary Calderone.[9]

In challenging *Fully Alive*, the writers in *The Interim* were fulfilling Hildebrand's prescription.

Our clear duty as Catholics is to resist this totalitarian enslavement and, above all, to protect the souls of our children from the damage which threatened them. If the response to the triumph of impurity, the shamelessness and the barbaric murder of modesty in our epoch is to introduce in Catholic schools this alleged sex education, then let us protest with every available means. Let us fight relentlessly all the Catholic schools which introduce such practices. Not one penny should be given to a pastor who tolerates or endorses this abomination.[10]

Hildebrand leaves no room for fence-sitting, timid, doubting parents.

We must ceaselessly inundate the bishops with the protests, so that if—which, may God forbid—we do not succeed in opening their eyes to the abomination of sex education, they will at least yield to the pressure exerted by truly Catholic parents. I mean those parents who are the glory and strength of the Church, who believe firmly the Credo of Paul VI, who believe in the infallibility of the Church in matters of faith and morals, and who, unlike the small but noisy group of avant-gardists, accept obediently and lovingly the teaching of *Humanae Vitae. It is these quiet millions whose parental rights are being usurped. It is their children whose souls are endangered.*[11]

The knowledge that such a state of affairs was propelled into being by our own dissident religious burdens the faithful Catholic with a tremendous grief. Those very religious whose obvious sacrifice had made our weak human wills bearable, now, having abandoned celibacy and chastity, are a source of derision for the essence of the Catholic lifestyle.

Marra writes:

> If we are agreed, therefore, that our fallen nature renders us extremely sensitive to the lure of impure sex, and if we are further agreed that all lingering with sexual matters may constitute a temptation and an occasion of sin for us, even though they be presented in a pure way, then we must denounce as satanically vicious a program that means to saturate children and youth with twelve years of sex.
>
> Have the clergy and other educators defending these programs gone mad? Do they not remember how, especially in their adolescence, the slightest allusion to sex was enough to set in motion persistent temptations to impurity? Why now do they wish to inflict these cruel gratuitous temptations upon youth already too sorely tempted? Why, to make matters worse, do they link these tasteless graphic instructions in anatomy with the subtle poison of a situation ethics that flatters the individual even as it dethrones or ignores any absolute moral commandment?[12]

Tarring the wheels of chariots of fire ..

Marra then reminds all of just how far we have fallen:

> Impurity means simply any sexual activity isolated from wedded love. What in the intimacy and earnestness of married love is chaste and pure become defiling and degrading outside of marriage. Instead of tender and irrevocable self-donation, there is a squandering of self and desecration of the act intended by God to serve love in its twofold mystery.[13]

Tender and irrevocable self-donation. How I wish I had heard those wondrous words in school! How I wish teachers today would avail themselves of such beauty of thought! I sincerely wish every teacher entering the profession today was given as mandatory reading that enrichment package of words by Deitrich von Hildebrand and William A. Marra. They would reject the sex-ed curriculum out of hand and the scandal would end.

The factories producing the sex-ed troops were generated by and attractive to clergy and theologians who harbored a hatred for Roman Catholicism.

Father John McGoey described the sex-ed factory for Ontario Catholic teachers between 1965 and 1985, specifically St. Jerome's College in Waterloo, as "a fiasco."

Back in the Sixties, the principles of SIECUS were brought to St. Jerome's by, among others, Oblate Father Leo LaFreniere.

McGoey put his finger on the exact device by which teachers were conditioned to adopt the material:

> This would have come to nothing except that for twenty to twenty-five years the unsuspecting, naive bishops of Ontario sent all family life teachers to St. Jerome's for specialized training.
>
> Was it not a Catholic College and the course taught by a priest? Surely, Catholic teaching would not only be protected but promoted there!
>
> Little did they know!
>
> Many teachers and students were shocked by what they heard. Suddenly sex was morally neutral; masturbation was normal and healthy...
>
> However, had not the shocked trainees been taught to respect, to defer to priests just as the bishops saw fit to defer to the 'professionals' teaching the course.[14]

Yes indeed. In spite of the great blurring that followed Vatican II, the bishops retained their power over lay professionals, their ability to intimidate, and seemed even more adept than usual at bullying tactics.

McGoey writes:

> The well of Catholic Family Life Education has been poisoned. Thousands of Ontario teachers who came to St. Jerome's College for Catholic Family Life Education were submerged in raw sex. They were told that morality is no

longer relevant to sexuality or family life education. However, shocked teachers were cautioned against making moral judgments. The Scriptural censor of judging one's neighbor was misapplied so that the worst scenario was for a teacher to imply that any other was doing wrong. They left the course assuming that basic Catholic morality was now different, nothing being right or wrong. All this because those in charge insist that moral theology be restricted to religious education.

Perhaps ten percent of the teachers joined the movement to total sexual license. They would lead a quiet campaign against the "sexually hung up old guard."[15]

Whatever their shock, the other 90 percent of the teachers were not used to leading a challenge to the bishops against their own priests. The bishops hearing nothing, assumed that all was going well.

Fr. Leo LaFreniere [yes, the Polka Dot Priest] readied the training for Catholic Life Education, offered it to the bishops who accepted it without questioning his sincerity or competence.[16]

TWO

COUNTDOWN TO THE NINETIES

IT IS HARD TO DO GOOD to a bishop who announces he will soon empty the sanctuary of all signs and symbols of the faith and if you don't like it—get out.

It is nigh on unthinkable to bless a bishop who makes fun of your orthodoxy while he allows ex-nuns to turn a Catholic Center into a New Age nest of lesbian poetesses, scoffing at the very idea that Jesus is God.

It is humanly impossible to resist tears when a bishop, succumbing to blackmail by his trendy, homosexual priests' council, excoriates then exiles holy priests defending the traditions that have cemented the faithful to the Church of Christ for two thousand years.

How then, Lord, to dredge up even an iota of respect for bishops who turn over to degenerate sexologists those innocents whose very souls Thou hast placed in their trust?

How then, Lord, do we comprehend right action when schismatic bishops throw the dice that will rend asunder Thy seamless garment?

Where, Lord, do we go for a shepherd when those Thou hast appointed fence us out of Thy fields by an inversion of the meaning of collegiality? Thy glens and glades have been turned into pastures of Asmodeus. Where do we look, Lord?

The ambush and sabotage of catechetics in the Sixties and Seventies was now paying off for the promoters of a contraceptive society. There were no longer nuns teaching catechism. In Vatican II's aftermath, spending time with children was beneath them. Priests were either no longer welcome in the schools or were no longer interested. But most important of all, sex and morality were no longer connected on the school curricula. The import of this mutilation of Catholic morality was beyond measure.

Alas, the Catholic school system was now promoting the notion that "family/sex education should be morally neutral leaving religious moral values to be taught by some other teacher in some other course."[1]

That "some other teacher" was by the Eighties more likely than not teaching that the greatest love of all, as Whitney Houston sings, "is to love yourself"!

Self, the private world of the child, was now isolated. God was set adrift, some benevolent investor drilling offshore who would fuel our plans for the future no matter what blueprint we followed.

Catholic bishops, for twenty-five years now, have been falling over one another to apologize for once preaching that the Catholic Church possessed the blueprint for the future—a.k.a. Salvation. Philip Scharper in *The Hidden Faces of God, pursuing what he gleefully sensed was the death knell for "extra Ecclesiam nulla salus"* ("outside the Church there is no salvation"), wrote: "It took the Second Vatican Council to brush aside the theological dust of centuries and restore an understanding of the steep grandeur of God's plan of salvation, the role of other religious within it and the relationship of the Catholic Church to the Kingdom of God."[2]

But it took the bishops of North America to fashion a focus on orgasm that said to children who could not spell the words, "outside of sex there is no fulfillment."

Like its counterpart—the American Conference of Catholic Bishops—the Canadian CCB is situated in its nation's capital city. It borrows from that political arena a pace, a posture, and a pretence it might not have were it found in Vancouver or Calgary or Halifax. To this body of men, the Canadian bishops, goes the responsibility for seeing that the Divinity of Jesus Christ and His mission as Messiah is taught to each and every child of every Catholic family in the land. How they respond to that challenge can be seen clearly by looking in on their behavior in the decade leading up to 1991. The scenario was the imposition on Catholic classrooms of a new program in which they, as creators, their bureaucracy, as producers, and their publishing houses, as executive producers, all had a vested interest.

The current chairman of the Canadian Conference of Catholic Bishops is Marcel Gervais, Archbishop of the archdiocese of Ottawa. In early 1991, Gervais began appearing in the secular press in a new photo portrait, styled, no doubt, for the purpose of impressing upon the general public a sense of stature, not so much of the office but of the man who held it. Critics feared he was posturing for a cardinal's red hat, which, like most archbishops, he was known to crave. More cynical observers simply accepted that he was proposing himself to be the first head of the Canadian Catholic Church when the schism between the CCCB and Rome would inevitably be announced. Invariably, jokesters would wonder if Gervais might not have a papier-mâché tiara waiting in the cupboard.

Whatever the purpose of his studied self-promotion program, one thing was clear—Gervais's was the only name appearing in press releases regarding the CCCB. The conference was in his grip. So, apparently, were the bishops.

It would have been natural then if the sex-ed scandal brewing pitted protesters against this figurehead. But, another fact made it positively justified: the sex-ed program in question was the creation of none other than Gervais himself.

The *Fully Alive* scandal filling supplements to *The Interim* in the Fall of 1991 and 1992 cast a much-needed spotlight on the goings-on. Father McGoey, in an article for *The Interim*, "The Poisoned Well," picks up the story in the early Eighties.

1980

"Bishop John Sherlock of London, Ontario, was in charge of

Family Life Education until he was elected President of the CCCB in 1983. Earlier in 1980 he had been given a highly respected auxiliary bishop, Marcel Gervais, whom he considered quite capable of supervising the production of the Ontario Family Life Education Curriculum."[3]

Writing in *The Orator*, Sylvia MacEachern, a Catholic mother and writer fighting for the recapture of the rights of parents by parents, outlined the movers and shakers behind *Fully Alive*.

"In 1980 Archbishop Gervais was serving as auxiliary bishop to the Diocese of London, Ontario. For some time, parents in Essex County had been valiantly fighting a wave of SIECUS-style secular humanist sex education launched within the Separate Schools under the guise of a Roman Catholic Family Life program. This anti-parent, anti-family curriculum, known as BAPP (*Becoming a Person* Program) was designed by Fr. Walter J. Imbrioski.

"Fr. Imbrioski held the dubious credentials of serving on the SIECUS Board of Directors 1968-70. In 1975, after many years of teaching and writing on human sexuality, Fr. Imbrioski decided to forego his vocation and his vow of celibacy to become Mr. Imbrioski; he married his BAPP co-author Frances Imzec."[4]

1981

"Eventually, Catholic Schools were presented with a rehashed version of BAPP, it was called the *Benzinger Family Life Series*. But parents weren't fooled. Again they protested the anti-parent stance of the program and its sparse reference to God, sin, and Holy Scripture....

"In response to the deluge of complaints, Archbishop Gervais did a critique of the *Benzinger* program. His minor criticisms of the program neglected to address parental concerns—and *Benzinger continued to corrupt the minds and morals of Catholic youth.*"

1982

Within a year of issuing the *Benzinger* critique, the Archbishop himself was listed as a speaker in a teacher training session for the sex-ed programs. Other speakers listed on the roster were:

"Dr. William Stayton: pro-abortion Baptist minister known to advocate homosexuality." (Dr. Stayton's name now appears as guest speaker at conferences promoted in the *Second Stone* ... a pro-homosexual national newspaper for gay and lesbian Christians.)

"Dr. Mike Barrett: founder of *SIECCAN Journal*, which promotes the usual SIECUS philosophy; wife Ann is heavily involved in Planned Parenthood.

"Peter Naus: well-known to parents for his heavy involvement with sex-ed programs, actively involved with SIECUS, member of the Board of Directors of SIECCAN, believes homosexuality is intrinsically equal to heterosexuality (a view shared by Fr. Andre Guindon, Professor of Sexual Ethics, University of St. Paul). Presently director of studies in Sexuality, Marriage, and the Family Program, St. Jerome's College, University of Waterloo, Ontario.

"Dr. John Theis: ex-priest married to ex-nun, contributor to *SIECCAN Journal*, Professor at St. Jerome's College, University of Waterloo, Ontario.

"Dr. Mike Carrera: executive member of SIECUS; known to express hostility towards the Roman Catholic Church's 'rigid views' on masturbation, homosexuality, and oral sex; known to believe that no one can masturbate too much." Known for brown-bagging ping-pong balls to teach genitalia to primary school children.

"Margaret Villamizer: known Marxist/Leninist, Essex County Separate School Board psychologist, who believed that baby boys should be turned over in their cribs and masturbated.

"Fr. 'Mike' Prier: Professor of Moral Theology at St. Peter's Seminary, London, Ontario, has advised seminarians that there are no moral absolutes; directs men to accept their homosexuality as part of their nature; promotes the feminist concept of androgyny, teaches that masturbation is seldom a serious sin. Assisted Archbishop Gervais with compilation of the sex-ed series *Fully Alive*."

McGoey describes those early days.

"With Bishop Sherlock's blessing, I visited Chatham to view the original material for *Fully Alive*, the new family education program which Bishop Gervais showed to me reluctantly. While he and Fr. Angus MacDougall, secretary of the Ontario Bishop's Conference, promised me a pre-publication copy, it was never sent, nor was I able to obtain it through proper channels.

"When I eventually did see the three first grades, I was appalled that it was going out in the name of the Ontario bishops and let them know so."[5]

SIECUS, Planned Parenthood, Zero Population Growth are the Establishment of the contraceptive mentality. It does not require a rocket scientist to figure out that sex education in the schools is the avenue along which merchants of contraception will exhibit, promote, and market their wares. The very word "Catholic" in a school system that pushes contraception is as out of place as a little red schoolhouse on a roller-coaster.

Something new on earth? Baum's new focus perhaps?

We pick up Father Alphonse de Valk's analysis in *The Interim*:

"A deplorable anti-Catholic, pro-Planned Parenthood bias had prevailed in them and had spread from them into the wider Catholic educational community in the province."

"Planned Parenthood," de Valk clarifies, "rejects moral teaching as Christians understand it, and mocks abstinence and chastity as 'Victorian,' totally unrealistic or useless. They accept promiscuous behavior, whether of teenagers or of adults, as normal and a fact of life one had better learn to accept."

As de Valk explains, "By the late Seventies, Catholic dissent on moral issues had reached major proportions in North America.

"*Human Sexuality*, a publication issued on behalf of the Board of Directors of the Catholic Theological Society of America ... endorsed by a prestigious group of theologians, flatly contradicted Church teaching on no less than thirty-five different specific topics.

"In short," de Valk concludes, "it represents the abandonment of a coherent Catholic moral theology."[6]

As early as 1987, Sabina McLuhan, then editor of *The Interim*, saw in *Fully Alive* "an absence of a context of specific Catholic teaching, an unhealthy pre-occupation with the children's ego, a program in which many of the lessons dealing with emotions and family and peer relationships 'could violate' family privacy and parental roles."

What was also obvious was an obsession with genitalia.

"Even at the grade one level children are expected to become familiar with correct names for genitals and to discuss genital differences between sexes. It is anticipated that children will ask questions about sexual intercourse following these lessons in grade 1 and 2 ..."[7]

Here, at this point, a troubling specter rises to cloud over the whole *Fully Alive* program, namely, a boardroom table surrounded by priests, nuns, and bishops discussing the genital differences between the sexes in language grade one children supposedly could understand.

"Penis. Vagina ..." the chorus echoes.

How were the bishops tricked into performing such a calamity?

Sylvia MacEachern dispels some of the murky camouflage SIECUS lowers over its involvement in schools:

> Catholics battling sex-ed programs over the years are well aware that all sex education materials are rooted directly or indirectly in SIECUS. SIECUS-style education in 'human sexuality' by its very nature (secular humanist) cannot—and will not—impart moral absolutes. In fact, the SIECUS philosophy, supported and promoted by feminists and Planned Parenthood alike, condones contraception, premarital sex, abortion, homosexuality and androgyny.
>
> Androgyny is a concept developed by the feminist movement advocating that gender is not fixed, or biologically based, but fluid. In consequence, the "whole" personality is seen as an amalgam of male and female characteristics. This catch-all gender is designed to counter so-called sexual stereotyping believed by feminists to be learned in the heterosexual environment of the nuclear family with its traditional male/female division of labor.
>
> Proponents of androgyny encourage boys to act like girls, men to act like women and vice versa. In natural consequence, androgyny extends its open arms.

> ... any activity that might imply that there are societal roles normally based upon one's God-given gender is subjected to the feminist process of role-reversal.
>
> ... compilers of the texts have gone to inordinate lengths to ensure that children aren't exposed to one smidgen of so-called "sexual stereotyping."[8]

McGoey notes:

> The contributors to and writers of the documents apart from Bishop Gervais were selected heavily from the inner circle of St. Jerome's. As the Archbishop [Gervais] announced, *Fully Alive* was not going to be integrated into Religious Education, but be a separate class [of five religious education classes a week]. In this class, Family Life was to be taught, stopping short of Catholic teaching on morality, rightness or wrongness, where it was claimed to have no relevance.
>
> The class text at St. Jerome's training course [several hundred pages] in use at the time contained less than two pages on love and one page on celibacy; but twenty pages with detailed erotic drawings on masturbation, thirty-five pages on homosexuality as an acceptable alternate lifestyle and many pages and explicit drawings of copulation and foreplay.[9]

Thirty-five pages on homosexuality? Erotic drawings galore? It sounded like an entire army of psycho-sexually immature dissident religious were having a field day with the teachers of the province. And this while pedophilia scandals rocked the Church from coast to coast?

"Ontario Catholics are stunned by the silence of their bishops on the vital matter of human sexuality," wrote McGoey.[10]

Clearly an agenda was reaching into the classroom, the desk, the mind of individual children in a way educators had never experienced before. Why? What were they after? What could possibly be so valued that marauding ex-religious would put at risk the minds and souls of children at such an innocent age? By what power mechanism were the bishops of Ontario coerced into not only not defending the souls in their trust against scandal, but actually enlisted to fuel and propel it all under a heavy blanket of silence?

McGoey's assessment was bleak, calling sex education as a whole "... the greatest con job perpetrated by the NEA [National Education Association] and the NCEA [National Catholic Education Association] bureaucracies in the United States....The public system in Canada bought this fraud, lock, stock and barrel, from self-anointed secular, humanist spokesmen....The Catholic system in Ontario did so by default of episcopal leadership and its canonization of the so-called 'professionals' in whom they put implicit but unwarranted trust."[11]

MacEachern wrote: "By 1986, the draft format of the new sex-ed program—*Fully Alive*—appeared in schools across Ontario. The final text bore the seal of approval of the Ontario Conference of Catholic Bishops.

"The introductory remarks in the [*Fully Alive*] grade one teacher's manual suffices to sound the alarm. Here, Fr. Leo LaFreniere is commended for his 'pioneering efforts' in sex education which were 'the beginning of *Fully Alive*.'

"This is one and the same Fr. LaFreniere credited with introducing the first Family Life sex-ed programs in Canada!"[12] And known for brown-bagging Dr. Carrera's ping-pong balls.

This human construct, this juggernaut of paint-by-number, join-the-dot genitalia obsessions created and propelled by dissenting priests, nuns, and bishops would roll relentlessly and ruthlessly over parental objections.

Parents daring to challenge the bishops were labeled a fanatical minority, vilified as Dark Age hysterics, and constantly treated with that "pharisaic elitist" pout of the dissenting clergy who had fashioned mini-careers out of their public attacks on the celibate priesthood.

Dooley says widespread consultation did not take place. "They [the guiding principles of *Fully Alive*] were the result of decisions by Bishop Gervais, Auxiliary Bishop of London, and a small group of consultants."[13]

Those who did ask questions, were told over and over again, "You are only a small minority. The vast majority of parents had no complaints."

One Toronto mother, Mrs. Catherine Balger, asked, "Would

parents violate the privacy of their children by calling them together for group sex education? Would the parent present sexually explicit programs and intimate matters to their children under such conditions? Surely, such programs would rightly be recognized as sexual abuse. Yet, programs are being presented in schools today under such conditions."[14]

De Valk pinpointed precisely the abrogation of parental rights.

"By setting a timetable grade by grade, the program undermines the rights of parents who wish to guide their children in sexuality on a one-to-one basis.

"*Fully Alive*'s sex-ed component appears to me contrary to custom, modesty, reason, and church teaching.

"*Fully Alive* ... is secular because its designers, on principle, decided to treat the subject of family education without the light of faith."[15]

Dr. Bernharda Meyer writing, in *The Orator*, points out:

> Catholic teaching is clear that it is the inalienable right of parents to be the primary educators of their child in sexual matters. Primary does not mean, as interpreted in *Fully Alive*, merely a right in time—chronologically first—but, even in this respect, the program forces parents, from Grade 1 on, to hasten according to its demands.
>
> In fact ... parents are not left free to decide when or whether, to enlighten their child.

She cites from Theme 3, "Created Sexual," the statement to parents:

> Information about sexual intercourse is not included in the school program until Grade 4 so that parents can introduce this intimate subject.
>
> In spite of the pretense of giving parents the power of discretion, they are forced into a deadline at Grade 4.
>
> In Grade 5, both the teacher and student books recognize the great differences in the development and the beginning of puberty of children in the age group from 10 to 17 (pp. 63-67 and 62, 64, 66). Ironically, the same program ignores the immense differences in their emotional, psychological, rela-

tional, and spiritual development and stability by offering the explicit sex-ed to all children of a grade alike.[16]

Fully Alive is not Catholic. The program lacks the most essential and basic Catholic knowledge about good and evil, its application and practical use for sexual behavior, and our Church's means of assistance through the Sacraments.

The program does not provide formation in chastity and sexual stability.

Dr. Meyer points to a directive teachers are given for grade one. It reads: "What did Ann's mother tell her (Ann) about boys and girls being different? (review the terms: penis, scrotum, vulva, vagina). Mention that the vagina is inside a girl's body. The vulva is the folds of skin on the outside of the body. A boy's scrotum is under his penis."

This is for grade one!

Now for grade four.

"In your discussion with the students, the following information should be included.... The husband's penis fits inside his wife's vagina ... during sexual intercourse sperm cells from the husband leave his body through his penis and go into his wife's body. The sperm cells travel through the wife's vagina and into her uterus."

Now for grade five.

"At certain times, semen can leave the man's body through the urethra; this is called an ejaculation, but an ejaculation cannot happen unless an erection occurs first. This does not mean that every time a man has an erection that an ejaculation has to follow. An erection occurs when blood flows into the soft tissue of the penis to become firm and larger. Afterwards, the blood flows back out of the tissues of the penis. Then the penis becomes soft again."

Grade six.

"During an act of sexual intercourse, the husband's penis is erect in order to fit inside the wife's vagina. After ejaculation, the sperm are released in the woman's vagina and from here they move into the uterus and then into the fallopian tubes."

Dad? Mom?

"When sex is discussed in the classroom," Meyer adds, "no child can escape."

> Sex-ed does not lead to peacefulness: when children are taught in a group about male genitalia functioning, erection, increase in size and volume, fitting inside the vagina, getting firmer and softer, it leads to arousal, upset, loss of self-respect, depression—and ... promotes sin because of the imaginative stimulation and peer communication such teaching engenders.
>
> If Catholic adults were taught from the pulpits, and through support groups at Catholic schools, about the Catholic modern teaching of the Theology of Human Sexuality—with emphasis on the Sacrament of Confession and Reconciliation—our Families could be restored to Christ.

Alphonse de Valk details the omissions:

> There is not an inkling of God as judge, or about the child learning to love God.... No discussion anywhere of sin.... In grade 7, for example, the questions discussed are mainly psychological and sociological ones: the difference between extroverts and introverts, the qualities essential for friendship, the responsibilities of a person within a family, the responsibilities of a person within the larger society.... Are repeated again and again with a seemingly never-ending emphasis on self, on me.
>
> We are the center. The child is the focus. God is a friendly satellite. There is constant self-examination, but not the kind which precedes the sacrament of reconciliation, which focuses on one's relationship with God first, then on that of society.

"On reading grade six and seven tests," de Valk says "... I had a growing feeling that this emphasis on emotion and feeling had strong feminine or, perhaps, I should say, feminist overtones. By grade 7 introspection and self-examination reaches an unhealthy level."[17]

Unbelievably, the entire projection of *Fully Alive*'s progress, through grades one to seven, deliberately avoided teaching about or even making reference to the Blessed Trinity.

God, in *Fully Alive*, appears in one-dimensional form, not as Trinitarian, three Persons in one nature, the very foundation of the whole of western thought. God the Father and God the Son play no role. But Spirit is given great play. Suffice it to say Spirit does not in any way mean the Holy Spirit. Spirit in *Fully Alive* is faceless, characterless, an entity bearing ominous overtones of the Spirit of "Women-Church." At last, after a millennia of meditation and theorizing and argument, the Spirit of God is given a face, one the feminists can live with—theirs.

And all of this implanted in the classrooms under strict controls and a never-ending veil of secrecy.

Bernadette Mysko of Saskatoon, Saskatchewan, cites, about classroom material being made as difficult as possible to inspect, "At one time in order to read newly developed 'religious' materials being taught to my grade seven daughter, I was put in a broom storage room next to a classroom because, the teacher couldn't allow the materials to go any further from her sight.

"We experienced firsthand a 'set-up' school board meeting with thirty principals walking in, attired in their business suits, to sit at the back of a meeting attended by about fifty parents."[18]

One pair of parents provide the following glimpse of Bishop Gervais in action.

"I pulled my children from the 'pre-piloting' of *FA* in 1986. In September of '87, when we learned that the program was to be piloted [in our schools] and no one was allowed to keep their children out of it, I pulled them out of school."[19]

Concerning the treatment of a trustee who sided with the parents at a public meeting with Gervais present:

> Well, the Bishop and his cohorts cut him to ribbons, and so totally disarmed him that he, like many people that night, left in a state of shock. The parents had wrongfully believed that with right on their side, it would simply be a matter of expressing our convictions and the program be dropped.
>
> No one could have been prepared for the onslaught of ridicule and verbal abuse that was heaped on all who opposed the program that night. Two things which Bishop Gervais said drew an audible gasp from the parents.
>
> One was, "Who are you to tell us what is good for your children!"

He spoke with such anger that he had to calm himself a few times, because he saw he was getting carried away.

But it was evident that he saw the parents as imbeciles whose duty was to shut up and obey.

The other quote was, "*On va le rentrer dans leur tête à coup de marteau s'il le faut.*"—("We'll hammer it into their heads if necessary.")[20]

Linda Britton, a Catholic sex-ed teacher, put her finger on a prime ingredient at work in the crisis.

"In my experience it is the contracepting and sterilized parents who are most willing to ... delegate to schools their children's sexual instruction. Because they are out of touch with their own gift of sexuality, they do not recognize the great importance of passing down to their children, personally, that great treasure which is the true understanding of sexuality."[21]

Brian Taylor, president of the Ontario Association of Catholic families elaborates:

"It is as Fr. Paul Marx of Human Life International mentions, over 70 percent of teachers practice contraception or are sterilized, they have temporarily or permanently made fruitless education regarding procreation within their own families, let alone in society's educational institutions. The witness to the teacher's chaste life is essential to the educational task."[22]

In the supposed attempt to sensitize the innocent to intimacy, intimacy is made commonplace; innocence is shot to shreds. The actual result is desensitization, evident in the increasing lust and violence in social life.

D. J. Dooley, writing for *Challenge* magazine, a traditional Catholic publication, revealed that some Catholic boards in the province "were defying Church teaching by giving out condoms. The excuse proffered in York Region, north of Toronto, and at a Catholic Central High School in London, right on the bishop's doorstep, was that the schools presented and upheld the position of the magisterium, but for those students who had made up their minds not to follow the official teaching the officials had provided contraceptive measures.

"In a very strong statement, Archbishop Ambrozic denounced

this shoddy kind of compromise. Contraception education, he declared, sells out the value of chastity, and what Catholic educators need to convey to young people 'is that they have faith in them as persons capable of responding to the truth of their lives, a truth that comes from God.'"[23]

What Ambrozic had inherited was the fruits of the *Winnipeg Statement*, that notorious betrayal of the Magisteriun and *Humanae Vitae* orchestrated by Gregory Baum and Remi de Roo of Victoria, British Columbia. The total denial of responsibility for upholding the truths of Catholic morality and doctrine conspired in by the bishops of Canada at Winnipeg had opened the door for every possible perversion of service by theologians, clergy and educators.

It is ironic that Ambrozic, in his role as Archbishop of Toronto, should in 1991 be staring down the smarmy face of dissent from the separate school board bunker in York Region North. That board contains at least two of the founding members of the Coalition of Concerned Canadian Catholics, the absolutely silly association of very anxious ex-nuns and ex-priests who, having betrayed their vows to marry and engage in sex, decided in the Eighties that it was not really fulfilling to have your cake unless you could eat it too. Now they are agitating for married priests and women priests. Not satisfied with destroying their own credibility in their agenda to obliterate the celibate priesthood, now they want the Catholic Church to deny itself to please them.

Michael Otis detailed the resulting clash of wills in *The Interim.*

> In April, of '91, Toronto Archbishop Aloysius Ambrozic issued a strongly worded "no" to condoms as a solution to the spread of AIDS or as a contraceptive. Yet, the York Separate School (Catholic) Board may place its stamp of approval on a revised policy that will contain an explanation of how condom use may prevent AIDS.
>
> "It seems like the York Region Separate Board is determined to circumvent the Archbishop's refusal to condone the teaching of 'safe sex,'" said Janet Smith, a parent living in the area.
>
> The chief architect of the "safe sex" policy appears to be

Religious Education Coordinator, (former priest), Noel Cooper who expressed the standard cliché "astonishment" by which modernists betray their true colors with Archbishop Ambrozic's "unrealistic" statement in an internal memo to [Program Superintendent] John MacRae and [Director of Education] Frank Baobesich.

At the direction of ... John MacRae and ... Noel Cooper, the ... [YSSB] Board had been trying to draft a "safe sex" policy since the fall of 1990.

When the Board was poised to formally recommend that sexually active students use condoms and spermicide, the bishop responsible for the York Region, Robert Clune, threatened "to make known ... that the notion is not in conformity with Catholic teaching and practice."[24]

An act of duty that required courage in 1990.

John MacRae has long been a fixture at the York Region Board. It was he who claimed that his role in program development made him the equivalent of a bishop in his own profession. It is not surprising, then, that the bishops get no more from him than the Pope gets from them.

Dooley comments on the educators involved in the Coalition of Concerned Canadian Catholics.

"These people are teaching teachers to hate and resist the traditional teaching of the Church. Is it any wonder that the Catholic school system is not performing satisfactorily?"[25]

Still, one can barely escape the suspicion that the sexologist in the classroom is a pawn of a larger game—an ideology being advanced castle by castle over and above the heads of the befuddled bishops, an ideology following the dotted lines on the map of childhood in pursuit of a treasure we cannot yet fathom.

THREE

A REMARKABLE TRIBUTE

THE THOROUGHNESS with which the sexologists invaded Catholic schools, supplanted catechetics, made fools out of liberated nuns and goofballs out of feminist priests demonstrated the organizational power of Planned Parenthood, while the legendary networking of radical feminism illustrated clearly their firm control over their pathetic bishops' bureaucracies. In their headlong drive to capture the innocents at their desks, the feminist Planned Parenthood forces shared the same vehicle—the bishops' egos. But if Gervais fancied that his teaching ability kept him in the sex-ed fast lane, he was to learn to his chagrin that compared to him the SIECUS/SIECCAN speedster was sporting racing stripes.

In the most scandal-ridden age in Church history, a creeping homosexualization of school curriculum left parents numb with disbelief. Everywhere the drive for equality and marriage rights and family benefits for same-sex partners was splitting Protestant congregations, fragmenting church councils, grabbing and holding headlines with ease. In June of 1990, the Gays of Ottawa sued City Hall for the right to have Father's Day declared Equality Day for Gays and Lesbians. And won!

What was the connection between the gay rights movement and the proliferation of homosexual attitudes that spread fungus-like into school texts down to the earliest level? What could possibly motivate such an assault on small children? What were they after?

Questions asked of the bishops brought answers from appalling heights of arrogance. A 1990 *Interim* editorial detailed parental response.

In 1987, a number of Catholic parents across Ontario formed the Ontario Association of Catholic Families (OACF) after their earlier protests against *Fully Alive* were rebuffed.

Prior to this, they had submitted three lengthy professional evaluations of *Fully Alive* by persons knowledgeable in the fields of psychology, catechetics, and the latency period. They never received a reply.

On May 31, 1990, Archbishop Gervais responded to a letter about sex education in the schools written by OACF's president, Brian Taylor:

> The term "latency period" is an artificial construct, based on superficial observation by Sigmund Freud, a questionable authority on children.
>
> The latency period ... is described as a stage in which sexual impulses are latent.
>
> If there is any truth to the "latency period," it is that at a very early age children ask questions with an innocence and a purity which allows parents and teachers to give correct answers without fear of disturbing them; this information is accepted with all the simplicity and trust of a child. There is no prurient interest.
>
> If parents insist that children have no interest at all in anything sexual (no parent would suggest such a thing) in anything having to do with the origins of life, it may be because their children have learnt that they will get no answers from their parents, and must seek them elsewhere.[1]

And so, with a stroke of the pen, Gervais dismissed two impediments to *Fully Alive*'s implementation. Latency did not exist. And the parents were to blame for children's lack of knowledge.

Father Alphonse de Valk responded: "If Archbishop Gervais believes that today there is no period of latency or innocence for children, then that's a private view he is entitled to hold. But we are entitled to disagree with it. When that private view is incorporated into a public program, we have the right to challenge that program."[2]

Murray McGovern, pediatrician and psychiatrist, states simply that:

> Virtually every practitioner of psychiatry agrees that between six and thirteen years of age, a necessary "latency" phase of development sets in to quiet the libidinous (sexual) and aggressive drives universally experienced unconsciously and consciously during the preschool period of development....
>
> Psychiatrists accept the opportunity of the "latency" style of psycho-sexual development as an imperative time to focus on the social, moral and spiritual dimensions of development. The mind develops the ability to abstract and shift from primary egocentricity and narcissism, to allocentric identification with idealized others (ego ideals).[3]

The so-called professionals who decided the latency period did not exist—a loose grab bag of ex-priests, ex-nuns, feminists, and Planned Parenthood agents—had succeeded in maneuvering the bishops under Gervais into publicly endorsing a complete falsehood and to deny Church teaching to boot.

Alphonse de Valk summarizes.

"If the Ontario bishops think that the best way to introduce little children to family life education is to say as little as possible to them about our Lord Jesus and to reply instead on a separate religious education course to integrate the various aspects, they are entitled to that opinion.

"But," de Valk added, "the bishops may not demand that the rest of us accept that pedagogical approach unless it can be shown to be in harmony with the Church's teaching on the subject."[4]

Writes McGoey in "The Poisoned Well":

> If Archbishop Gervais accepts full blame for what has come through St. Jerome's and SIECCAN and through him, to the Catholic schools, he could begin decontamination.
>
> The Archbishop sees the problem when he reminds the children of how much God loves them, but he misses the

answer when he fails to teach them how much they need to love God for their own well-being.[5]

On October 17, 1991, Bishop O'Mara wrote a letter to the directors of the sixty-two separate school boards in Ontario calling the *Fully Alive* program "a remarkable tribute to what enlightened collaboration can achieve for our home and school community."

He then addressed criticism of the program as follows: "Recent criticisms of *Fully Alive,* as aired in *The Interim,* should be simply ignored. It is an irresponsible mixture of misguided zeal, error, misrepresentation, half truths and innuendoes. It undermines the total credibility of the editors of *The Interim.*"[6]

The letter was followed by pressure on Catholic schools to cease advertising in the pro-life *Interim,* and a tidal wave of public relations dictated by Archbishop Gervais aimed at erasing from the map any credibility *The Interim* might have left.

The credibility of the bishops needed no such attack. It had crumbled into loony-tunes sparkle dust long ago. While excoriating the Catholic writers who challenged their scandals, they turned a blind eye to the mess they had erected in the wake of the once-respected Catholic schools:

- a director of religious education in Alberta who refuses to bless herself because she claims it is "sexist";
- a nun who teaches children Bible stories in the basement during Mass on Sunday and hosts a lesbian outreach circle on Wednesday;
- a parish in Alberta whose feminists rewrite what they call a new version of the Our Father as Earthmaker, Painbearer, Lifegiver;
- and homosexual and pedophile scandals washing in a murky surf from coast to coast.

O'Mara's letter was dated October 17, 1991. Never one to miss a beat, Planned Parenthood of Toronto sent out a letter dated October 21, 1991 to school board chairpersons, citing their mandate of "encouraging and facilitating responsible, informed decision-making regarding birth planning and sexual health issues. It is only natural then, that one of our concerns is the status of sexuality education in our school system."[7]

The letter acknowledged resistance to its goals and advises the school board chairperson, "Those holding public office must act cautiously in addressing this subject."[8]

Then it spelled out its anti-life anthem:

"The rate of unintended pregnancies, especially among teenagers, remains seriously high. Consider the anguish of a teenager having to choose from among parenthood, abortion and giving a child up for adoption. Postponing or even canceling education and career goals, and dealing with the other tumultuous family and emotional issues present in this situation. As well there is the financial burden to the province in health care costs related to those pregnancies, and welfare and social services costs which tend to be higher for single and/or teenager parents."[9]

The letter ends with the plea for school board chairpersons, "... to work with us for the implementation of mandatory sexuality education in our province."[10]

This anti-life, anti-family, anti-God, anti-love declaration of war on Christian morality bears the signatures of Jeff Gill, President, and Ray Tomalty, Vice-President.

In an attached complaint package, Planned Parenthood states: "the variation in the number of students actually taking the courses and programs is 'worrisome.'"[11]

It lists that any Planned Parenthood "Mission and Purpose" statement must indicate the extent to which the program is oriented toward birth planning, toward the prevention of teen pregnancies, toward the prevention of sexually transmitted diseases, and toward the promotion of healthy sexual attitudes and values.

As opposed to?

In typical inverse, reverse jargon Planned Parenthood rolls out its demand for mandatory uniform sex education in the following masterpiece of double-speak:

"No teenagers in Ontario should have to suffer the consequences of receiving inadequate education in the crucial area of sexuality, health issues and birth planning.

"Attendance should be mandatory for sex-ed programs. It should start in kindergarten and continue to grade 12."[12]

Hands-on instruction in the new phallic religion.

"For example, with regard to condom use, simply lecturing students is not sufficient to ensure understanding. Unless the students are actually given condoms in class, asked to open the packages and allowed to practice on an artificial model how to put it on correctly, we will be negligent in protecting them from sexually transmitted diseases and unwanted pregnancies.

"We recommend that the Sexual Health Education program be a pass/fail course." Then, in the next sentence schizophrenically adds: "Students should not feel academically threatened by this all-important course."[13]

These guidelines for the hunting and killing of babies and the spiritual mutilation of teenagers is drawn from the mental firing range of Maureen Jessop and Ellen Rosenblatt, authors of the 1981 *Adolescent Birth and Planning Needs, Ontario in the Eighties*, published by Planned Parenthood of Ontario, and Ronald and Juliet Goldman's 1982 *Children's Sexual Thinking.*

FOUR
THE NEON BISHOP

RECENTLY, on a television talk show, I remarked how I had been surrounded all my life by priests—how I had served them as an altar boy, sought them out in adolescence, and enjoyed their friendship in adulthood—and I added that I had never met a bad man among them.

The interviewer responded with, "You haven't?"

Of course, I should explain, the interview took place in Canada where, by 1991, twenty priests and brothers in Newfoundland alone were in the spotlight for abusing youths in their trust. Forty other cases dotted the rest of the country.

The interviewer reminded me of that, as interviewers are wont to do, and asked me if I thought it was because the clergy had been having an identity crisis. I could tell she had recently interviewed a bishop.

What then, she wanted to know, had gone wrong with the Catholic Church?

I thought about being at church that day, watching the liturgy that once was the glory of the ages now reduced to "vaudeville" without the slapstick, liturgical dancers flopping and flapping here and there like latter-day Druids in need of deep personal therapy and pompous deacons behaving as if they had been trained by Inspector Clouseau.

I answered, at last, that the scandals she mentioned had nothing to do with Roman Catholicism, for the Church in North America had not been Roman for thirty years, and no part of it was Catholic any more.

Only later did I fully realize what I had said, and I thought, "Can this possibly be true?"

Oh, yes, it's true. The bishops of North America have dethroned Christ the King, dismantled the culture of His Kingship, and turned His throne room, the sanctuary of the Roman Catholic Church, into a tarmac for jet-set, dissenting clergy

You remember the sanctuary, don't you. It was the 1925 encyclical of Pius XI, *Quas Primas*, symbolized in color, light, and shape. From inner-city marble-columned basilicas to prairie plywood Gothics, the sanctuary always managed to be a compelling evocation of the Patriarchs, Prophets, the Word Made Flesh, the Apostles, Evangelists, Fathers and Doctors of the Church, and Founders of religious orders. And there among the saints, there was always Mary, the Mother of God, the intersection of the Old and the New, living tabernacle of the Incarnation, living altar of the Crucifixion, living partaker of the Resurrection. And there, among the choirs of angels was the man-made tabernacle of the Blessed Sacrament, foyer of the faith, hearth of heaven, pedestal to paradise.

Alas, now, in entire archdioceses the sanctuary of the living God is a thing of memory only. And, as Joseph de Maistre would say, "never has a crime had so many accomplices."

In his breathtakingly satisfying book on Saint Thomas More, Richard Marius writes, "More died for an ethereal vision of the sacred that has faded quite away in the electric glow of our modernity."[1]

That electric glow, which has lured the religious out of convents and monasteries and rectories, has redefined martyrdom for our age of modernity. The refusal to abandon religious habits, to pursue degrees in secular universities, to seek appointments in secular professions, to accept individual incomes, the rejection of patty-cake theology and the unswerving loyalty to the vision that won them to Christ, are now sufficient to ensure for victims of the revolution a living martyrdom for the Faith. The new headsman is the neon bishop, who will actually boast of his zero tolerance for any subordinate harboring even minimum allegiance to the vision of the saints.

What comprised that vision? Calvary. What was the source of

that vision? Calvary. What sustained the vision? Calvary. What was the outcome of living by that vision? Calvary. How did Calvary come to have such a hold over our hearts, minds, souls? By a simple show of authority. And by simple, I mean that all the encyclicals ever written, all the workings of all the holy and wholesome minds this side of the dead, all the good intentions of all the Fathers and Doctors of the Church combined would not have been inspired into existence were it not for one action of Christ—namely, that Christ did not ask anyone's permission to Redeem us. He did not ask anyone's permission to die. He did not ask the Apostles what they thought of the idea, did not break the disciples into groups so they could go off and workshop it, did not send the Holy Women off to endless sensitivity workshops to see if they had originated such ideas themselves in their youth, and did not arrange for the publication of a newspaper out of the Upper Room headquarters with His picture on every second page to let the city know what a consummate organizer He was. He just did it. Did it with complete and total authority—the authority that started and stopped the Flood, the authority that stopped the sun at noon for Joshua, the authority that parted the Red Sea—and we are here today on dry land because of it.

Symbols of authority, throughout sacred and secular history, have varied for myriad reasons, according to the nature of the authority, the degree of authority, the character of the one in authority. The authority of Christ is by nature the authority of love, a tough love that demands we carry our cross and go to our death for our own good. In degree it is total; Christ accepted total responsibility for our sins, and the character of Christ makes His authority noble.

The symbols employed by Christ to represent His authority are unchanging. They were not thought up on the spur of the moment. They were not conclusions drawn from a weekend seminar, were not the subject of a cut-and-paste felt banner Saturday morning workshop, were not submitted to any council, committee, specialists, facilitators, animators, experts, or consultants. Yet they have served Christianity and western civilization for two thousand years.

The abandonment of honor to the Kingship of Christ by the hierarchial Magisterium of North America has led to the dismantling of the sacramental, hierarchial, dogmatic Church that is our sacred heritage. Under cover of Vatican II, the blueprints of the fortress were switched. The Rock was cleared and upon it began to rise a Church of purely human construct.

In the end, the bishops who were at the Council must accept total responsibility. We must acknowledge, however, that those who are still alive have little of the energy needed to mount a defense of the true Faith. This is not, after all, the Elizabethan age, when the eighty-one-year-old John Southworth considered it his sacred duty to risk and ultimately be awarded the ignominy of death by being drawn and quartered, naked, in the public circle of Tyburn Arch in defense of the sacraments.

The bishops of Vatican II bought the claptrap of the Sixties, lock, stock, and guitar. No longer navigators for the Bark of Peter, they smilingly surrendered their seniority to become cruise directors on the beached, post-Conciliar Love Boat, while on shore the shards of that civilization they betrayed crumbled into dust.

I am continually struck, as I contemplate the dissent in the Church, by how even the bishops act and speak as if the encyclicals of the popes of the past are meaningful only to the age in which they were written.

Pius XI wrote *Quas Primas* on the Kingship of Christ in 1925. Yes, it was a mere three years after the Fascists marched on Rome. Yes, it was the year the tentacles of communism reached into Italy. Yes, it was already very much a sure thing that Pius XI would sign the upcoming Lateran Treaty of 1929 thereby solving at last the Roman Question, the troubled relationship between the state of Italy and the Vatican, and accepting, after almost sixty years of refusal, that the earthly realm of the Church had been reduced to a few acres. But, surely no one expects to be taken seriously who says his "Kingship of Christ" encyclical was just an effort to stare down the Fascists, and thumb the papal nose at Lenin's executors, claiming that no matter what politicians and armies might do, Christ was Emperor over all souls "anyway."

Those who would say such things are of the school who cry

"triumphalism" at every solemnity, who think Pius IX reached the declaration of the dogma of infallibility because he had been reduced to landlessness by the Piedmontese. This kind of talk is the jejune omniscience of the Political Science 101 coffee room. Yet, today's dissenting clergy dismiss *Quas Primas* as a mere political stratagem on the part of Pius XI. And, of course, they echo relentlessly the refrain that that encyclical was meaningful "only to the age in which it was written."

Notice how, when a pope's thoughts coincide with the spirit of the age, they are so easily disposed of. That is the reason, you see, why everything that has happened between the days of the primitive Church and the post-Conciliar Church must be treated as eminently forgettable. Get it?

It will be sweet judgment upon the significance of the conceited ruminating of the current dissenters when their writings are proven not to have any meaning outside of this sad and silly age in which we are living.

By the time of the release of *Humanae Vitae* in 1968, the bishops, in the words of Anne Roche Muggeridge, "had become dependent upon and intimidated by the modernist skills of their revolutionary experts." "The bishops," she notes, "had been the first converts of the proselytizing periti."[2] Soon it was tricolor cockades for every bishop.

The revolution's success in becoming indispensable to the bishops, too set in their ways to cope smoothly with the sophisticated demands of Vatican II, made the revolutionary leaders the "de facto government of the Church on the local and national levels."[3]

"By the time *Humanae Vitae* appeared, dissenters held all the key posts in the new national bureaucracies."[4]

Dissent from *Humanae Vitae*, propelled by the revolution through the workings and the sayings of the completely hoodwinked and completely converted bishops, effectively separated the bishops from Rome. Now, Muggeridge says, "having divided the bishops from Rome ... the Revolution proceeded to conquer them."[5]

Collegiality, the sharing of responsibility for decision-making by a broader base of bishops, became the cement by which the dissenters ensured the bishops would not break ranks and return to Rome.

The *Winnipeg Statement* effectively established the principle of the right of dissent for individuals measuring their sexual ethics against the standards of Rome. "The revolution separated the mass of the governed from its allegiance to the government by using the issues of birth control to separate the bishops from the Pope and the laity from both."[6]

All that now remained was to fragment the laity. Separate and govern. The laity, traumatized by the change in the rules of prayer and worship, by the rebellion against rubrics and the devaluing of the sacred, were now prey to a new imperative, straight out of the Sixties: apply the principle of democracy to everything. Consultation, councils, committees were needed to ensure the participation of the laity—in place of what, in squint-eyed hindsight, was seen as their "impassive" participation of the past.

The ebb and flow, ascents, descents, flights, and fires of the interior life were now to be replaced by amateurish liturgical aerobics in the aisles, around the "chopping block" altar on the Shakespearean thrust stage superimposed over sanctuary floors.

Self-interested committees, parish councils, an endless multiplication of ministries, presiders, conciliators, animators, facilitators now separated the laity not only from the priest but from one another, all under the lie that it represented much-needed democratic structures. The once-shatterproof Church had been fragmented into uncountable mini-shatters. Now it would lie there, shards of belief from a vessel of faith that had lost its balance and toppled from the out-of-control potter's wheel, bleached, parched into dust by the relentless, glowering, electric glow of our modernity, awaiting only a good sweeping, so that in its place could be erected a new Church, founded by and for man.

Now that they had separated the bishops from Rome, all that was left was for the so-called reformers to conquer them one by one. Proven already was the bishops' absolute and total inability to resist any trend that was newsworthy, media-grabbing, trendy. All that was needed then was a slogan that, like pixie dust, would reduce the bishops to a sentimental mass of do-gooderism and assure them the sympathy of the public. That was achieved by the emergence of two words which, when linked together, would overnight cause bishops to cast off the last vestiges of loyalty to the King at whose command the priesthood had fought and died for two thousand years. The two words were "social justice." The axe had been laid to the base of the throne.

The bishop, the priest, the nun, the fem-thought bureaucrats in fact and in deed were suddenly acting as if social justice could not be achieved under the Kingship of Christ. With their agenda ever in mind they preyed on the homeless, the oppressed, the aged, the battered, the illiterate, using them as curriculae staples for the school of social redemption, using every cause of the week as fodder in their attack on the seat of power. They had reduced the Good News of Salvation to, in Cardinal Ratzinger's words, "the Jesus Project."[7] When you see only the man and not the Christ in man you are blind to Christ. You are only a social worker. Justice blind to Christ is not justice. It is bogus. False. Phoney.

"Only the fear of an all-seeing and all-powerful God can control the individualism of human desire," wrote Joseph de Maistre. "Nations have never been civilized except by religion.... religion accompanied the birth of all civilizations, and the absence of religion heralds their death."[8]

Even the arrogance of Robespierre had to yield to that reality. Like many of the theologians of today, Robespierre found out that being the center of the universe is never easy. As he learned amid the snickerings on the Champs de Mars during his Festival of the Supreme Being, a religion inaugurated out of the spirit of the age does not survive the age.

FIVE

THE SPIRIT OF THIS AGE

BY THE MID-SEVENTIES, the furnishings of the throne room of the Only-Begotten had been auctioned off and replaced by good buys from that same K-Mart where the sisterhood—liberated of the tight purse strings of the mother house—had gone to price short skirts after cashing their first pay-checks.

The removal of these externals of the Kingship of Christ were done under the pretence of updating the sanctuary to make it more suitable for the revised liturgy. Anyone questioning the removal of a statue, a reliquary, a bank of votive candles was met by the blank-eyed gaze and elitist attitude of one of the sisterhood, who would invoke "Vatican II" with the expression of long-suffering compassion reserved for the poor, uninformed, ignorant things who had asked the question, "Why?" But underneath it all was the simple formula—move the furniture, trick the blind.

In *Cranmer's Godly Order*, Michael Davies points out Confucius's dictum that to interfere with the public rites is to interfere with the very fabric of government.[1] The government being interfered with was the dogmatic, sacramental, hierarchical government of the Church founded by Christ. Anyone who has watched the Bible being carried overhead at a slant, supposedly to instill in us some never-before-understood significance of it, must have long ago realized that banal innovation was the work of people who would have us convinced that the worship at hand was Bible-worship, that the man in the pew should immerse himself in it, or he would never know what he was worshipping. This, of course, completely ignores the fact that for two thousand years men who could not read saved their souls by worshipping the fruit of the womb, the Upper Room, Golgotha and the Empty Tomb, the Body and Blood of Christ truly real and truly present in the Holy Sacrifice of the Mass.

"In the past," writes Anne Roche Muggeridge, "liturgical reform was always in the direction of an intensification of the Catholic idea of the sacred."[2]

What reform has meant since Vatican II has effected a radical alteration in belief resulting from a radical devaluing of the sacred! And, I hasten to add, it has effected a long-lasting loss of contact with the beginnings of the Church, with its Founder, with His rights over us by reason of His being King of hearts, King of minds, King of souls.

The new law of worship could have no truce with the old. Out went those prayers from the Mass that acknowledged the hierarchical, sacramental nature of the Church. Prayers at the foot of the altar, The Last Gospel ...

But our theologians, and their tableservers, the bishops sensing that the Church they would build to usurp the Rock of Roman Catholicism should look sort of Catholic and act sort of Catholic, perpetuated their great deception.

The person with the printing press printing funny money is a bogus banker. The theologian publishing his watered-down rewrite of the Gospel is a specious and cunning forger. The enemies of the Magisterium trading in trends and sex and smarmy smiles are trying to recast the very shape of the key to the throne room. The bishop, the priest, the nun who serve the fem-thought bureaucrats' need to dismantle the signs and symbols of the Kingship of Christ are trafficking in falsehood. But one must admit, they have a knack for passing their phoney currency.

After all, had the laity not stood idly by without protest while the altar was moved out from the wall, the tabernacle was sidelined to a dingy unlit corner, the hymns of glory to the Trinity and to the Mother of God were replaced by jingles and political sloganeering delivered in singsong, hand-clapping, campfire, cheerleader, group hug smile-a-thons?

Neutralizing any stubborn lay person who harbored a fondness for pre-revolutionary notions, such as that alarming union that took place between Christ as King and even the lowliest penitent on his knees, would be handled in the same way that, throughout the 1800s and 1900s, monarchy had been successfully replaced by so-called people's governments, at the insistence of the tyrant of the day, in France, Germany, Russia, or Mexico. Simply devalue, deny, debase the worth of anything that came before. With this directive in place, the Kingship of Christ came under direct assault from modern Committees for Public Safety set up overnight by the networking dissenters. Their determination was to ensure that soon there would be no place either in private affairs or in politics for Jesus Christ and His Holy Law. Few would have believed that by 1992 the effort to eradicate the Kingship of Christ would have been so successful that Mathew Fox would be able to accuse anyone who still thought of Christ as God to be guilty of "Jesusolotry,"[3] and the bishops hearing it would do nothing, say nothing, take no action whatever to comfort or support the accused.

Symbols are the visual language of Truth. They are Truth. Isaias unveiled one of His name symbols, "the Prince of Peace." "His empire shall be multiplied ..." "He shall sit upon the throne of David and upon his kingdom ..."[4] Jeremiah foretells that He "shall be wise and shall execute judgment and justice in the earth."[5] Daniel announced that He came to the Ancient of Days and was given "power and glory and a kingdom," and added, "His kingdom shall not be destroyed."[6] Zachary labeled Him "the Merciful King," entering Jerusalem upon an ass as "the just and savior."[7]

At the very moment when the New Testament was being conceived out of the Old, the Archangel Gabriel announced, concerning the child to be born, "of His Kingdom there will be no end."[8] That He would reign in the house of Jacob, forever. Now, if you do not give much significance to the house of Jacob, then that will matter little to you. If the throne of David is merely some chair on which David sat to exhibit his authority, well, you could have one of those set up for yourself. If a kingdom is just an archaic metaphor for people for whom you are responsible, well, heavens, isn't that what a parish is? Power and glory are simply a question of having a well-heeled, efficient, hardworking bureaucracy, and every bishop with any savvy at all has had all that, ever since Vatican II.

What then of the words to the Roman magistrate? It was before the power of Rome, from within the depths of the deepest rejection, suffering, and humiliation, that Christ chose to make the point, "My Kingdom is not of this world."[9] To disregard that, to disbelieve it has significance, to overlook acknowledging that the time, location, and audience for that announcement were deliberate, purposeful, precisely chosen—why, a person would have to suggest that anything not of "this world" is mere fancy, that "kingdom" is a melodramatic metaphor, that the man saying them was just that, a man, deluded, disillusioned, worthy of pity and merely prone to saying memorable words accidentally at well-documented moments in history. The words, then, do not indicate the greatness of His power; they are merely the pretentious utterances of a man stubborn to the end. Noble perhaps ... but powerful? No.

As for the authority and mandate He passed down to His chosen few, His Apostles, well, they are eminently dismissible considering their source.

Such a near-incomprehensible abuse of the truth would betray a mentality ignorant of even the most rudimentary knowledge of history and the Scriptures, a self-centeredness of heart akin to that of a teenage skinhead arrested in his emotional development and a soul completely untouched by the gift of faith. Either that or a soul admitting a complete loss of faith. Evidence of such abuse, such overwhelming, deadening ignorance, such a complete and total loss of faith is not only in evidence in the highest Church offices in the land, but has been commandeered in the last decade to fuel a war of extermination against the faithful adherents of Roman Catholicism. The blueprints for the assault were drawn up and approved by none other than the bishops of the Catholic Church in North America.

Ottawa, Canada, is a capital city in thrall to its own heritage. On the northern shore of the Ottawa River a new Museum of Civilization, memorializes the racial forces that have made my country. Above the cliffs on the opposite shore, the Gothic arches of Parliament Hill echo the clamor and rhetoric of an electorate agitating for a rescue of the Canadian dream.

As you are no doubt aware, the Canadian dream is badly in need of rescue. We are a country that had it all and let it slip away.

We had "that greatest meed [reward], a heart that feareth God."[10] We had the immemorial altar of sacrifice where we went to be set free from "sin's foul tyranny." And there, rich in goodwill, we begged in acquittal of our human, worthless, sinful selves more fear of God. *Thy Kingdom come, Thy will be done.*

Then we turned our back on all of that. We were distracted by the sound of something scratching in the shadows.

Now we are home to "that mystical itch" that Chesterton identified as the strangest secret in hell—the itch of the evil man to make all men evil.[11]

It was our theologians, our Gregory Baums, our modern bishops, our very own Remi de Roos who took their itch to Winnipeg in 1968 and broke the back of the hierarchical Magisterium of North America so that from there the word went out that "he who could no longer follow the teaching of the Church on contraception, but must pursue his sexuality in the way he saw fit was doing so in good conscience." Gregory Baum, prime promoter of Dignity, a support group for Catholic homosexuals not approved by Rome, and Bishop Remi "transubstantiation-is-a-thing-of-the-past" de Roo.

It was the "good conscience" of our dissenting religious that drove the supernatural from our shores and left "the unnatural," as Chesterton would say.

Now we have convents subject to the spiritual colonialism that is the driving delirium of radical feminists. Now we have seminaries dominated by "Looking for Mr. Good-Baum" theology. Now our church basements are home to demonic squatters rehearsing witch-priest masses for the lewd trinity of Naturalism, Rationalism, Liberalism.

Now our Sunday liturgies are little Remi de Roo festivals where, in place of the Word made Flesh, we have homilies right out of the

Sixties.

All well and good as long as it doesn't mean liturgical dancers chasing butterflies, deacons bobbing for apples, and a playground presider tapping his toes to the baleful guitar jingles of Mother Doo-Wop and the Superiors.

On Nepean Point, adjacent to Sussex Drive, stands the brand new National Gallery of Canada, acclaimed as a brilliant showcase of masters old and new. Were one aiming to commit an act of violence against a nation, people, cultures, art, and belief systems, one could find no better showcase than this particular intersection of heritage and hope. On the other hand, a terrorist intending to dismantle the patrimony of an entire civilization would consider the style and location of Notre Dame Basilica across from the National Gallery a fulfillment of all his most crucial requirements.

The interior of Notre Dame Basilica (where I took readers once before in *The Last Roman Catholic?*) was designed by the gifted architect Bouillon in imitation of the treasure houses of faith in France. Beneath a star-studded, royal-blue ceiling, a high altar rises mid-sanctuary, a veritable catechism in sculpted figures—a three-dimensional confirmation that Christ is King of minds, hearts, and souls, with legislative, judicial, and executive authority over all creatures because of the perfection of His knowledge, love, holiness, by the power of His Redemption of mankind, by the right of His being One Person with God.

If you do not believe that we are created, do not believe in sin, and do not believe in sacramental grace, then none of this matters. You are blind to the vision that fueled the Church for two thousand years. You might as well take a sledgehammer and reduce it all to dust, sweep the place out, put in a new carpet and maybe an imposing chair—something to hold people's attention while you instruct them in what you do believe.

In this sanctuary on Holy Thursday, 1990, I listened in disbelief as Archbishop Gervais announced that on the first Holy Thursday Christ washed feet to "elevate us to the dignity of the divine." On Good Friday, he announced this was the day "the Church in Her wisdom concentrated on the Crucifixion, the rest of the year she concentrated on the Resurrection." On Easter Sunday, he announced that "Christ died on the cross to immerse Himself completely in our humanity." What, I wondered, would become of this great sanctuary now that it had an archbishop who was inside out, upside down, and backwards?

Recent announcements of planned changes to the interior brought a thoroughly justified howl of rage from Ottawa's heritage authorities, prompting the planners to cancel a proposed press conference and drop an iron veil of secrecy around their plans. Notre Dame planners had apparently told Heritage Ottawa that Vatican II's liturgical changes demanded the alterations. That, of course, was a blatant lie. The *Constitution on the Sacred Liturgy* states emphatically that no innovations must be allowed unless the good of the Church genuinely and certainly requires them. As one who has attended Mass at Notre Dame for over a year I can attest that no such need is apparent, except perhaps to provide a runway ramp for the five women who race helter-skelter all over the sanctuary during the English Mass on Sunday.

When called for comment, Notre Dame's rector, Father Huneault, seized up, directing the caller instead to Monsignor Lavergne, Archbishop Gervais's secretary. Of course, Monsignor Lavergne was unavailable for comment.

The philosophy at work seemed to be summed up by the motto, "Do it first, worry about heritage busybodies later." Archdiocesan telephone voices were quick to substitute the word "restoration"—a word implying respect for designated heritage requirements (and used for the initial announcement)—for the word "renovation," which has been the byword for loot and pillage ever since parish councils, priests, and nuns used Vatican II as an excuse for a rampage of destruction that denuded our sanctuaries of any evidence of Roman Catholicism.

I never doubted that the trail would lead to the Archbishop's door. This was to be an act of authorized vandalism, a demonstration of power from a spoiled elite acting as a law unto themselves, who continue to thumb their nose at tradition, sacred art, sacred music, and architecture.

The Archbishop mumbled sweetly about making room for concelebrants, peppering his response with the usual mention of Vatican II and renewal.

Alas, the archdiocesan properties, as evidenced by a decade of "renovations" to our churches, are in the hands of those whose taste in art and architecture runs to Ramada Inn modern.

The Basilica of Notre Dame is not theirs to mutilate. It is the sacred heritage of every Frenchman and Irishman whose blood-roots stretch back to the very parishioners who paid for it, and of everyone with faith-roots in Roman Catholicism. They'll get their way eventually, of course. They will simply lock the doors, devastate the interior, and rejoice in their *fait accompli* when the doors reopen to the horrified citizens of Ottawa.

Were a terrorist to impose all at once on the great basilicas all of these ingredients of the Christ-less Church of the modern age he would have no more vital act to perform than to remove from this exquisite throne room of Christ the King the very mountain of the King, the high altar. Christ the lawgiver to whom obedience is due. Christ the judge by whom all reward or punishment will be allotted, Christ the all-powerful who justly owns the right to have all his commands carried out would be hard to call up in the heart, mind, and soul of even the most learned or the most pious faithful if all imagery proclaiming His rightful attributes were upside down, inside out, or backwards. Or simply removed.

In their place—to focus all attentions on the man ruler, the man judge, the man executive—the Presider, would be located a single but glamorous, awe-inspiring chair. Man replaces God in the holy place.

Imagine such a glorious house of the Lord looted and emptied of the symbols of Kingship, denied the very colors of royal right, the purples, crimsons, blues, and gold of the throne room buried under a layer of grey. Imagine a bishop, seated there in his Presider's chair reading his beliefs aloud to a seated or standing assembly. Such is the profit of all our years of not resisting manipulation.

History will record that in the Church in North America, the cult of the Presider was begun so his basilica would provide an extension of the ideology of his bureaucracy, a showroom of the power of the dissenting bureaucrats.

By denying public adoration of the Blessed Sacrament, intended, as Pius XI stated in *Quas Primas*, "to raise the minds and hearts to the mystery of Christ forever and truly with us Body and Blood,"[12] the enemies of the Church are saying either we are not capable of having the mind and the heart raised to such wonders or that there is nothing really there.

By forbidding recognition of Christ in His role as Divine King, they are saying that He is not truly wonderful in all His works, or, we don't have any right to Him.

By extolling and magnifying the purpose, function, and importance of a Presider, the enemies of the Church are denying the sacramental nature of the priesthood and ignoring the right of true believers to "proclaim and extol the glory of Him who triumphs in all the Saints and in all the Elect."

By enthroning the creature in place of the Creator, these enemies of the Church echo the original lie from Genesis: "You will be like God ..."[13] Free of the Creator, free of the laws of nature herself, absolute Lord of one's own destiny.

As Cardinal Ratzinger states, "Man continually desires only one thing; to be his own creator and his own master.

"Christianity," he adds, "is not our work. It is a revelation and we have no right to reconstruct it as we like or choose."[14] In the context of the reconstructed Christless Church of today, the Spirit-of-the-Age Church, the Presider's chair is a counterfeit throne!

"They sit in the chair of Moses and expect the very manner of papal deference that they themselves worked so hard to destroy," wrote Salvany, and "Liberalism is the enthronement of the creature in place of the Creator."[15]

With the enthronement of the creature, the Church of man has arrived. Its lamentable fruits are our reward for not resisting its theological manipulation, its liturgical manipulation. Its manipulation of our heritage, our culture. Its manipulation, abuse, and mutilation of the One and Only Truth, that Christ is King.

In place of the Kingship of Christ, would emerge a whirlwind of egomaniacal human pretenders, our own bishops spouting new rituals, new creeds, new religions, all for and from the pleasures of man, all for and from the insistence of total freedom of man to choose for himself, to become the master of all he surveys, while still calling himself Catholic.

Liturgical manipulation is striving to uncouple the Church from Christ—to serve twenty years of theological manipulation aimed at uncoupling the Only-Begotten from the Father, Jesus, denied as the Christ, removed from His being one substance with the Father.

Cardinal Ratzinger cites as one of the roots of crisis in the Church that, "many no longer believe what is at issue, [the Church] is a reality willed by the Lord Himself."[16]

Those many who no longer believe have not believed it for a long time. It remains only for the little people, the faithful, to be liberated from all restraints by Vatican II's misinterpretation, to be free to enjoy the new shape, to revel in the "collective conscience" made up of the new faithful to cart off the remnants of the True Faith. How to convert, subdue the stubborn? Attack them at their weakest point. Their bodies. The spirit may be willing to resist change, but the body now and then must rest, Make them stand. Get them where they rest and where they sleep. Make them tired. Wear them out. Minds are susceptible when the body is drained of its power to resist. Bombard them with glaring light, blaring sound, frenetic action.

If Christ reigns in the hearts of men, then let's chill the hearts of men, simply remove from sight those things that warm to melting the penitent, overflowing, or broken heart. Get rid of that heart-quickening music of the ages. Throw out Gregorian chant, banish it, silence it forever. Rip down those murals, those images of the Ascension, the Coronation, the Resurrection, and level those architectural lines so the heart can never be pulled upward by the searching, seeking eye. Lower the ceiling, shorten the spires, empty the church of pillars, all those things that make the heart soar, that make man want to be born again, not of the will of the flesh or of blood or of man, but born again of God.

If He reigns in the wills of men then liberate the will of man so every act, thought, and deed can be justified by his right to a freedom of choice, thereby removing him for all time from the will of He Who sent His Only-Begotten to live and dwell amongst us.

If He reigns over all souls by reason of His death on the cross,

His victory over sin, and His redemption of mankind, then get that cross out of the Church, make them forget all that sacrifice stuff by forcing them week after week to look instead at a resurrection apparatus, something that shows that man and woman are equal, preferably some floating figure with breasts and a waistline.

As for shows of obedience, reverence, acknowledgment of sinfulness before the all-pure, all-holy Son of God, that is easy to discourage. Cancel genuflections, put out the word that the Sign of the Cross is sexist, pack up the Stations of the Cross, and watch for anyone who unravels a rosary. Keep an eye on them. Or an ear. Some are still bold enough to let their beads rattle against a pew.

But to undermine all these stubborn remnants of the old, dogmatic past there is one simple action that is unmatchable for its effectiveness. Remove the kneelers. People who cannot kneel to say the rosary will stop saying it. People who cannot kneel at the consecration will stop affording it any consideration at all, then we will have no resistance when this consecration-transubstantiation business is buried once and for all. And don't forget to introduce the term "outdated spirituality."

Thenceforth, the so-called kingdom of Christ on earth will no longer be able to "with every token of veneration salute her Author and Founder as King of Lords and as King of Kings."[17]

SIX

CLASS ACTION HARVEST

DISSENTING BISHOPS, placed in the presider's chairs by dissenting theologians, express astonishment at the refusal of traditional Catholics to accept their every word at face value. They are reaping what they have sown. Cardinal Ratzinger explains, "whoever practices a certain contemporary theology, lives its consequences to the utmost, as the almost complete loss of the usual certitude that marked the priests, religious."[1] What are the consequences of this contemporary theology?

• "A Church that more and more shows a 'female face' and is increasingly manned by homosexuals, perhaps already to the point of their dominating it at least here and there."[2]

• A Church of which the rector of old St. Mary's Seminary in Baltimore went on record as saying "such is the undeniable appeal of today's American Church to homosexuals" that "he feels obliged" to limit their number at his institution, as, if did he not, there might be no one else preparing for the priesthood.[3]

• A Church that by December 1988 had "some 200 episodes of sexual abuse of minors involving priests or members of American religious orders." According to the Register, court proceedings of this kind have cost U.S. Catholic dioceses at least $30 million.[4]

• A Church where Archbishop Rembert Weakland, a man as far removed from reality as any archbishop actually could be, suggested that children are sometimes responsible for seducing the clergy.[5]

• A Church where a pastor in Lafayette, Louisiana, "successfully transferred by the Diocese to head several different parishes within ten years had sexually molested well over thirty boys under his supervision and had engaged in such activities during all these years. Suits brought in court by the parents of these boys resulted in a jury awarding the parents well over $10 million which the Diocese is required to pay. This is in material compensation for the moral havoc wreaked upon these boys by the pastor."[6]

"There is still no end in sight to the continuous retreat in which they [the bishop of the United States] have been so long engaged."[7]

• A Church about which Cardinal Ratzinger says: "Whoever practices a certain contemporary theology, lives its consequences to the utmost..."[8]

Such as Father Neils Rasmussen, fifty-three years old, a tenured member of the Notre Dame Theology Department and "world class liturgist," whose descent into the abyss of homosexuality ended when he fired a .357 magnum through his heart, Saturday, August 29, 1987. At the hour of his suicide he was clothed in a red tank top and blue-jean shorts, wearing a "wide metal-studded leather wrist band, and was lying amidst an array of guns, whips, handcuffs, and unusual paraphernalia—leather clothing as for motorcycling or sadomasochism." His suicide note "specified that he wanted no form of Christian burial."[9]

Rasmussen was found by Rev. Thomas F. O'Meara, O.P., Professor of Theology at Notre Dame, who figures in the Father John O'Connor battle with the homosexual mafia of the Dominicans.

• A Church which Randy Engle characterizes bleakly: "The growing number of homosexual and pedophile priests and brothers and lesbian nuns, including homosexual bishops have formed a Sixth

Column within the Catholic Church in the United States. Many of these individuals have played important roles in the development and promotion of the new sexual catechetics in the parochial schools."[10]

• A Church from which on July 19, 1989, Alphonsus Penney, Archbishop of St. John's, Newfoundland, resigned after the arraignment of twenty priests and brothers under his jurisdiction for child molestation.[11]

"When the Canadian Bishops' Ad Hoc Committee on Sexual Abuse was initially established, one Paul McAuliffe ... a member of the pro-women, anti-priestly celibacy, dissident organization known as the Coalition of Concerned Canadian Catholics [an organization fuelled by the frantic demands of married ex-priests and married ex-nuns] sent a personal brief to the committee [criticizing] the patriarchal structure of the Church and ... the Church's 'misuse' of power which 'seems' to support child abuse.

"For this bold attack, McAuliffe's reward was an invitation to act as chairman for one of the four Ad Hoc sub-committees stockpiling information for the bishop's document on sexual abuse!" (Needless to say his committee's twenty-one recommendations suggested "reviewed parish and diocesan structure and ... an informed community!" As if we didn't have enough of that!)

The hierarchy-hating, Rome-bashing, feminist juggernaut surrounding McAuliffe trashed male dominance in the Church and promoted feminist-oriented clichés about "informed community."[12]

In fact, none of their criticisms fit Alphonsus Penney, a man with "a great reputation for personal piety." His great error, according to various of his former subjects, was to allow his priests to "do their own thing," (just as McAuliffe suggested) "with little or no supervision."[13]

• A Church so swamped with sex abuse charges against homosexual priests and bishops, that the *National Law Journal* wrote an article about it as a new legal specialty.

"The suits are catching on like wild fire.... litigation against dioceses for the emotional havoc pedophiliac priests wreak has been prevalent enough to allow some personal injury lawyers to develop a speciality.... As cases have proliferated, an informal network has developed among some of the plaintiff's lawyers handling them. A few are even talking about creating a formal group within the Association of Trial Lawyers of America to exchange information on their common experiences."[14]

"Potentially," the article said, "the Church also could be faced with a class action against a diocese where many children have been abused and with the indictment of a bishop who failed to report a crime."

Meanwhile, back at Notre Dame, Richard McBrien continues to push for the recognition of married homosexual couples and for a homosexual priesthood.[15]

• A Church where bishops themselves are caught half in and half out of the closet door.

Bishop Ferrario of Honolulu is accused of providing the services of a homosexual male prostitute lover to other bishops.

Bishops Hughes, Untener, and Gumbleton get all bleary-eyed while holding a mock Mass using Gallo wine, sitting down at a table surrounded by gays and lesbians at a Chicago Gay Conference. Cardinal Bernardin, in whose archdiocese twenty-one priests stand accused but have not yet faced trial because of Bernardin's maneuvering, sent his congratulations to the three bishops upon their "outing."

Therese Ickinger comments, "The Bishops who took part in the sodomite circus, Hughes, Untener, and Gumbleton, should be immediately defrocked and excommunicated. Cardinal Bernardin should be deposed and the Chicago Archdiocese placed under interdict until a public rite of purification is performed by a special legate of the Pope."[16]

• A Church analyzed by a spokesman for Concerned Catholic Parents of Philadelphia in terrifying terms:

"Behind all these putative 'dissenters' and 'feminists' 'causes' are determined, unrelenting, militant, incorrigible homosexual clergy and 'theologians.' Most of the faithful laity (those who won't or can't read between the lines) will be left in the dark as to exactly who (homosexual clergy) and what (church-sanctioned sodomy) they're dealing with—and (to repeat) that is: inveterate, militant, heretical homosexual priests, nuns and 'theologians' who will go to any length to attain their singular dream of complete Church acceptance of every aspect of their homosexual deviancies, including clerical homosexual marriage, adoption, divorce, and eventually pedophilia, etc., ad infinitum."[17]

• A Church for which Father Enrique I. Rueda, foremost analyst of homosexuality in the institutional Church, prescribed:

> We need a comprehensive program designed to extricate the Church from even the appearance of compromise with homosexualism.
>
> 1) Making automatic the reduction of clerics and religious to the lay state the first time they are known to be homosexual.
>
> 2) Seminarians and novices need to be told that they should leave the seminary if they feel same-sex attractions.
>
> 3) We need another commission to clean up seminaries and to make sure that homosexuals either don't apply to enter the seminary or leave before ordination.
>
> 4) Lay people who are in the employ of the Church should be let go if they are known to be practicing homosexuals.
>
> 5) It would be a good idea to require all teachers of moral theology to take an oath in which they affirm their personal adherences to the tending of the Church and a formal promise to teach them as their own. Those who refuse should be summarily dismissed.
>
> 6) No one who disagrees with the teaching of the Church concerning the abominable nature of the homosexual vice should be granted a degree in theology, religious education, and other religious discipline.
>
> 7) No priest who disagrees with the teachings of the Church—as presented in an oath to be taken on a regular basis—should be granted faculties to preach or hear confes-

sion.[18]

But Therese Ickinger reminds us that there is another issue in which the betrayal of the bishop cries to heaven for vengeance.

"Still it is the sell-out of the pro-life movement by the American Hierarchy that must stand as one of the great cowerings of history. Twenty-seven million children are dead, over an eighteen-year period, in a country that hypocritically boasts 'liberty and justice for all.' The bishops' outcry against this barbarism has been like the wind of the western sea, soft and low.

"Msgr. James MacKay [attorney in fact] for the Archdiocese [San Francisco] does not condone, encourage or approve ... speaking to any individual at any abortion clinic ... for the purpose of harassment, threat, or persuasion [note this] or offering any literature to any clinic worker or patient."[19]

After excoriating the Connecticut bishops she goes on, "Their brother bishop in New Jersey, in 1981, had mandated sex education in all the New Jersey Catholic Schools and actually endorsed the State's Board of Education curriculum which includes the diseased outpourings of some of the world's most degenerate perverts.

"In Indiana, the bishops have come out in favor of withholding food and water from those persons who are not dying quick enough ..."[20]

Francis B. Schulte (Archbishop, New Orleans), having been, while he was just Monsignor Schulte, Assistant Superintendent of Schools in the Archdiocese of Philadelphia, imposed "outrageous anti-Catholic texts" upon the schoolchildren of Philadelphia.[21] Ickinger cites *Growth In Christ*, one of the *Light and Life* series, as an example of anti-Catholic teaching imposed upon schoolchildren, quoting, "While condemning abortion as a whole, Catholic theologians admit to the exceptional case where expelling the fetus may be the better thing" and when faced with parental outrage ... his reply to a Catholic mother was, "If you don't like it, get out."[22]

- A Church where
  We no longer have prayer, we have performance.
  We no longer have wisdom, we have word games.
  We no longer have worship, we have wall to wall self-esteem.

We no longer have saints, we have social workers.

We no longer have *Ave Maria, Pater Noster, Gloria Patri.* We have handshakes.

We no longer have *Agnus Dei,* we have clap your hands.

We no longer hear *Domini Non Sum Dignus,* we hear Nicaragua, El Salvador, and Original Goodness.

We no longer have Christ the King, we have a Presider.

We no longer have shepherds, we have cruise directors.

We no longer have God. We have only us.

PART TWO

TARGET ZERO

ONE

A HOLY ACQUISITION

IT IS SO EASY to forget that God is always there somewhere. In childhood, we know He is everywhere. Then the dark time overtakes us and in His apparent absence we worry.

Years ago, we lived in a white house on a sloping hill. At the bottom of the slope was a cedar log fence and beyond that a pasture. Once, I dreamed of a lane running parallel to the log fence and from the lane came a noise. I slipped out a window in my nightshirt and hurried down the slope so I could spy on the lane through the log fence. What should I see there but a cart being pulled by a donkey. In the cart sat a woman and a man. He wore a hat, she a green kerchief. I saw only their backs as they had already passed by. In the cart were tree trunks, twisted and bent. Four or five of them. Running behind the cart, playing as he went, was a boy my size and age.

Leaning against the log fence was a window with eight empty frames, a perfect ladder. I climbed it to the top of the fence and called out, "Where are you going?"

He stopped, not the least bit surprised by the sound of my voice, pointed in the direction the cart was moving and said, "To the King."

I understood immediately the cause of his playfulness. His joy would soon be complete. He would find the throne room of the King, climb into his lap, and fall asleep in total safety. It was his destiny.

Mine, too. I knew it was to be my turn someday. For I knew, as a child, traveling through earth time with loving and devout parents, that our journey would lead us to the throne room; everywhere were invisible road maps and blueprints showing us the way. We, too, would reach the safety of our loving master. Yes, I knew, the lap of Christ the King was my destiny.

The Catholic child knows it without being told. Or used to when he was allowed to be a child.

Now, however, he is confronted with an invasion force determined to establish a beachhead on the shores of his innocence.

What are they after? I know in my heart it is something vital to the child's world. Something to do with the very means by which a child copes, some blueprint visible to the child that adulthood causes us to lose sight of.

But what?

Bombarding a child with the propaganda that there are no norms to sexuality could not be the result merely of maladjusted, dissenting religious trying to find understanding for himself or herself in a tiny-tots classroom. Think, then—what target to be found only in children between the ages of six and twelve would be so tantalizing that it would draw together in one agenda the feminist movement, Planned Parenthood, gay-lesbian equal rights activists, abortion advocates, pedophiles, jackbooted ex-nuns, dissenting clergy, and renegade theologians?

Says pediatrician and psychiatrist Murray McGovern, "Social institutions should consciously recognize the inherent natural importance of the 'latency' stage of psycho-social, psycho-academic, psycho-moral and psycho-spiritual development."[1]

"During the latency phase of psychosexual development, the foundation for an optional hierarchy of values can be remarkably reinforced, and an excellent Old Testament super-ego (conscience) empowered by fear and shame can acquire New Testament insight and a commitment to be 'good.'"[2]

The small white coffin floated down the aisle. Walter was leading the pall bearers. He was in complete control, in complete charge of his emotions, his destiny.

"You know they found Ronald?" I had said.

"Yes," Walter said.

You know he won't be back?

"He's dead, I know."

The boy in the bag. A boy cut out of the herd, culled from the very order of things he had been born into, his senses, instinct for truth, instinct for justice all telling him that there was no order of things. That there was no systematic series of groups, no class, no family, no genera, no species to which he belonged. No Kingdom. The road maps and blueprints leading to the throne room were visible to him, but no one was leading the way. Instead there were self-absorbed pretenders to the throne, eyes glazed over with self-interest, blocking the way, blinding him to a future in which he, too, would assume his rightful place in the chain of obey and command reaching from the street corner all the way up to the choirs of angels. Because something had gone wrong, somehow the order legislated for the good of society no longer ensured good for that society. For at the very moment in his young life when what he needed most was an acknowledgment of that holy knowing of his own desire to be good, his fortress was betrayed by those very ones commissioned to defend it. His teachers, priests, nuns, and bishops were all propagandizing that the thing of greatest value was not the commitment to be good but the inevitability of being orgasmic. Those very adults selected to ensure the care and control of holy or sacred things had looted the sanctuary of his soul, scraped it clean of all signs and symbols of victory over evil, scoured it bare of any reference to a nature above human nature. Said in fact that the most important thing in life is not death, but sex. Ronald pulled a bag over his head and proved them wrong.

To invade the soul of a child and abort the process of reinforcing an optimal hierarchy of values is to assault order, rank, system, government, rule. It is to sever the ties, and separate from all that came before, the child who, in his isolation, no longer knowing where he came from, cannot believe in where he is going. It is to guarantee despair. Without the *pull of the future*, the human being is sentenced to incarceration in the present. Without self-discipline and self-denial, there is only the present. Inundated with voices telling him self-gratification and self-fulfillment are the optimum, the chances of discovering the value of self-denial are minimal. Without control—no order. Without order, into which we are all born, there can be no belonging. Except maybe in a garbage bag, where the voices of dissenting priests and liberated nuns repeating "penis, vagina, penis, vagina" cannot be heard. The bag at least is a guarantee of silence.

"An Old Testament conscience ... can acquire New Testament insight."

That holy acquisition is the entrance into the heart, mind, and soul of the child, the truth children were born to receive—that Jesus Christ, the Son of God, Divine, truly God and truly man, came to earth to guarantee for that child a life after death, a victory over sin, and that to do so He gave His Body and Blood to us for all time, presenting it to the world first in a cup, the Grail, the sacred cup of forgiveness.

To the apostasized ex-nuns and ex-priests who for the last twenty-five years have indulged their obsession with genitalia by playing doctor with the children of the community, one can only offer condolences. In the prolonged pre-orgasmic, middle-aged delirium in which those particular cave-dwellers have grown old, they have usurped the natural dwelling place of the Holy Spirit and decorated the walls with pornographic sketches. They know what fate awaits them. There never has been a society on earth that considered the sexual exploitation of children forgivable. To the educators who mutilated a system born of the exhaustive holy labors of bishops of ages past to accommodate the agenda of the agents for a contraceptive society, they have already secured their reward; the separate school system which has not been Roman for thirty years and is now only laughably referred to as Catholic is within a few short years of being completely dead and buried. It will not enter the twenty-first century. Before the clock chimes the last midnight of this horrendous century, Catholic teachers will no longer have to wonder if they have pay equity with public school teachers.

To the bishops of North America who betrayed Christ, His sacraments, His holy Church, His Commandments, who denied Him His Divinity and His mission as Messiah in their wholesale betrayal of Roman Catholic catechetics, one can only stand back and give them room to exhaust the torment their betrayal has ensured for them. They, alas, have been warned that at the moment of their death, they will be the subject of a lightning-swift swap—their pectoral cross for a millstone. Their plummet to the depths will not occur in silence. They will be engulfed in the cries of a Niagara of lost souls cataracting into the abyss.

TWO

MEETING MR. B.

THE ARRIVAL OF THE SIXTIES coincided with my first year away from home. I did not notice that God no longer walked in the garden until several months had passed. The bleakness of college life, I discovered, had nothing in common with home, family, or the orchards of adolescence. The desert of academe shifted and sifted memories of the sacred as the steady, relentless aridity of secularism eroded the joyous shoreline of youth. Faith in anything above our earthbound human nature was derided, scorned, scoffed at. An "F" or "F+" might decorate any paper bearing reference to the sacred. But even in the darkest hours of the darkest age, man has heard His voice.

I first hear "The Voice" in an English tutorial in late September, 1961. Eight of us sat around a boardroom table in the office of Professor Gale listening to a 33 rpm recording of *Juno and the Paycock* coming from a portable turntable atop the file cabinet at his shoulder. The recording was not yet done when he lifted the needle off the disc and turned to me.

"Well, now, Mr. Demers, what are your thoughts on that?"

I was afraid he would ask me first. It has been my lot throughout life to be mistaken for someone brimming over with answers. Alas, try as I might, I had not been able to make out one word of it. Then, too, I had been five minutes late.

"Actually," I said with not a little nonchalance, "I couldn't understand a thing the old man was saying."

A great collective gasp emptied the room of air. The other seven around the table stared at me in various stages of arrested horror.

I was about to ask, "What did I say?" when I looked toward the professor and my nonchalance fled. He was sitting in a perfectly rigid imitation of a praying mantis, hands arrested in midair, one over a coffee cup, another over a notepad. His eyes were attempting to focus in my direction, but could not. A stranger entering might have guessed he was trying to swallow his face. Best thing to do was leave, I thought, and I slipped out of the room, a great sucking sound filling the space I vacated as air rushed into that vacuum and resuscitated the motionless assembly.

To this day, I do not know if Professor Gale has ever forgiven the elements of Time and Space that conspired to affront his ears with the words of a freshman referring to Siobhan McKenna, Ireland's greatest living actress, as "that old man." He may very well be sitting there still.

Shortly after, feeling I owed it to "The Voice," I borrowed from the lending library the album set of Shaw's *Joan of Arc* recorded by Siobhan McKenna. That was in September. I returned it in April, having had "The Voice" conquer my heart and soul daily again and again for months on end. I feel quite guilty about the possibility that there may be university alumni of my vintage who do not even know that the recording exists, seeing as I hoarded it for the full term. But, there you have it. I held Joan of Arc captive in my apartment, turning, turning, turning on the turntable at my bedside for seven months, listening past many midnights to "The Voice" that could make the world turn the other way, Siobhan McKenna, Jehanne La Pucelle, racing the wind that whiskered the wheat that waved in the fields of Domremy to rendezvous anew with St. Michael, St. Margaret, St. Catherine. Announcing her purpose at Vaucouleurs. Crowning Charles at Rheims. Taking the arrow at Orleans. Defying the subtleties of corrupt Couchon with the very Protestant and very Shawvian, "Whose judgment shall I judge by if not my own?" Yet repeating her loyalty to the Church, to Rome, to the Pope. Converting the cynics round the pyre in Rouen as through the flame came from a heart so pure it would not burn, "Jesu. Jesu. Jesu." That voice filled with certainty about the life hereafter, consistently loyal to the end to the Master of life, the object of her passion, He who was represented through the smoke by two crossed sticks held above the flames.

Not all the tutorials in the calendar of all the months ahead caused to dim the glow left in the soul by the voice of Siobhan McKenna. From the suffocating secularism of college agendas, it was possible to take sanctuary within the exquisite cathedral of sound that was her voice. A season of sighs, a summer of perfect passion, a harvest of matchless purity that voice laid at the tabernacle of the heart's desire. If Time allows all traces of higher learning to fade from memory, that voice will echo still, to and beyond entombment.

"The Voice" returned November 25, 1989. The setting was ironic, a Sacred Heritage Conference in a renowned heritage site. The Elizabeth Bruyere Family Medical Center had originated from and literally grown out of the convent of the Grey Nuns, or Sisters of Charity, founded in Ottawa in 1846 by Elizabeth Bruyere, a sister of the order founded by St. Marguerite d'Youville.

Bruyere had not wanted to come to Ottawa at all when she was originally ordered there, but being of the disposition that honored obedience as well as poverty and chastity, three factors today very little in evidence in our so-called religious women, she set out from Montreal with several other nuns in a horse-drawn cutter driven by a priest. It was February and that meant a journey through two days of winter. They stayed the first night at Montebello, then, rising early, struck out for their destination, which was then called Bytown. Throughout the journey Bruyere questioned why she had been chosen. She was only twenty-six and felt ill-equipped to deal with the task of serving in a town known for its brawling drunken timber rafters from the Ottawa River and bitter anti-Catholicism fuelled by Orangemen of the region.

Yet, she was a soldier in the ranks of the elect fighting to secure in the world the reign of the Kingship of Christ, the just rule of the Redeemer over our minds, hearts, and souls by virtue of His being the Son of the Father, Wisdom Incarnate, and by the power of His victory over Death.

We seldom hear clergy speak of Christ in these terms today. The bland cream of modernism sours at the notion of the Kingship of

Christ. Nuns and priests trained in the Sixties and stuck theologically and philosophically in the liberal swampland of that era haughtily flaunt all the latest buzzwords about social justice with that two-fold dishonesty that betrays the forked tongue of modernism, the inference that social justice could not be achieved under the Kingship of Christ, and the blatant lie that the pre-Conciliar Church had no interest in social justice.

Such felonious presumption is turned to ashes by the likes of Elizabeth Bruyere. Her arrival on Pointe Gatineau that February day, from which she could see the threads of chimney smoke rising from the rooftops of Bytown across the frozen Ottawa River, echoes of the uncountable Catholic women and men who gave their lives in the service of establishing the social justice of Christ the King—Vincent de Paul in recent times, the cream of the Church during the plagues of the Middle Ages, the silent, unsung benefactors of the poor inspired by Christ's Sermon on the Mount, all the way back to the unrecorded charity of Jesus during his hidden years.

What Elizabeth Bruyere saw from Pointe Gatineau was nothing less than an acknowledgment that social justice and the religious of the Church of Christ the King went hand in hand. Racing across the frozen river to welcome her to Bytown were no fewer than eighty-one horse-drawn cutters crammed with well-wishers from the city. By their rampaging, racing, whip-cracking, bell-ringing welcome they were proclaiming that now in their muddy, sprawling, bickering city on the Ottawa, the hungry would be fed, the sick cared for, the orphans mothered, the French would have a school, the Irish arriving from under the clouds of the famine and plague would have love and care, and the poor would have the Gospel preached to them and lived to the fullest right before their eyes.

Today, while many of Bruyere's spiritual daughters live exemplary lives of self-sacrifice in imitation of their founder, many Grey Nuns now wear natty little executive suits, drive the latest cars, and live in their own apartments. Upon Marguerite d'Youville's canonization, they made more out of the fact that Marguerite had survived an abusive husband than they did that great French soul's rescue of unwanted illegitimate French babies from the bayonets of their English soldier fathers. (Finding a bayoneted baby, the soldiers' answer to birth control, prompted Marguerite d'Youville to undertake her great mission).

In Rome, snappily dressed mod squad Grey Nuns had stood with their backs to the Pope to deliver the readings of Marguerite d'Youville's canonization Mass. They had demanded the right to sing the mind-numbing banalities from the *Glory and Praise* Handbook of Dreadful Jingles but were refused. Naturally, they had used the canonization ceremonies to protest this refusal of Rome to pander to their latest women-on-the-altar demands.

A conference on Sacred Heritage held on their premises was, therefore, an event with tantalizing possibilities. The opening address by the keynote speaker discussed the preservation ethic of restoration programs for sacred places and spaces in relation to the immanence or transcendence of the religion housed within.

Speakers came and went, lamenting the destruction of sacred interiors that had continued unabated, sanctuary after sanctuary, ever since Vatican II, yet continually referring deferentially to the notorious document singularly responsible for the destruction since 1978, that series of renovation guidelines entitled *Environment and Art in Catholic Worship.* No one mentioned that the document had no official status whatever in the Catholic Church, that the American Bishops Conference for whom it was workshopped never adopted it, that it was basically the result of a group of liberated nuns and priests who got together and ordained themselves interior decorators.

But then, a priest stepped up to the microphone. He was fifty perhaps, white-haired, Irish-handsome, in a black suit and roman collar. Had anyone told me this peaceful looking man was "Red Mike," one of the Berrigan gang, a so-called socialist who during the upheavals of the anti-war movement in the United States had had his own day and more in court, I would have disbelieved them. Yet indeed it was Father Michael Doyle from the Sacred Heart parish in Camden, New Jersey. For long, he would be thought of by the orthodox Catholics of the United States as one of those clerics responsible for the shambles to which the once solid Church of Rome had been reduced, the liberal Left of the clergy who were for all intents and purposes deliberately leading the Church in America away from Rome. Yet, that day, as he stood in front of the microphone in an understated, self-effacing manner, he brought the focus of the conference back to the presence of the sacred in our lives.

That evening at a social held on the upper floor of the old building, I sought him out. I don't now recall exactly how we came to talk about theater and poetry and film, but isn't that the way with Irishmen? You say "g'day" and the first thing you know you're keening along with the cast of *Riders To The Sea.*

It was not long before he uttered those two words of Celtic magic, "Siobhan McKenna." The name of that great Irish actress with a voice that could make the world turn the other way was uttered in answer to a question I don't recall asking.

He had known her as a personal friend, in some ways as a confessor, but evidently as true mates of the soul. He described the last evening he had seen her alive. She was in Philadelphia to appear on stage and visited him at Sacred Heart in Camden. She had encouraged him to write about life, about Ireland, with the words, "The wetlands need ye." Then, he related, she bid him farewell in Gaelic. Father Michael looked far off and shaped the sound of her farewell:

"*Eawaugh,*" he said. "*Oice Mait.*"

But it was her voice I heard.

"*Eawaugh.*"

Transfixed by that voice I had once kept turning and turning on my bedside turntable back in college, I lost track of the time passed in silence. Then I rose to retrieve from the bar nearby a refill of Ottawa Valley Lager. I was perhaps no more than three steps away when I heard "The Voice" again.

I wobbled, struggled for balance, and glanced instinctively at the ceiling. Around and about the room, people continued conversations as if I alone had felt the earth move.

Perhaps "The Voice" had startled my senses into picking up vibrations. At any rate, the reality was that the earth had moved. The time—6:45 p.m., Friday, November 25, 1988, the precise moment of the earthquake measuring 6 on the Richter scale whose epicenter was Chicoutimi, Quebec. Six aftershocks would follow, each greater than 2 on the Richter scale, the last one being at three o'clock the next morning. It was felt as far west as Sault Ste. Marie and as far south as Virginia.

"*Eawaugh.*"

The earth had moved.

Hearing "The Voice" unexpectedly again after decades of silence prompted a change in direction I would not have foreseen even hours earlier. In the intervening twenty-five years, the world, in general, and the Church I loved, in particular, had turned itself upside down, inside out, and backwards. Biological manipulation forever striving to uncouple us from nature had reached the bizarre outer limits of sanity. Men could be changed into women and back again if so desired. Theological manipulation, ever striving to uncouple the Church from Christ, had flooded Catholic schools with counterfeit catecheses in which the Trinitarian nature of God was ignored, the Son of God who took on our flesh to lead us to our Father had been replaced by the god within, the god of self-esteem, who simply led you backwards through a black hole in the self. Societal manipulation, ever striving to uncouple sex from morality, had spawned a pedagogical manipulation striving to uncouple the child from his parents, separate justice from God, and separate civilization from anything to do with family. Surely, it could not go on much longer. There was already so little left of our beginnings. It was time to go back in search of old roots, to find out where this betrayal of father, mother, child, and God had begun.

It would take two years before I could dismantle an extended lifestyle and strike out in search of answers. Two years before, I found myself driving westward to the border town where so much lay unanswered. The very night I arrived a phone message was relayed from someone who wanted us to get together for old times' sake. It was from Mr. B.

Twenty years had passed. While, I had left the system and watched it and society crumble from the outside, he had remained inside the education system and survived, on his own terms. Mr.

B. now taught at an outdoor education center. There he was confronted with a new class each morning and afternoon who came to him from across the city to learn outdoor survival, snowshoeing, trail-blazing, maple syrup tapping, junior forestry, and wilderness training. I stood in a snow-draped field before his education camp and awaited his return down a forest road.

In twenty years since the boy in the bag marked with a full stop my interest in classroom teaching, I had seen the full fury of devils from the abyss unleashed on the young. A babysitter and her boyfriend experimenting with angel dust before a fireplace presenting the parents with a roasted baby upon their return. Sex abuse nightmares destroying day-care credibility in California, the Carolinas. In Ontario, children being grilled for months about their Hamilton parents' satanic human sacrifices. A teenage boy killing his mother and eating her heart. A teenage lesbian, in an effort to appear as an acceptable suitor to the parents of a girl she obsessed over, killing a taxi driver and using crazy glue to affix his genitals to her body. In Detroit, a killer burying twenty-six young sex victims under his house. In British Columbia, a crazed killer being paid $100,000 by the Mounties to tell where he had buried eleven sodomized teenagers. Adult human sacrifices by satan worshippers being reported the length and breadth of North America. Parents suing school boards because their adult children couldn't spell. Children suing parents for disciplining them. Abuse hotlines opening so children could report on parents and teachers. An entire profession, an entire society living in terror.

The hum of a truck engine cleared the trees. Soon, the vehicle entered the field, pulling behind it a wagon piled high with children making noises reserved for children on a God-given winter's day. They circled the field, then pulled to a stop before the camp and disembarked with the organized chaos of kids who know how they must behave in order to get more of the same.

Mr. B. advanced across the roadway, and with a casual serenity we picked up from where we'd left off all those years ago.

"A lot of factors come into play," he said later that night in front of the fireplace of the hillside retreat he had built for himself north of the city.

I had asked what he considered the root of the crisis in teaching.

"Mothers entering the work force en masse. The resultant guilt trip because they aren't there to greet their kids any more. The concern of 'How do I compensate?' The easy answer is—compensate materially. Buy the kid everything money allows. The child must not be deprived of what others have. Consumer goods become the new god. Grade five and six students suddenly have their own snowmobiles.

"Children," he said, "are led into a change of attitude from the parent's change of attitude. A new litany emerges to replace those long ago discarded. Thou shalt not suffer thy child to be deprived. Thou shalt indulge every whim of the child. Thou shalt never suffer thy child to be centered out for any reason but especially not as a have-not.

"Eventually, the child senses anything can be bought. Anyone can be bought. Once a child sees his parents can be guilted into doing what he wants, the parents become targets, the child becomes a terrorist. Along with that comes the extremes of physical and verbal abuse.

"Now physical abuse will heal, but what someone says lasts forever. So parents and teachers come to watch everything they say. The very nearness of a child is a cause for editing, for the child, supported by misguided social service agencies, can use anything and everything against them.

"We have replaced the true values of love and nurturing with an envelope of protection around the child on his pedestal. The healthy code of self-denial has been replaced by the comfort zone of the excessive.

"The child has inherited the Big Me mind-set of the Sixties. He is the ultimate authority on everything. Such a system has robbed teachers of their authority; the parents have forfeited theirs just to have peace on the home front. Authority now belongs to the child by default. He is the center of the universe. A monster at the center of the universe of family and social chaos and disillusionment. A terrorist in full control of those around him.

"The innocent forces, innocent only through ignorance, are the sociologists and their program mandate. They are the scourge of the home and school. The social worker is God's way of saying 'I told you so.'

"Non-innocent forces deliberately fanning the egos of adolescent tyrants include the totally irresponsible film and television media. Against these forces the parent is helpless, the teacher compromised every way he turns.

"What kids need and no longer have is a healthy fear of parents. When the bills start arriving in the kid's name, then he can start taking charge of his own life, but as long as the parents are paying, surrender of authority is suicidal.

"One of the biggest deceptions of this century came with the invention of the slogan 'peer pressure.' Peer pressure simply comes from an absence of parental pressure. Kids should be worrying about what their parents think, not what their peers think.

"But parents are to blame here. They pander to the notion of peer pressure by turning authority over to the child. They want to be friends with their children. That is a grave mistake. An adolescent doesn't need a friend, he needs a parent who will take their responsibilities in hand and make sure he gets out of adolescence in one piece.

"Of course this won't please the sociology experts. Experts treat answers that are too simple as necessarily lacking.

"We have been duped, teachers sold down the drain. A compromise was made between wanting to promote Catholic values and the politics of education. Funding is the deciding factor. Catholic boards rolled over for government funding, and Catholic education went with it. Boards are now controlled by the 'Me generation' of the Sixties. They can't teach Catholicism because it is contrary to their philosophy. The resulting restlessness of a system that has lost its reason for being reduces the teacher to having only one certainty in his professional life—his salary. Teachers are excoriated for striking for better pay. The critics may very well be justified, but strikes in teaching shout out one sad truth, the figures on the paycheck are the only reality left over which the teacher has any say at all."

We continued the talk the following night, warming homemade red wine before the fireplace.

"A fellow teacher and I considered an option. Art and I sat down and composed a bit of a manifesto—based on the hope that it is not too late to try to regain one's ground in the classroom by saying it's time all teachers across the province took a united stand, we don't stop until the schools meet these two simple criteria:
1) the teacher controls the classroom, with no interference from Children's Aid, resource departments, and all else to meet the needs of one child, for there is too much interference for one student to handle. The reality is the child becomes professional at handling consultants; 2) the position of the principal must be one of authority and not that of the diplomat. The rules are spelled out. Yet the principal is the first one to bend the rules, because of outside pressure, it being easier to go this route than to challenge the pressure. Without support from the board through the principal, the teacher is adrift, lost.

"Responsibility and accountability of teachers is only as real as their board's determination to support the authority of the teacher in the classroom. But these intervals are threatened daily by a system that panders, out of guilt for abandoning its Catholic mandate, to the child. The teacher is daily humiliated by being just an extra on the set. The child is the superstar.

"But the necessary externals are also gone. Order. Regimen. Schedules. Grading. There are no demands on the child any more. Why should a child respond to any authority when he runs no risk of failing, of disciplining for wrongdoing? Unsatisfactory behavior is tolerated because of totally non-existent standards. Unacceptable behavior is made acceptable because the only criterion is the student's need to be appeased.

"The sociologists put a loaded gun into the students' hands—the term 'abuse.' Psychological, sexual, physical, verbal abuse are the new scoring lights on the pinball arcade school has become. Couple that with the boards' driving obsession to be politically correct and you have a snake-ridden swamp of compromise luring the teaching profession deeper and deeper into the mire.

"Remember. Most parents have to adjust to just one teacher. A teacher of thirty students has to adjust to sixty parents. He has to be in complete control of his agenda or be putty in everyone's hands. The teacher who only thought he knew where he was going loses his certitude. That teacher perhaps entered the profession with only two questions as his guide. For whom am I responsible? To whom am I accountable?

"In those days, a simple formula was at work. The teacher stood between the home and the world. He had the parents' confidence because of a simple formula. R + A = M. Responsibility plus accountability equals maturity. There was never any question of the teacher's autonomy. He was supported by the home and by the system. Today, he can rely on neither."

I unveiled to Mr. B my estimate of the damage—that the prime ingredient of the Catholic classroom no longer exists. The Divinity of Christ and His mission as Messiah was the beginning and end of the teacher's task. It was why parents entrusted their children to Catholic schools, why the early bishops struggled against incredible odds to win the right to have separate schools, and it inspired teachers daily, consciously and unconsciously, to go the extra mile to fulfill their mandate.

The liberated nuns, dissenting clergy, and theologians stole that holy mission from out of the school curriculum to supplant it with an agenda of secular humanism. The Catholic classroom without Christ at its center is a war zone. The teacher defenseless. Every adolescent ego a land mine.

For a hundred years, the role of male and female teachers leavened the education system. The women teachers met the spiritual stress of their times with the internals of the faith, imparting prayer, the tenets of the faith, the truth about life, about death, in short, mothering. The male teacher, by nature, assumed responsibility for the external working out of those mysteries, discipline, the externals of authority, fathering. Mr. B. summed it up, simply: "I guess it all boils down to a simple question and answer for both teacher and parents. Do you believe in Christ? What have you done to impart your belief to your children? What will you say to Christ when he asks you 'What did you tell your children about me?' On the answer on those questions depends the whole issue of teacher and parent authority."

THREE
HOLY GROUND

I SUSPECT THE WRITER of the movie *Alien*—featuring a life form that grew to maturity within a host body, had acid for blood and a lewd locomotive jaw where lips should be—had once been a teacher and was committing to celluloid, albeit unconsciously, a meticulous metaphor for the thing that today inhabits the space in our children where the sacred should be.

The monster inside pushed those other long-standing symbols of childhood right off the marquee: the Scarecrow, the Tin Man, the Cowardly Lion. No brain, no heart, he's much too shy. Oh my, how they used to satisfy when teachers needed help to categorize a student. "There's no place like home, no place like home," said that over-the-rainbow declaration of unadulterated childhood.

Today, the spirit inhabiting the runaway child heart has been twisted out of all recognition by the lust of adult sexologists.

"There's no place like home," the alien says as he takes up residence within the child. But he doesn't click ruby slippers, he snaps a condom.

No, Toto, I don't think we're in Kansas any more.

In their wake, the sexologists, obsessed with planting their agenda in the cribs of the nation, have left behind a child crippled by their ugliness, a child who now plays landlord to the tenant from hell.

There is a monster inside. It rages and roams, now ruling the mind, now the tongue, now sitting behind the eyes, now coiled in the fists, fists raised in anger, framing the ancient mask of rage borrowed from time to time from its original owner and worn by tyrants intent on re-ordering the world to serve them.

This is a vulgar tyrant. There is no modesty of purpose in its performance. It is arrogant, boastful, disrespectful, deceitful, manipulative, loth to obey, quick to strike, prepared to play any game to get its way.

Its way is the destruction of all authority, all order, all peace. It is content amid tears and turmoil. It employs threats, sneers, jeers, taunts, jibes. It is certain that it will remain secure, totally independent. Stress follows in its wake from room to room, burdening everyone with whom it comes in contact.

It's anthem is, "I will not serve."

Family, friends, school, church, and community. These are the sources of physical, mental, emotional, and spiritual growth for the child. Ask a child what are the causes of stress in his life and if he has not yet been made a captive of the monster inside, he will provide telling yet innocent answers. John, aged ten, answers, "When you are doing a test and you have to go to the bathroom. When you tell on something your friends did bad and they all get mad at you. When you get tackled and hit hard in football and you tell the teacher and the kid who done it beats you up after school. When the bully from class throws snowballs at your window at night. When you catch your fitness teacher smoking and she marks you down." Oh, for such innocent days again.

Daniel, aged twelve, answers, "When you get five bucks allowance and your friends get ten. When Christmas comes and you have to get something for Dad. When you're not there when the rules are explained for a test and you have to ask again and everybody calls you 'suck.' When you do stuff wrong and you want to go back in time to change it, but you can't—like egging that old man's window at Halloween. When you think of dying and there's nothing there after you're dead. I tried to talk to the guidance teacher and I asked him about what comes after death and he just looked at me and said, 'C'mon kid, get a life.'

"People don't want to be bad, like stealing Christmas lights, but you do and it's over before you have time to say 'No, I'm not gonna.' There's no time to say no any more."

No time to say no any more. Daniel, you said a mouthful.

William de Marois, as early as 1974, warned:

> Child analysts are beginning to get firsthand contact with results of these [sex-ed] programs. Beneath the verbal facility, they are finding anxiety, guilt and confusion. The knowledge is turning out to be pseudo-knowledge which has in no way been helpful.
>
> Religiously educated children suffer incomparably more than others because of the irreverent nature of the thoughts and fantasies aroused in them by this type of instruction. A host of erotic and unseemly fantasies about their teachers, ministers and family members will be evoked no matter how calmly the material is presented. Sexual drives are stimulated in school and the truly religious youngsters will have to make superhuman efforts to suppress such disturbing fantasies. It is painful to think of the torment to which these children will be so helplessly subjected, and of their ultimate and inevitable need for intensive therapy in order to undo the corroding and distorting effects of guilt, anxiety, loss of self-esteem and feelings of alienation from the family.

The pilgrimage to the street corner where Ronald died was shrouded in a mid-January snowfall. The school from whose second-floor window I had watched the searchers come and go was now closed up. Just one more of the seemingly endless line of Catholic school properties now abandoned for one simple reason—there were no more children.

Across the street still stood the weathered woodshed where they had found the boy in the bag. Ronald would be thirty-two or -three now, the perfect age, had he lived. Why did he not live? Why was the pull of the future not strong enough to keep him going? To make him roll out of that bag and struggle for life?

The catechetical scandal of the Sixties and Seventies was aimed at marginalizing catechetics altogether to make room for the new absolute, the "divinization of orgasm."

When a school teaches sex education, it is no longer Catholic. It is serving that phallic religion whose followers practice its contraceptive principles with a conscientiousness they never lavished on the Faith of their fathers. The fruits of a contraceptive society do not include children. Schools close, neighborhoods die. Fitness studios open. A lot of people jog. Others panic over the environment. Condemn seal hunting. Wear buttons that say, "Plant a Tree. Be." When all the questions are tabulated about what went wrong in my generation, I suspect they can all be honestly addressed with one explanation—we got what we wanted.

I never cease to marvel at a phenomenon that occurs without fail whenever the Baltimore Catechism is mentioned in adult Catholic teachers' seminars. The room turns into a raucous caldron of scoffing, tsk-tsking sounds, and almost invariably the loudest condemnatory comment will be volunteered by a liberated nun.

This perplexes me. What is it about the Baltimore Catechism that modern nuns dislike so fervently? The fact that it is a veritable road map of the dogmatic, sacramental, and hierarchical Church for two millennia administered by the male religious? So much has changed. One spends these twenty-five post-Conciliar years arduously attempting to be considerate of the female religious point of view, then, lo and behold, in a crowded room someone cries out "*Baltimore*," and the first person on her feet will be a nun who snorts "... to be happy with Him in the next, indeed!" as if the male in question was the least likely prospect a liberated nun would want to know, to love, to serve in this world, let alone surrender all options to in the next.

She's as likely to exit the room and return in clown make-up as she is to remain and hear even one more Q and A excerpted from the much-maligned *Baltimore.*

What darkness their silliness has brought to the world.

One afternoon in 1989, a chance to sit at a teacher's desk for an afternoon prompted me to browse through the daybook which contained the curriculum agenda day by day.

I could not resist looking over the notes on what was once called religion. What it is called today, I still have not determined.

It appeared from what I could see in the daybook that the course most closely aligned with religion had something to do with old people. In one week, the class had written letters of introduction of their own precious little persons to the elderly they were going to visit, then the next day they went to visit them and presented these thoughtfully compiled credentials. The third day, they discussed their visit describing what they thought of old people in general and those old people in particular. The fourth day, they discussed what they could do to make old people happier, like writing them letters of thanks and appreciation with nice little animals on them, then the fifth and final day, they wrote letters of thanks and appreciation and drew nice little animals on them.

Years ago, H. G. Wells wrote *The Time Machine*, a novel about a man who acquires the ability to live in the future, visit the present, and know the past. What Wells did not say was that he was his own time machine, if only he could have lived a little longer.

We have in existence on earth today a species of life form the likes of which has never existed before in the history of the world—the human who has lived long enough to pass the age of sixty-five. These people are the living past who make up the perfect present because they have lived through so much they have no fear of the future.

In the first to tenth centuries, a man could live his entire life without ever seeing a written word in print. In the eleventh through the eighteenth centuries, a man could spend his whole lifetime never knowing for sure the look of a culture fifty miles away from the place of his birth. But a person born in this century knows what all the other centuries knew and more besides.

A person over sixty-five today has lived through more social changes, more economic demands, more psychological stimuli than experienced in the last two thousand years combined. People over sixty-five were born in the adolescence of the Industrial Revolution, saw the birth of the automotive age, movies, and radio. They have watched men learn to fly. They have seen the spread of the telephone, the hula hoop, the frisbee, and Communism. They have seen the fall of the British Empire and the rise of feminism. They have witnessed the growth of advertising, the invasion of the electric can-opener, the dictatorship of television, and have searched the ocean floor from their sofa. They have lived through the slaughter of millions in different wars, the mass sterilization of Indian women, the first test-tube baby, the first man on the Moon. They have mourned an assassinated President. They have fought pornography, won and lost battles on abortion, and been alive to see the economic unification of Europe. They have survived jogging mortgage rates, running bank rates, racing gasoline rates, trotting inflation, galloping consumerism, and the skid of recession. They have seen the depressing paganism that was ancient Rome rise again out of Moscow and collapse.

They have seen caviar made in Manitoba. They have learned the names of villages in Korea and street corners in Saigon. They have wondered at the Jonestown massacre. They've lived through so many front-page tyrants they can spot an Idi Amin growing ten years off. They endured McCarthyism, Watergate, and Alice Cooper. They tapped toes to honky-tonk, jazz, swing, rock, rock and roll, acid rock, and punk. They might like Anne Murray. Might remember Helen Morgan or Enrico Caruso. And the Beatles. They are immune to fads and social plagues so they will survive the humiliation of lotteries, the banality of soap operas, and the hysteria of TV evangelism. But, most stunning of all, they will witness and endure that one force determined to tell them they can now die when and how they want to.

It is strange but true, that minds made strong by sixty-five years of adapting to the most radical changes the human race has ever undergone must rely on yet more patience and resort to yet more humor to wait out the arguing of those who think they know what senior citizens need to make their lives complete: the right to die. I have a sneaking suspicion that these living, breathing, walking treasure houses of knowledge that have survived two world wars, a baby boom, a baby bust, the poisoning of the Great Lakes, the dawn of the solar age, the losing of the *Titanic* and the finding of the *Titanic* know what they want. Having for years fought off salesmen at the door, the senior is now confronted with smiling ethics consultants selling them death and smiling knowingly and patiently at mention of "God's will." But they need not despair.

The upcoming generation knows how to make thank-you cards with nice little animals on them.

With no religion taught in the schools and children at the grade-three level learning to use computers, the names of which they cannot spell, we can be assured that before the next century is half over, one will have to go to a religious archive to research the meaning of the quaint phrase "Immaculate Conception." Ask a child these days what is meant by the Incarnation and his response will fill your heart with sorrow. Yet, we crave to know more of our beginnings.

Trilobites that accomplished nothing more than lying eyebrow-deep in swamp water millions of years ago still tyrannize the imagination of paleontology students today; the laying of a whooping crane egg in the Yukon can earn a free charter airplane ride to Florida where it will be guaranteed to hatch; park developers labor in concrete to simulate herds of dinosaurs that once roamed Alberta; and communities craving to touch the past are adept at opening museums every time somebody falls off an old chair or trips over a hydro insulator—all proofs that gone from our planet are life forms that thrill us because they were here and scare us because they are gone.

The Blood Indians of southern Alberta believe that before the pyramids of Egypt were built their ancestors were meeting their Provider face to face at a cliff called Head Smashed in Buffalo Jump. There they developed an entire culture around the 360-some uses they found for the buffalo driven over the cliffs to their death.

Today, the federal government subsidizes the operating of an interpretive center at the foot of the cliff, where their descendants can learn of their heritage.

At the rate our heritage is disappearing, Catholic children will consider themselves singularly blessed if, in some future time, they can learn of what their parents lost through an interpretive center at the foot of Head Smashed in Catholic Jump.

"The only kind thing about the future," writes Anne Roche Muggeridge, "is that not one moment of it is foreseeable."[1]

Yet, about the future there is one thing of which we can be certain: that He who has on His garment and on His thigh written, "King of Kings and Lord of Lords," "will reign until at the end of the world He has put all His enemies under the feet of God the Father."[2]

And where will the bishops be that day? At the airport flying off to a tribute dinner? Dictating their memoirs? Out of town? At the cottage hoping no one will drive up?

In our eternal smugness we thought the *Baltimore Catechism* old-fashioned. We thought of it as a primitive, crude tool of learning. We know better now.

As George Bernard Shaw said about politicians, "It is time for some mad ones, look where the sane ones have landed us." I say it is time for some homemade lessons, look where the experts have brought us.

When the armies of Imperial Rome finally defeated Carthage in 146 B.C. and thereby ruled the known world, they prided themselves on having triumphed over a barbaric civilization that made a religion out of sacrificing children. The Carthaginians worshipped a god imported to their North African shores from Tyre and Sidon, a close relative to Moloch, that fellow who has come down to us through artists' renditions, the giant eating his children. Each time the Carthaginians went to war, they killed children in ritual sacrifice to appease the gods of war and bring them victory. Rome ended all that when it stomped Carthage into the sand, where it remained until Caesar began a Roman colony there a hundred years later. Rome then went on to subjugate the entire world as they knew it, patting themselves on the back for having erased the worshippers of Moloch from the earth.

It has taken the human race two thousand years to return to the banquet table and appease Moloch's appetite. In this decade, as in the last, western civilization will continue to abort the unborn in the sickening rampage of child slaughter that has made of the twentieth century an abattoir. When we fall, and what civilization that countenances free abortions could hope to survive, erased from the history books will be all the good we have achieved, and we will be remembered in time only as the worshippers of Moloch that were vanquished.

It seems unthinkable now that in the next century children will know no more about us than we know about Carthage. But it was also unthinkable in 1939 that millions of our human brothers and sisters would be slid into ovens and sent up in fire as offerings to the god of hate. This has been and seems destined to continue to be the Unthinkable Century.

Is it criminal or merely sinful to be so pessimistic? I put the question to the manipulators of the present-day economy—bankers, realtors, and industrial bluebeards who have made our modern society a dreaded place for the young. Surely, there is no more tragic symbol of the twentieth century than the young woman facing motherhood in an inflationary world where the economic survival of the child might spell the economic ruin of the parents and the marriage. There is nothing in our society today that gives to young parents the faith and fortitude of those parents of the Thirties and Forties who raised ten and fifteen children believing that God would provide food for them. We have slid back into the new serfdom, where only mortgage payments and rent payments made on time are treated as virtues. Instead of devoting manpower and resources to the development of those staples that can support the human race, the human race has decided to terminate itself.

Yet, there is hope. Imperial Rome grew to be the greatest all-smothering monolith the world has ever known. It ruled the world for hundreds of years. Then it began to shake. For, forty-four years after Caesar began his colony in Carthage, the sound of a child crying at birth filled a cave on the outskirts of a town five miles south of Moriah. That cry carried out of the cave, echoed over Judea, and reverberated through every corner of the Roman Empire. It has been heard in barnyards and courtyards and hamlets and kingdoms, countries, continents, and hemispheres for two thousand years.

That child's cry did to Imperial Rome what trumpets once did to Jericho. It was heard at the end of the Mongol Invasion, the French Revolution, and the Third Reich.

And it will be heard again.

Children are the pull of the future. They generate their own survival by demanding that we work for them, provide for them, stretch ourselves to the limit to give them a just existence. They will, given the breath to do it, be the downfall of the modern thieves who tyrannize our marketplace. A child's needs are so great, he forces the most unlikely aspects of the world to provide for him.

Western civilization began in the dead of that night when loving parents secreted a child into Egypt—ancient, pagan Egypt chosen by God to safeguard His Son's right to live. Out of Egypt, He called His living Son. God will thank Egypt someday. Perhaps out of Egypt, at heaven's summons, will come a bishop to truly champion the right of all to life.

But what will children live on when we can't provide for them? What the human race has always lived on—on love. It changed the world once. It can do it again. Luckily, children come into the world entirely helpless. If they could look after themselves, who would possibly have any interest in them? They're noisy, unkempt, ill-mannered, and odious at the least provocation. They survive only because they are so totally needy that they force everyone to think about them, care for them, plan for them. They consume imagination, melt the heart, and illuminate the spirit. They are the stuff that revolutions are made of.

If we put children first, our society will upend itself. The banks will end up where they belong—serving society, not doubling its interest every snowfall. When we devote ourselves once more to the family and its offspring, we will feel again the irresistible promise of the future.

The future, too, is like a newborn, and demands we make provision, develop resources, invent shelter. It carries its own promise, as once it was indicated in that cave of long ago. Five miles south of Jerusalem's rock called Moriah lies the town where an expectant mother was once denied lodging by an innkeeper with the bank deposit on his mind. And nearby lies the earthen shelter where her child uttered his first cry.

Every Christmas card is a reminder that we are, as William de Marois said in 1974, "enlisted in an army in this world, the Church militant. Let us also remember who in this 'day of battle,' is our commanding officer, and that He is, eschatologically speaking, already victorious."[3]

There may be no Catholic children soon. Catholic schools and Catholic bishops have seen to that. What then of the heritage the Son of God died to give us?

Time and again, all teachers wonder why they entered the profession. My decision to do so came in 1961. It was on one of the first Sundays of winter when the voice of Joan of Arc crying from amidst the flames was still in the process of vanquishing all my callow purpose.

It happened as I listened to a fellow boarder detail over the table between us the events of a savage day.

Karl was twenty-four, an apprentice at McAfferty's Mortuary, a pursuit that seemed totally at odds with his casual, buoyant nature. This particular evening he appeared aged and spoke mechanically. His eyes followed his own hands as he spoke as if from their clenching and unclenching he was pulling the words one by one. Occasionally, he would draw in the air the events of the story, or reach out to touch them as if they were unfolding before his eyes. What details he could not possibly have known or seen he imagined, dramatizing his guesswork as if to test some new-found ubiquity, then continuing on.

Twelve hours earlier, he related, in a town a hundred miles away, on a bleak winter morning, a man had backed his red half-ton down the driveway onto the street, then proceeded toward a white wood-frame church several blocks away. In the back of the half-ton, his nine-year-old daughter, in blue mitts and yellow parka, sat playing with the family dog. They were the only movement in an otherwise still, silent town of two thousand people in the northern part of the province.

It was one of those crisp winter days when the smoke from chimneys rose straight and taut toward the sky, not giving as much as a shudder, until just before it joined the grey cloud blanketing the earth for as far as the eye could see. Here and there the glow of mid-morning television animated a living-room window but any other movement was concealed from view behind drapes and blinds.

At the same time, outside of town, there was taking place a gathering that occurred every seven years or so, it seemed, in that part of the world. Dogs who did not really belong to anyone, big dogs for the most part, had gathered in a pack just inside the tree line beyond the fire ditch that separated the houses of the town from the forest.

As all packs do, this one had a leader. He was the first to leave the shelter of the trees and descend the sloping bank of the fire ditch. A raid on garbage cans was in order, hunting and foraging bearing meager returns that month.

The fire ditch caused Main Street to break at a right angle and turn south; through time and tradition it was called, from that corner on, Church Street. The red half-ton, already traveling slow, scarcely altered its speed as it cut the corner and then rolled southward. It drew to a stop before the white church with the steep bank of steps.

The girl in the yellow parka jumped down to the earth. The dog complained gruffly at her departure then looked at her stupidly, the way dogs do when the cold winter air drunkens them.

At the edge of town, the dog pack blanketed the fire ditch, first the downward then the upward bank in the wake of the lead dog, until they were all huddled together on the tip of civilization a few short strides from where Main Street became Church Street.

The half-ton paused in front of the church long enough for the girl to climb the steps, then it pulled away, the dog in the back continuing his low, throaty growl to no one in particular.

At the top of the steps, the girl reached up to find the door latch. It rattled in her blue-mittened hand, but the door did not open. It took a moment for her to realize that a note had been stapled to the door. It began, "No Sunday School today ..."

There was more to the message, but it was in longhand and not so easy to read. The girl was still trying to read it, whispering the words under her breath, when she sensed she was not alone.

The dogs had not encountered any human beings nor even town dogs after crossing the fire ditch. They had progressed down Church Street in perfect silence behind the leader. Now they were standing still, all of them in the street below the steep flight of steps. At the top, a young girl in a parka stood looking down at them. She was trying to speak, but no words came out.

The lead dog sniffed the air. The girl had the smell of the family dog on her parka. The leader padded softly up the first steps. The other dogs followed in his wake. The smell of her parka was overpowering now. The hunger within drove the leader over the last few steps. The girl screamed and covered her face. The dogs thundered up the steps. Soon the sound of their devouring filled the air.

"All they found was a piece of her skull, the brow, the size of the back of my hand," Karl said.

He held up his hands to demonstrate the size of the fragment. His forearms touched together; the fingers of both hands were curved to form a cup, the imaginary fragment balanced invisibly on his fingertips. His arms and hands shaped a chalice of bone and flesh. He looked into the empty chalice for a long time, as did I, knowing what men have dreamed of knowing for more than a millennium, what it felt like to look into the Grail.

To know, to love and to serve God is the highest honor to which man can aspire here on earth. To teach others how to do so is man's greatest calling. To lead us to that knowledge is why two thousand years ago, after filling with His actual blood a drinking cup for all mankind, Christ went out and submitted body, blood, soul, and divinity to the slaughter of His innocence. The Divine Example setting the standard for all teachers to come, the Divine Lesson blueprinting for all future architects of the will, the form, shape, and dimension of the sacrifice required of them.

"Suffer the children ..."

Allow, permit, assist, guide, instruct, teach, fill with your own being the Grail that is each child on earth.

Is it not noticeable to you that the child who knows of the Immaculate Conception differs from the child who does not? He must differ. That glimpse of the holy is like a spark in the dark. It reflects and multiplies in the many mirrors of the soul, dispelling doubt, exiling shadows, so that not a sparkle will be dimmed of the incandescent, youthful heart.

So tell him early, when purity is king, before he leases out the mansion of his soul to worthless squatters.

Teach him early in the simplest terms. Wonder, gratitude, and awe will be his starting point to sexual wonderment if he hears at precisely the right time, in precisely the right way, from precisely the right voice, that greatest of mysteries so simply sung "Round yon virgin, mother and child."

The mysteries of the Immaculate Conception, the Incarnation, the Nativity are the cloud of holy knowing within which the wonders of sexuality attain the greatest dignity and the realities of our sexual nature are most perfectly taught. In the mystery of the Virgin birth, there is a limitless wonderment for the child who hears "How can this be since I have not known man?" and a holy forum in which to impart answers to those who wonder aloud.

So stop there, you who are to teach this child. A child's place of learning is a precious space. Remove your shoes. This is holy ground.

The child comes to you hungering for certainty, consistency, loyalty. All that has come from the mother, until now, must now come from you. You will sanctify that hunger by teaching him of sacred truths.

You will empty yourself to the last drop to fill the child. Yet, surprisingly, you will refill. Our nature abhors the vacuum left by removal of the sacred. Violence and despair rush in when sacred truths depart. So you must refill. And you will. It is the charism of the teacher, the giver of truths, that the more he gives, the more he has to give. Yours will be the secret of the bush that burns but does not consume itself. It is a mystery. It is grace.

Snow had fallen twenty years on Ronald's grave the day I reached it. I laid multi-colored flowers on the snow and not a petal was white. For he who lies beneath the snow was colored inside. He died from the colorlessness we drew as a fence around his young life, early winter imposed on a child in the springtime of his belief by a system bleached empty of God.

Winter to a God-starved child is bleak and sub-bleak. The child needs to see reflected in the world around him all the wonder his instinct for God tells him is there. That is how snow angels come to be imprinted in our yards.

We are creatures who need to cast our multi-colored shadows on the snow. We are driven to shatter a blizzard's colorlessness with electric-blue snow machines and crimson shovels, scarves the color of neon bananas and tams and toques that might have fallen from a carnival carousel. We fight white. For we know inside that sooner or later we all have the blindfold tied over our eyes when the color of faces we love moves out of our lives.

We live for the multi-colored mysteries of the "abyss of divinity" where our most earnest cravings for God start and, with His blessing, end. The cruelty of white when you are colored inside is unmatched.

But pray that your flight may not be in the Winter or on the Sabbath.

—*St. Matthew* 24:20

AFTERWORD
BY MALACHI MARTIN

IN MORE WAYS THAN ONE—some of them terrifying—this last decade of the second millennium is a time for hard-nosed reckoning and, inevitably, for calling in long-overdue debts: ethnic, regional, ideological, and religious. Witness the travail of the new South Africa; the tortuous seeking of peace in the Middle East; the rising revolt of the "South" against its exploitation by the "North"; the agony of a multifaceted Islam appraising its place in an alien New World Order; the bloody internecine strife of some thirty nations morally bastardized and culturally mongrelized by the Soviet party state for nearly half a century. Most poignantly, we are now also called to witness the crimes of those Roman Catholic bishops who, with their non-Catholic allies, continue to go along with an obvious attempt to liquidate the Roman Catholic institutional organization that visibly clothes the Mystical Body of Christ.

I say "most poignantly," because their gross betrayal and abandonment of the traditional Church of Rome was in no way necessary. It was not etched on monumental brass or graven in everlasting granite. They were not forced by any superior power. They had all the means of recognizing the threat and of foiling it. Maybe, just maybe, it might have cost some of them their blood, or their sociopolitical privileges, or both. But wasn't that the promise they made to the Vicar of Christ and to Christ Himself on the day of their consecration as successors to the Apostles and as servants of the Servant of God?

And, now, well into this last, fateful decade, their awesome debt to Christ, to the sacred Church organization, and to this generation of children has been plastered across their faces by Almighty God's unforgiving debt-collector: irreversible time. The damage they have done—the souls lost to salvation, the extinction of faith in millions of our young citizens—all is irreparable by these ecclesiastical perpetrators.

Anyone acquainted with the facts can immediately verify the overall statement of *Children of Winter*: that the Bishops of North America collaborated, individually and collegially, in robbing one whole generation of children of their God-given right to be educated as Roman Catholics. Jim Demers has concentrated on describing the damage done and on conveying the dastardly behavior of bishops in not merely allowing but collaborating to create this terrible winter of ignorance and unfaith. He offers his own life experience in teaching children as the prism through which we can perceive, in both human and supernatural terms, what the condition and the promise of Roman Catholic religious teaching were in North America up to the Sixties. And he highlights the truly diabolical strategy—he calls it the "greater design" behind the whole movement—employed by the enemies of religion and adopted holus-bolus by the bishops from the late Sixties onwards to our day.

The target to be attained by that strategy is found only in children between the ages of six and twelve. It is the latency stage of psycho-social, psycho-academic, psycho-moral and psycho-spiritual development. In that stage, the child needs above all other things "an acknowledgment of that holy knowing of his own desire to be good."

It is devastating but salutary to read how Roman Catholic bishops collaborated with the extraordinary phalanx of "the feminist movement, Planned Parenthood, gay-lesbian equal rights activists, abortion advocates, pedophiles, jackbooted ex-nuns, dissenting clergy and renegade theologians," collaborated in teaching the child in that latency period that "the thing of greatest value was not commitment to be good but the inevitability of being orgasmic."

The author hurts your soul with his crisp summary of the evil done in Roman Catholic schools under the orders of bishops: "They looted the sanctuary of the child's soul, scraped it clean of all signs and symbols of victory over evil, scoured it bare of any reference to a nature above human nature." For this is precisely what they did, knowingly, willingly, using all the sacred power delivered to them as supreme local pastors of souls. We know it; we need only accept the testimony of our own eyes in our own neighborhoods.

There is no sign of any change of heart in these guilty pastors, no sign of any panic, no sign of any realization of the damage done and being done. Ancient Nineveh in the sackcloth and ashes of repentance will not be imitated by the bishops' conferences.

From the policies of individual state educational departments, including the imposition of multiculturalism, of Outcome Based Education, of "feed-back" techniques and "rainbow" curricula in public schools; from the new governmental squeeze on the burgeoning home-schooling efforts of concerned parents, and the concerted opposition to any "voucher system for parents"; from the close coordination between United Nations educational agencies and individual state educational systems, it is quite clear that a massive design is being implemented to achieve complete homogenization of all educational systems, at least in the major industrialized countries. All this is being conducted according to a new code of "human values" morally and religiously "neutral," which is deemed a strategic necessity by the intending builders of the New World Order.

Truly a great design! And one which is destined to produce the new citizens of a world bereft of the supernatural message of salvation and holiness coming to mankind from beyond this material cosmos through our Lord and Savior, Jesus Christ, and His Roman Catholic Church.

The crime of neglect committed against children fits very aptly into this greater design, which ultimately stems from a greater evil—in fact, from the greatest evil, the mortal enemy of our human race who wars against Christ. Roman Catholics know that Christ has already won the war, but that we will lose many individual battles. We have already lost the educational battle for this generation of children.

All our trust and hope must now be placed in Christ's healing grace, and in the advent of an age dominated, the Church tells us, by the person and the power of Her through whose immaculate womb our salvation was first introduced into our world two thousand years ago.

APPENDIX

OATH AGAINST MODERNISM

By His Holiness Pope St. Pius X
September 1, 1910

To be sworn to by all clergy, pastors, confessors, preachers, religious superiors, and professors in philosophical-theological seminaries.

I, ___________, firmly embrace and accept each and every definition that has been set forth and declared by the unerring teaching authority of the Church, especially those principal truths which are directly opposed to the errors of this day. And first of all, I profess that God, the origin and end of all things, can be known with certainty by the natural light of reason from the created world, that is, from the visible works of creation, as a cause from its effects, and that, therefore, His existence can also be demonstrated. Secondly, I accept and acknowledge the external proofs of revelation, that is, divine acts and especially miracles and prophecies as the surest signs of the divine origin of the Christian religion and I hold that these same proofs are well adapted to the understanding of all eras and all men, even of this time. Thirdly, I believe with equally firm faith that the Church, the guardian and teacher of the revealed word, was personally instituted by the real and historical Christ, when He lived among us, and that the Church was built upon Peter, the prince of the apostolic hierarchy, and his successors for the duration of time. Fourthly, I sincerely hold that the doctrine of faith was handed down to us from the apostles through the orthodox Fathers in exactly the same meaning and always in the same purport. Therefore, I entirely reject the heretical misrepresentation that dogmas evolve and change from one meaning to another different from the one which the Church held previously. I also condemn every error according to which, in place of the divine deposit which has been given to the spouse of Christ to be carefully guarded by her, there is put a philosophical figment or product of a human conscience that has gradually been developed by human effort and will continue to develop indefinitely. Fifthly, I hold with certainty and sincerely confess that faith is not a blind sentiment of religion welling up from the depths of the subconscious under the impulse of the heart and the motion of a will trained to morality; but faith is a genuine assent of the intellect to truth received by hearing from an external source. By this assent, because of the authority of the supremely truthful God, we believe to be true that which has been revealed and attested to by a personal God, our creator and lord.

Furthermore, with due reverence, I submit and adhere with my whole heart to the condemnations, declarations, and all the prescripts contained in the encyclical *Pascendi* and in the decree *Lamentabili*, especially those concerning what is known as the history of dogmas. I also reject the error of those who say that the faith held by the Church can contradict history, and that Catholic dogmas, in the sense in which they are now understood, are irreconcilable with a more realistic view of the origins of the Christian religion. I also condemn and reject the opinion of those who say that a well-educated Christian assumes a dual personality—that of a believer and at the same time of a historian; as if it were permissible for a historian to hold things that contradict the faith of the believer, or to establish premises which, provided there be no direct denial of dogmas, would lead to the conclusion that dogmas are either false or doubtful. Likewise, I reject that method of judging and interpreting Sacred Scripture which, departing from the tradition of the Church, the analogy of faith, and the norms of the Apostolic See, embraces the misrepresentations of the rationalists and with no prudence or restraint adopts textual criticism as the one and supreme norm. Furthermore, I reject the opinion of those who hold that a professor lecturing or writing on a historico-theological subject should first put aside any preconceived opinion about the supernatural origin of Catholic tradition or about the divine promise of help to preserve all revealed truth forever; and that they should then interpret the writings of each of the Fathers solely by scientific principles, excluding all sacred authority, and with the same liberty of judgment that is common in the investigation of all ordinary historical documents.

Finally, I declare that I am completely opposed to the error of the modernists who hold that there is nothing divine in sacred tradition; or what is far worse, say that there is, but in a pantheistic sense, with the result that there would remain nothing but this plain simple fact—one to be put on par with the ordinary facts of history—the fact, namely, that a group of men by their own labor, skill, and talent have continued through subsequent ages a school begun by Christ and His apostles. I firmly hold, then, and shall hold to my dying breath the belief of the Fathers in the charism of truth, which certainly is, was, and always will be in the succession of the episcopacy from the apostles. The purpose of this is, then, not that dogma may be tailored according to what seems better and more suited to the culture of each age; rather, that the absolute and immutable truth preached by the apostles from the beginning may never be believed to be different, may never be understood in any other way.

I promise that I shall keep all these articles faithfully, entirely, and sincerely, and guard them inviolate, in no way deviating from them in teaching or in any way in word or in writing. Thus I promise, thus I swear, so help me God . . . .

PROFESSION OF FAITH

I, ________________, with firm faith, believe and profess all and everything that is contained in the Symbol of Faith, that is:

We believe in one God,
the Father, the Almighty,
maker of heaven and earth,
of all that is seen and unseen.
We believe in one Lord, Jesus Christ,
the only Son of God,
eternally begotten of the Father,
God from God, Light from Light,
true God from true God
begotten, not made, one in Being with the Father.
Through him all things were made.
For us men and for our salvation
he came down from heaven:
by the power of the Holy Spirit
he was born of the Virgin Mary, and became man.
For our sake he was crucified under Pontius Pilate;
he suffered, died, and was buried.
On the third day he rose again
in fulfillment of the Scriptures;
he ascended into heaven
and is seated at the right hand of the Father.
He will come again in glory to judge the living and the dead,
and his kingdom will have no end.
We believe in the Holy Spirit, the Lord and Giver of Life,
who proceeds from the Father and the Son.
With the Father and the Son, he is worshipped and glorified.
He has spoken through the Prophets.
We believe in one, holy, catholic, and apostolic Church.
We acknowledge one baptism for the forgiveness of sins.
We look for the resurrection of the dead,
and the life of the world to come. Amen.

I firmly embrace and accept
all and everything which has been either defined by the Church's solemn deliberations
or affirmed and declared by its ordinary magisterium concerning the doctrine of faith and morals,
according as they are proposed by it,
especially those things dealing with the mystery of the Holy Church of Christ,
its sacraments and the sacrifice of the Mass,
and the primacy of the Roman Pontiff.

NOTES

BOOK ONE — THE GRAIL

PART ONE — AUX BARRICADES — THE SIXTIES

CHAPTER 1: DIVINING

1. Joseph de Maistre, *Soirees II*, in Will and Ariel Durant, *The Age of Napoleon*, p. 335.

CHAPTER 2: CATECHISM COAST

1. Robert Renison, in Thomas Boon, The Anglican Church: From the Bay to the Rockies (Toronto: 1963).

2. The Baltimore Catechism No. 1, Lesson 34, Question 22, p. 120. All further references will be to Lesson and Question numbers in this edition.

CHAPTER 3: ELUSIVE BUTTERFLY

1. Archbishop Marcel Lefebvre, Canadian Layman, vol. 2, no. 9, May 1976.

2. Catholic Encyclopedia (New York: Robert Appleton Company, 1908).

3. Father Felix Sarda Y. Salvany, Liberalism (Rockford, IL: Tan Books, 1979), pp. 21, 27.

4. Pope St. Pius X, "Pascendi," in J.B. Lemius, O.M.I., *A Catechism of Modernism* (Rockford, IL: Tan Books, 1981).

5. M. Loisy, quoted in *Catholic Encyclopaedia.*

6. Ibid.

7. Pablo Neruda, *Time* Magazine, 1980.

CHAPTER 4: THE MEDDLING CLASS

1. *The Baltimore Catechism No. 1*, pp. 106, 107.

2. Anne Frank, *The Diary of A Young Girl* (Garden City, NY: Doubleday, 1967).

CHAPTER 5: THE THING

1. Sister Mary Alexander, "Open Letter to Bishops," *Canadian Layman*, vol. 1, no. 11, June/July 1973, p. 7.

CHAPTER 6: HATPINS AND HERESY

1. Joseph de Maistre, from *Soirees II*, in Will and Ariel Durant, *The Age of Napoleon.*

2. Frank Kennedy, *Insight*, a special supplement to *The Interim*, August 1991.

3. Robert Hoyt, *National Catholic Reporter*, July 10, 1970.

4. William de Marois, "Our Continuing Catechetical Scandal," *Canadian Layman*, vol. 2, no. 6, July 1975.

5. Sister Mary Alexander, "Open Letter to Bishops," *Canadian Layman*, vol. 1, no. 11, June/July 1973, p. 7.

6. Robert Hoyt, quoted in Sister Mary Alexander, "Open Letter to Bishops."

7. De Marois, "Our Continuing Catechetical Scandal."

PART TWO — BRICK ROADS — THE SEVENTIES

CHAPTER 1: HANDMAIDS OF THE REVOLUTION

1. Pope Pius XI, in Derek J. Holmes, *The Papacy in the Modern World* (New York: Crossroad Publishers, 1988).

2. James Hitchcock, in Sister Mary Alexander, "Open Letter to Bishops," *Canadian Layman*, vol. 1, no. 11, June/July 1973.

3. Sister Mary Alexander, "Open Letter," p. 2.

4. William de Marois, in Sister Mary Alexander, "Open Letter to Bishops," *Canadian Layman*, vol. 1, no. 11, June/July 1973, p.5.

5. Hitchcock, in Sister Mary Alexander, "Open Letter," p.5A.

6. De Marois, in Sister Mary Alexander, "Open Letter," p.4.

7. Hitchcock, in Sister Mary Alexander, "Open Letter," p.5A.

8. Sister Mary Alexander, "Open Letter."

9. Cardinal Joseph Ratzinger, with Vittoria Messori, *The Ratzinger Report* (San Francisco: Ignatius Press, 1984).

10. Isaias, ix 1-7.

11. Jeremiah, xxiii 5.

12. Daniel, ii 44.

13. Daniel, vii 13-14.

14. Zachary, ix 9.

15. Rev. Ronald Rolheiser, in Rick Bell, *Western Catholic Reporter*, June 10, 1991. Rev. Rolheiser is the Oblate provincial superior of Saskatchewan.

16. Pius XI, *Quas Primas* (Berlin, NJ: Gregorian Press). Encyclical Letter of Pope Pius XI.

17. Pius IX, *Syllabus of Errors*, quoted in *The Catholic Encyclopedia.*

18. De Marois, in Sister Mary Alexander, "Open Letter."

19. Gregory Baum, O.S.A., *Faith and Doctrine: A Contemporary View* (Paulist Press, 1969).

20. De Marois, in Sister Mary Alexander, "Open Letter."

21. De Marois, in Sister Mary Alexander, "Open Letter."

22. Msgr Vincent N. Foy, "Tragedy at Winnipeg," newsletter, *Human Life International* (Gaithesburg).

23. Rev. Joseph H. O'Neill, *Catholic Register*, quoted in de Marois, "Our Continuing Catechetical Scandal," *Canadian Layman*, vol. 2, no. 6, July 1975, p. 7.

24. De Marois, "Our Continuing Catechetical Scandal," *Canadian Layman*, vol. 2, no. 6, July 1975.

CHAPTER 2: HAVE-A-NICE-DAY THEOLOGY

1. William de Marois, "Our Continuing Catechetical Scandal," *Canadian Layman*, vol. 2, no. 6, July 1975, p. 14.

2. Bishop Paul O'Byrne, in de Marois, "Our Continuing Catechetical Scandal."

3. De Marois, "Our Continuing Catechetical Scandal."

4. Ibid.

5. Cardinal Suenens, in Peter Hebblethwaite, *In the Vatican* (London: Sidgwick and Jackson, 1986).

6. Sister Mary Alexander, "Open Letter to Bishops," *Canadian Layman*, vol. 1, no. 11, June/July 1973.

7. Ibid., p. 17

8. Ibid.

9. De Marois, "Our Continuing Catechetical Scandal," p.18

10. Sister Mary Alexander, "Open Letter to Bishops."

11. Ibid., p.3B.

12. *Catholic Encyclopedia.*

13. Sister Mary Alexander, "Open Letter to Bishops."

CHAPTER 3: SEX AND THE SINGLE CHILD

1. J. B. Lemius, O.M.I., *A Catechism of Modernism* (Rockford, IL: Tan Books, 1981).

2. Ibid.

3. James Likoudis, "Fashioning Persons for a New Age," *Social Justice Review*, December 1971.

4. Pope Paul VI, "General Address to the Bishops," Vatican City, 13 September 1972.

5. Francis J. Conklin, "In Defence of the Family," *Canadian Layman*, vol. 2, no. 3, January/February 1974.

6. Ibid.

7. Ibid.

8. Dr. Melvin Anchell, *National Review*, June 20, 1986.

9. Msgr. Eugene Kevane, *Canadian Layman*, vol. 1, no. 11, June/July 1973, p. 3.

10. Likoudis, "Fashioning Persons."

11. William A. Marra, "On Becoming A Plumber," *Canadian Layman*, vol. 1, no. 11, June/July 1973.

12. Conklin, "In Defence of the Family."

13. Kevane, *Canadian Layman.*

14. Conklin, "In Defence of the Family."

15. Sean O'Reilly, "Formal Sex Education: Fact or Fancy," reprinted in *Canadian Layman*, vol. 1, no. 11, June/July 1973.

CHAPTER 4: PARENTS, FIRST AND FOREMOST

1. Francis J. Conklin, "In Defence of the Family," *Canadian Layman*, vol. 2, no. 3, January/February 1974.

2. Ibid.

3. James Likoudis, "Fashioning Persons for a New Age," *Social Justice Review*, December 1971.

4. Ibid.

5. *Gravissimus Educationis.* The Declaration of Christian Education of the Second Vatican Council.

6. Sean O'Reilly, "Formal Sex Education: Fact or Fancy," reprinted in *Canadian Layman*, vol. 1, no. 11, June/July 1973.

7. Ibid.

8. Conklin, "In Defence of the Family."

9. Pope Pius XI, *Divini Illius Magistri*, On the Christian Education of Youth (Vatican City, 31 December 1929).

10. Conklin, "In Defence of the Family."

11. Msgr. Eugene Kevane, *Canadian Layman*, vol. 1, no. 11, June/July 1973.

12. Cardinal Joseph Ratzinger, with Vittoria Messori, *The Ratzinger Report* (San Francisco: Ignatius Press, 1984).

13. William de Marois, "Our Continuing Catechetical Scandal," *Canadian Layman*, vol. 2, no. 6, July 1975.

14. Conklin, "In Defence of the Family."

CHAPTER 5: POLKA-DOT PRIESTHOOD

1. Msgr. Eugene Kevane, *Canadian Layman*, vol. 1, no. 11, June/July 1973.

2. James Likoudis, "Fashioning Persons for a New Age," *Social Justice Review*, December 1971.

3. David Dooley, *Insight*, a special supplement to *The Interim*, vol. 2, no. 6, December 1991.

4. Dr. Michael A. Carrera, in *Canadian Layman*, vol. 2, no. 3 January/February 1974.

5. Sean O'Reilly, "Formal Sex Education: Fact or Fancy," reprinted in *Canadian Layman*, vol. 1, no. 11, June/July 1973.

6. Archbishop Joseph Aurele Plourde, from the *Ottawa Citizen*, June 5, 1973, p. 4.

CHAPTER 6: SOMETHING NEW ON EARTH

1. Paul VI, General Address to the Bishops, Vatican City, September 13, 1972.

2. Ibid.

3. James Hitchcock, in Sister Mary Alexander, "Open Letter to Bishops," *Canadian Layman*, vol. 1, no. 11, June/July 1973, p. 7.

4. Sean O'Reilly, "Formal Sex Education: Fact or Fancy," reprinted in *Canadian Layman*, vol. 1, no. 11, June/July 1973, p. 2.

5. John Steinbacher, *The Child Seducers* (Fullerton, CA: Educator Publishers).

6. James Likoudis, "Fashioning Persons for a New Age," *Social Justice Review*, December 1971.

7. James Likoudis, "Sex Educationists and Theorists of the Sex Revolution," *Social Justice Review*, vol. 2, no. 1, 1973.

8. Viktor Frankl, *Man's Search for Meaning* (Freiburg: Herverbwechere's Band 430, 1972).

9. Louise W. Eickoff, "Sex Ed Programs Are Wrong," *Canadian Layman*, vol. 2, no. 1, September/October 1973.

10. Likoudis, "Sex Educationists."

11. Francis J. Conklin, "In Defence of the Family," *Canadian Layman*, vol. 2, no. 3, January/February 1974.

12. Anna Freud, quoted in O'Reilly, "Formal Sex Education."

13. Msgr. Eugene Kevane, *Canadian Layman*, vol. 1, no. 11, June/July 1973.

14. Conklin, "In Defence of the Family."

CHAPTER 7: CHARIOTS

1. Peter Hebblethwaite, *In the Vatican* (London: Sidgwick and Jackson, 1986).

2. Anne Ross, *Canadian Layman.*

3. Ibid.

CHAPTER 8: THE ROAD FROM UTOPIA

1. James Daly, Canadian Layman, vol. 2, no. 3, January/February 1974.

2. Ibid.

3. Ibid.

CHAPTER 9: PHANTOM

1. John McCrae, "In Flanders Fields," from The New Oxford Book of Canadian Verse (Toronto: Oxford University Press, 1982).

BOOK TWO — A HISTORIC BETRAYAL THE EIGHTIES AND THE NINETIES

PART ONE — AMBUSH OF THE INNOCENT

CHAPTER 1: THE CULT OF THE PRESIDER VERSUS THE FAMILY

1. Rev. John McGoey, "The Poisoned Well," Insight, a special supplement to The Interim, vol. 2, no. 4, September 1991, p. 13.

2. Ibid.

3. Rev. Alphonse de Valk, Insight, a special supplement to The Interim, vol. 2, no. 7, 1992.

4. Ibid.

5. Ibid.

6. Dietrich von Hildebrand, *Sex Education: The Basic Issue I* (Butler, NJ: Roman Forum).

7. William Marra, *Sex Education: The Basic Issue II* (Butler, NJ: Roman Forum).

8. Hildebrand, *Sex Education.*

9. Ibid.

10. Ibid.

11. Ibid.

12. Marra, *Sex Education.*

13. Ibid.

14. McGoey, "The Poisoned Well," p. 13.

15. Ibid.

16. Ibid.

CHAPTER 2: COUNTDOWN TO THE NINETIES

1. Alphonse de Valk, "Editorial Note, 'The Poisoned Well,'" *The Interim,* September 1991, p. 13.

2. Philip Scharper, *The Hidden Face of God,* p. 12.

3. Rev. John McGoey, *Insight,* a special supplement to *The Interim,* vol. 2, no. 4, August 1991, p. 5.

4. Sylvia MacEachern, "Will Morally Bankrupt Androgyny Be Fully Alive?" *The Orator,* November/December 1990. All further references are to this issue.

5. McGoey, *Insight,* vol. 2, no. 4.

6. De Valk, "Editorial Note."

7. Sabina McLuhan, editorial, *The Interim,* 1987.

8. MacEachern, "Will Morally Bankrupt Androgyny..."

9. McGoey, *Insight,* vol. 2, no. 4.

10. Ibid.

11. Ibid.

12. MacEachern, "Will Morally Bankrupt Androgyny..."

13. David Dooley, *Insight,* a special supplement to *The Interim,* vol. 2, no. 6, December 1991.

14. Catherine Balger, letter to the editor, *The Interim,* May 1991

15. De Valk, "Editorial Note."

16. Bernharda Meyer, "Teaching Children Modesty and Purity: Pt. 1," *The Orator,* March/April 1991. All further references are to this issue.

17. De Valk, "Editorial Note," p. 4.

18. Bernadette Myski, letter to *The Interim.*

19. Jeanne Arcand and Marc Arcand, letter to *The Interim,* December 1991, p. 8, letter 8.

20. Ibid.

21. Linda Britton, letter to *Insight,* a special supplement to *The Interim,* vol. 2, no. 6, December 1991.

22. Brian Taylor, "A Defence of Randy Engel," *Insight,* a special supplement to *The Interim,* August 1991, p. 3.

23. David Dooley, "Catholic Schools—Do They Serve a Purpose?", Challenge, vol. 18, no. 2, November 1991.

24. Michael Otis, "RC School Officials Press for Condom Policy," *The Interim,* September 1991, p. 1.

25. Dooley, *Challenge.*

CHAPTER 3: A REMARKABLE TRIBUTE

1. Archbishop Marcel Gervais, *Insight,* a special supplement to *The Interim,* vol. 2, no. 6, December 1991.

2. Alphonse de Valk, "Editorial Note, 'The Poisoned Well,'" *The Interim,* September 1991.

3. Murray McGovern, *The Interim,* vol. 2, no. 6, December 1991, p. 6.

4. De Valk, "Editorial Note."

5. Rev. John McGoey, *Insight,* a special supplement to *The Interim,* vol. 2, no. 4, August 1991, p. 5.

6. Bishop John O'Mara, in David Dooley, *Challenge.*

7. Letter from Planned Parenthood, citing Maureen Jessop and Ellen Rosenblatt, *Adolescent Birth and Planning Needs* (Planned Parenthood of Ontario); and Ronald and Juliet Goldman, *Children's Sexual Thinking* (London: Routledge & Kegan Paul, 1982).

8. Ibid.

9. Ibid.

10. Ibid.

11. Ibid.

12. Ibid.

13. Ibid.

CHAPTER 4: THE NEON BISHOP

1. Richard Marius, *Thomas More* (New York: Alfred A. Knopf, 1984).

2. Anne Roche Muggeridge, *The Desolate City* (Toronto: McClelland & Stewart, 1986), p. 91.

3. Ibid., p. 92.

4. Ibid., p. 93.

5. Ibid., p. 92.

6. Ibid., p. 102.

7. Cardinal Joseph Ratzinger, with Vittoria Messori, *The Ratzinger Report* (San Francisco: Ignatius Press, 1984).

8. Joseph de Maistre, from "*Works,*" in Will and Ariel Durant, *The Age of Napoleon,* pp. 163, 177.

CHAPTER 5: THE SPIRIT OF THIS AGE

1. Michael Davies, *Cranmer's Godly Order* (New Rochelle, NY: Arlington House, 1976).

2. Anne Roche Muggeridge, *The Desolate City* (Toronto: McClelland & Stewart, 1986), p. 127.

3. Fr. John O'Connor, "Homo-OPs Expel Priest After 42 Years," *The Eternal Call* (Chicago: VNI Ltd., Spring 1991).

4. Isaias, ix 6-7.

5. Jeremiah, xxiii 5.

6. Daniel, vii 13-14.

7. Zachary, ix 9.

8. Luke, i 32-33.

9. Matthew, xxv 31-40.

10. Erasmus of Rotterdam, quoted by Zsolt Aradi, "Vow of Our Lady of Walsingham," *Shrines to Our Lady Around the World* (New York: Farrar, Strauss & Young, 1954), p. 68.

11. G.K. Chesterton, *The Everlasting Man* (Rockford, IL: Tan Books, 1979).

12. Pius XI, *Quas Primas:* Encyclical Letter of Pope Pius XI (Berlin, NJ: Gregorian Press).

13. Genesis, iii 5.

14. Cardinal Joseph Ratzinger, with Vittoria Messori, *The Ratzinger Report* (San Francisco: Ignatius Press, 1984).

15. Father Francis L. Filas, S.J., *St. Joseph After Vatican II* (New York: Alba House, 1969).

16. Ratzinger, *The Ratzinger Report.*

17. Pius XI, *Quas Primas.*

CHAPTER 6: CLASS ACTION HARVEST

1. Cardinal Joseph Ratzinger, with Vittoria Messori, *The Ratzinger Report* (San Francisco: Ignatius Press, 1984).

2. *30 Days,* no. 7, December 1988.

3. Ibid.

4. Ibid.

5. Fr. Enrique Rueda, "Vigorous Action Needed," *The Wanderer,* 18 August 1988.

6. John Molloy, "Reaping What You Have Sown," *Dawson Review.*

7. Charles A. Coulombe, "Wayward Shepherds," *Christian Order,* vol. 33, no. 1, January 1992.

8. Ratzinger, *The Ratzinger Report.*

9. E. Michael Jones, "Requiem for a Liturgist," *Fidelity,* January 1988, p. 28.

10. Randy Engle, "*Sex Ed: The Final Assault,*" (Gaithesburg: Human Life International, 1990).

11. Coulombe, "Wayward Shepherds."

12. Sylvia MacEachern, "Dissident Chairs Committee on Sex Abuse," *The Orator,* November/December 1991.

13. Coulombe, "Wayward Shepherds."

14. Rorie Sherman, "New Legal Specialty," *National Law Journal,* April 4, 1990.

15. *30 Days,* no. 7, December 1988.

16. Therese Ickinger, "The Gullet of the Wolf," *The Remnant,* July 15, 1992.

17. Letter to Fr. Enrique Rueda from Concerned Philadelphia Catholic Parents and Faithful, November 4, 1986.

18. Rueda, "Vigorous Action Needed."

19. Ickinger, "The Gullet of the Wolf."

20. Ibid.

21. Ibid.

22. Ibid.

PART TWO — TARGET ZERO

CHAPTER 1: A HOLY ACQUISITION

1. Murray McGovern, *The Interim,* vol. 2, no. 6, December 1991, p. 6.

2. Ibid.

CHAPTER 3: HOLY GROUND

1. Anne Roche Muggeridge, *The Desolate City* (Toronto: McClelland & Stewart, 1986).

2. 1 Corinthians, xv 25.

3. William de Marois, "Our Continuing Catechetical Scandal," *Canadian Layman,* vol. 2, no. 6, July 1975.

BIBLIOGRAPHY

BOOKS AND DOCUMENTS

Baltimore Catechism No. 1.

Boon, Thomas. *The Anglican Church: From the Bay to the Rockies.* Toronto: 1963.

Catholic Encyclopedia. New York: The Robert Appleton Company, 1908.

Davies, Michael. *Cranmer's Godly Order.* New Rochelle, NY: Arlington House, 1976.

de Maistre, William. *Works.*

de Maistre, Joseph. *Soirees II*, vol. 24.

Durant, Will and Ariel. *The Age of Napoleon.*

Engle, Randy. *Sex Ed: The Final Plague.* Human Life International.

Frank, Anne. *The Diary of A Young Girl.* Garden City, NY: Doubleday, 1967.

Frankl, Viktor. *Man's Search for Meaning.* Freiburg: Herverbwechere's Band 430, 1972.

Gravissimus Educationes (The Declaration of Christian Education), Second Vatican Council.

Hebblethwaite, Peter. *In the Vatican.* London: Sidgwick and Jackson, 1986.

Lemius, J.B. *A Catechism of Modernism.* Rockford, IL: Tan Books, 1981.

Marius, Richard. *Thomas More.* New York: Alfred A. Knopf, 1984.

Marra, William. *Sex Education: The Basic Issue II.* Butler, NJ: Roman Forum.

Muggeridge, Anne Roche. *The Desolate City.* Toronto: McClelland & Stewart, 1986.

Paul VI, "General Address to the Bishops," Vatican City, September 13, 1972.

Pius X, Pope Saint. *Pascendi Dominici Gregis* (On the Doctrines of the Modernists).

Pope Pius XI, *Divini Illius Magistri* (On the Christian Education of Youth). Vatican City, December 31, 1929.

Pius XI, *Quas Primas* (Encyclical Letter of Pope Pius XI). Berlin, NJ: Gregorian Press.

Ratzinger, Cardinal Joseph, with Vittoria Messori. *The Ratzinger Report.* San Francisco: Ignatius Press, 1984.

Robson, Christopher. *The French Revolution.*

Salvany, Father Felix Sarda Y. *Liberalism.* Rockford, IL: Tan Books, 1979.

Scharper, Philip. *The Hidden Face of God.*

U.S. Conference of Catholic Bishops (1982). *Liturgy Documentary Series 2.*

Vatican II. *Constitution on the Sacred Liturgy.*

Vatican II. *Documents of Vatican II.*

von Hildebrand, Dietrich. *Sex Education: The Basic Issue I.* Butler, NJ: Roman Forum.

Zsolt, Aradi. *Shrines to Our Lady Around the World.* New York: Farrar, Strauss & Young, 1954.

JOURNALS

Canadian Layman. Vol. 1, no. 11; vol. 2, nos. 1, 3, 6, 9.

Challenge. Vol. 18, no. 2, November 1991.

Christian Order. Vol. 33, no. 1, January 1992.

Dawson Review.

Faith.

Fidelity. January 1988.

The Interim. May, September, December 1991; *Insight,* a special supplement. Vol. 2, nos. 4, 6, 7; Vol. 1.

National Law Journal. 4 April 1990.

National Review, 20 June 1986.

The Orator. November/ December 1990; March/ April, November/December 1991.

Remnant. 15 July 1992.

Social Justice Review, December 1971; vol. 2, no. 1, 1973.

30 Days. No. 7, December 1988.

The Wanderer. 18 August 1988.

Western Catholic Reporter, 10 June 1991.